To

Jessie Gladys Murray,
high-spirited ever
faithful,
with all good wishes &
affectionate regard,

George A Gordon.

Oct. 3, 1925.

MY EDUCATION AND RELIGION

AN AUTOBIOGRAPHY

George A Gordon

MY EDUCATION AND RELIGION

An Autobiography

BY

GEORGE A. GORDON, D.D.

With Illustrations

BOSTON AND NEW YORK
HOUGHTON MIFFLIN COMPANY
The Riverside Press Cambridge
1925

The Riverside Press
CAMBRIDGE · MASSACHUSETTS
PRINTED IN THE U.S.A.

NOTE

THIS book would not have been written but for the persistent encouragement of two friends, both of Boston, William F. Whittemore and Ferris Greenslet. I am indebted for valuable assistance in reading the proofs to my wife, my daughter, my sister Mrs. John Gordon, and my friend Miss Ella L. Stacey, and to the vigilant proofreaders of my publishers, to all of whom I hereby express my sincere thanks. Thanks are also due to my friend William B. H. Dowse for the excellent views of the surroundings of my early life in Scotland.

GEORGE A. GORDON

CONTENTS

ILLUSTRATIONS

MY EDUCATION AND RELIGION

CHAPTER I

DEFINITIONS AND IMPLICATIONS

TWO objects have been before my mind since I was a young man, education and religion. The measure in which I have been able to gain an educated and a religious mind is for others to say, if indeed they should care to consider my unimportant life. Since I have, whether wisely or foolishly, allowed myself to be persuaded to write a sketch of my existence, the thread on which the events of that existence is strung, viewed in one way, is the aspiration after an educated mind; viewed in another way, the desire for a spirit heartily in the service of God and at peace in that service.

The history of a man's mind is largely to be found in the family to which he belonged, the teachers he has had, the friends he has made, the aspects of nature he has loved, the books he has read, the work he has tried to do, and the free play of spontaneity. These educational and religious forces will appear in the sequel. Here and now we are concerned with definitions and implications; the consideration of these will perhaps clear the way for what follows.

By education I mean the methodical, wise, and unremitting development of latent mental power. The educated person is one who more and more finds his mind a ready and an availing servant. Perhaps this definition will do to begin with. It is, of course, implied in education that there is something to educate; it is taken for granted that one has mind. The philosopher Kant says that if a man has not mother-wit, he cannot be taught it.

Here is a desk with pigeon-holes all properly labeled, and here are papers all properly addressed; if one cannot find the right pigeon-hole for the right paper, he is simply hopeless. The farmer does not create the earth or the soil. He may improve it, enrich it, but he cannot create it; that is given. Education is of no use to a mindless human being. Education takes what is given; that is the first implication in education.

The second implication is that education must train to a high degree of efficiency the actual powers of the mind. Accuracy in observation, and in telling a story, is a mark of an educated mind. Carlyle says that his father, an Ecclefechan stonemason, was apt to exaggerate — most of us can sympathize with him — and the old man, when he had made a statement, would go back and revise it, and thus bring it into accord with fact; to that extent he was an educated man. Carlyle said that he found in himself the same tendency to exaggerate, and we can well believe it. In speech he was one perpetual torrent of humorous, or quasi-humorous, exaggeration; but when he wrote a book he was one of the most accurate men of his age, and thereby he showed his education. The Apostle Paul showed in the same way that he was an educated man, when he said, 'Of the Jews five times received I forty stripes *save one*.' Only a good education in Tarsus, supplemented by the Holy Spirit, could have led him to make such a careful statement.

Education trains the memory in tenacity, in wealth, in

reliability; and the memory is one of the great powers of the human mind. Knowledge is impossible without it; one cannot make a rope out of sand; there must be cohesion. In knowledge there is cohesion and continuity of experience. Thus we find another apostle saying in a crisis, 'Then remembered I the word of the Lord.' That word was in his memory; that memory was rich, tenacious, trained; when he faced a certain crisis there was a call for wisdom, help, and out of the depths of memory came the shining word of wisdom.

Judgment is, of course, profoundly affected by true education. When I was a boy on the farm of an intimate friend of my father, there were no scales on which to weigh the oxen that we intended to sell. How could we ascertain their value? We could not altogether trust to the judgment of the man who wanted to buy them. We measured the oxen; we put a line down the whole length of the animal's back, and then took his girth, and, taking the length and the girth as premises, from these figured out the weight and the value of the animal. That farmer had a very great influence on me. I remember to this day his formula, 'Measure with exactness, calculate with caution, and in that way you will reach something like a sound conclusion.' And again, 'Look out for your premises, and then look out for your processes, and when you do that, you can be fairly sure of your conclusion.' That farmer was an educated man.

There should follow the discipline of the imagination, one of the greatest faculties of the mind. Those who read Swift with care must note his marvelously trained imagination. His Lilliputians, and the world of the Lilliputian, are in scale perfectly conceived and expressed; one meets with no disproportion or jar; and when one comes to Brobdingnag, everything again is on the right scale, carried out by an imagination under perfect discipline.

When we come to science we face the same educational necessity. Who ever saw a molecule, an atom, an electron, those physical forces that constitute the background of our ordinary physical universe? No man has seen them at any time, no man can see them; but the scientific man, working through experiments which guide his imagination, realizes by that faculty the existence of those infinitesimal forces. And in no way other than through imagination can the results of science be appreciated or new progress be made.

In ethics we are under the same law. Paul's heavenly vision was invisible; it was in his imagination. Every young man who longs to lead a decent life must carry in his imagination a picture of what he would like to be; in his imagination he makes, paints, frames, and hangs up the great banner of the life that he would like to lead.

When we come to God, it is the same. The great faculty by which we become sensible of the being, the pulsing tides and power of God, is imagination. We think of Him as the Absolute Soul of the universe; then by the force of imagination we draw near, we speak to Him as to a friend, we bring our life to Him as we do to those who love us in our own homes. Therefore, one of the greatest, philosophically greatest, lines in the New Testament is this: 'He endured, as seeing him who is invisible.'

The third implication of an educated mind is knowledge. Our powers are trained in the acquisition of knowledge, and this begins with the very beginning of life. Probably

an infant learns more in the first year of its existence than
in any ten succeeding years. Think for a moment of that
little mind three or four weeks old, to which everything is a
wonder, an interminable tangle; colors crowding upon its
eyes, sounds pouring in through its ears to its brain, flowers
with their perfume, foods with their taste! 'What kind of a
conglomeration is this?' the baby would say, if it could
speak. 'Who put me into this unintelligible confusion?'
The baby does not despair; it asserts itself, it begins to
work, and by the time it is a year and a half old, it has actually reduced its world to something approaching order;
it has achieved more, I believe, in that first year of reflection and classification than in any succeeding ten years of
its life. This process goes on through childhood, and when
we think it is old enough to bear systematic training, we
send the child to school, primary, high school, perhaps
college.

Plato stands in the ancient world for the most amazing
of all educational systems. For ordinary citizens, music,
which included literature, and gymnastic; there must be
from three to six years at that. For those who were qualified he had another programme. Arithmetic, by which he
meant the science of number; plane geometry, solid geometry; astronomy, the science of motion in the heavenly
bodies, or what he called 'harmonics'; dialectic — that is,
question and answer, the soul itself moving up from the
realm of shadows and unrealities closer and closer to the
realm of truth, beauty, and goodness in themselves; and
last of all, the vision of the heart of the universe, the
sovereign good, the light, life, fire, and glory of the whole
universe. When his elect citizens had seen that great sight,

they were ready to come back and be politicians. Reflecting on this, I have many times cried out, 'My God, how far we have fallen!'

Business has been brought into the realm of education in the last ten or fifteen years in the finest sort of way. A school of business administration is now to be found in almost every university in the land. Business itself is one of the great universities of the world. If a man is not accurate, if he has not a memory rich and reliable and becoming more and more so, if he is not sound in his judgment, careful about his premises, his processes and conclusions, and if he has not an imagination that can open up the future for his business in a sound way, his name will swiftly be found among the failures.

Another implication of education is that he only is a properly educated man who takes pleasure in the right things and feels pain toward the wrong things. Plato and Aristotle gave this as a sign, a fundamental mark of a properly educated person, that he should take pleasure in the things in which he ought to take pleasure and feel disgust toward those things for which he should feel disgust. And those men and the best of their race had truth of feeling toward all our great human interests; they are still teachers and examples that the modern world cannot forget without immeasurable loss.

Victorious moral purpose is implied in genuine education. Ever since Fichte taught the German nation more than one hundred years ago, thoughtful men all over the world have seen that the will cannot be left out of education. Consider, for example, Edgar Allan Poe, a man of genius if any American ever had genius, a man who accomplished wonderful things. What might he not have achieved if his intelligence and his marvelous sensibility had been under the control of a victorious moral purpose!

Enough has perhaps been said to indicate what I mean by education, and it is time to ask what I mean by religion? My answer is the vision of God, and life lifted into moral power, freedom, and joy by that vision. It is my experience that the Christian religion is the greatest educational force in the world. It makes life worth living; therefore, under its administration all knowledges that illuminate life become of increased value. It lays sovereign emphasis upon the truth; 'Ye shall know the truth, and the truth shall make you free'; therefore it honors every intellect fitted to lay hold upon the truth. It gives the vision of Absolute Worth and thus brings to bear upon feeling an unmeasured power. It educates the mind in discrimination between seeming good and real good, between incidental good and essential and eternal good. It brings a man out through that discovery into intellectual self-reliance and freedom; and finally Christianity coalesces with moral power, it is known as victorious moral power.

My purpose in the following pages is to exhibit certain permanent principles of human life through some of the experiences of an individual who early set his heart upon an educated mind. One hears a great deal about auto-suggestion, but what troubles me in this sketch is auto-intoxication. Madam Hardy, one of the most dignified, one of the most beautiful women of the Old South Church when I became its minister, the wife of Alpheus Hardy, chairman of the committee that called me, sent me at the time of my marriage, among other things, a bottle of Madeira wine, bottled in 1800. I put it away, thinking that as it had lived ninety years it might well live to be a century old. Later, having had an attack of grippe and not feeling in my usual health, I thought of the wine, but felt that I must not touch it because I did not know whether it would agree with me. I called in our beloved family physician, one of the best of physicians and one of the best of friends, and I said, 'I am going to open this bottle now and you must take a little of it.' I gave him only about two tablespoonfuls. He sat for about five minutes and then said, 'I am going home, lest I give away professional secrets.' This sketch that I am to write stands before me very much like that bottle of wine.

There are mountains in Scotland, and there are hills, and knolls; the elevations of the earth's crust are divided into these three classes, mountain, hill, knoll. From each of these, with its own atmosphere, one can look up and see the steady, glorious, everlasting lights. My purpose is to invite my reader to a knoll — not a mountain, not even a hill, but a knoll — and to ask him to look up with me at some of the permanent forces and splendors that guide, make, and bless human life. Forget the knoll, forget the atmosphere as much as you can, fix your gaze upon the things eternal.

CHAPTER II
STOCK: EDUCATION BY INHERITANCE
I

IN the greatest of the songs of Israel we read, 'We bring our years to an end as a sigh,' or, as the Scottish version puts it, with inimitable music and pathos, at least to Scottish ears, 'Our days wear awa' like the sough of a sang,' surely a counsel of perfection for any man about to write the story of his life. It is reported that in arranging for his funeral, while evidently dying, the poet Burns issued one prohibition, referring to a company of ill-trained volunteers, 'Don't let that awkward squad fire a salute over my grave.' How many awkward salutes have been fired both by biographers and autobiographers over lives that should have been spared these humiliations. The best thing for small and great alike would seem to be to sink one's history and one's life in the being of the Eternal Silence, and if this may not be, to come as near to it as possible.

In the many miseries of my first year in Boston I found, as many another youth has found in similar thoughts, a strange solace in a passage in Byron's 'Lara,' which has clung to my memory ever since:

> 'The crowd are gone, the revellers at rest;
> The courteous host, and all-approving guest,
> Again to that accustom'd couch must creep
> Where joy subsides, and sorrow sighs to sleep,
> And man, o'erlabor'd with his being's strife,
> Shrinks to that sweet forgetfulness of life:
> There lie love's feverish hope, and cunning's guile,
> Hate's working brain, and lull'd ambition's wile;

O'er each vain eye oblivion's pinions wave,
And quench'd existence crouches in a grave. . . .
Glad for a while to heave unconscious breath,
Yet wake to wrestle with the dread of death,
And shun, though day but dawn on ills increased,
That sleep, the loveliest, since it dreams the least.'

There is another view, called, in Israel, the Kingdom of God, in Greece, the State, and among ourselves, social good, and the delight of service rendered, however small, to this nearest and most real of all human causes. Thoughts, impulses, instincts in this direction, the majority of persons have or may have, by a little training, and these overcome all ordinary inertia, wipe the board clean of popular pessimism, and write in its place a healthy if moderate optimism. The City of God in time and in the universe, whether preached by the New Testament, by Marcus Aurelius, or by Augustine, has in it an immeasurable power of appeal, and wins to the service of civilized life alike the splendid gifts of the wise and mighty and the humble, no less beautiful, and infinitely moving sacrifices of the poor.

There is as every thoughtful man knows a profounder discouragement. The eminent person, much more one who fails of that distinction, who begins to set his poor individual existence in relations with universal human history, is like a mote in the sunbeam about to describe its relations to the interstellar spaces. No undertaking could possibly be vainer. Moment by moment changes come; oblivion inevitably claims its own, and seals it 'within the iron hills.' The dust under one's feet, or 'blown about the desert air,' is the symbol of external life, vanished intellect, unremembered goodness, forgotten genius. The stellar universe presents a crushing contrast to the brevity and vanity of man's existence on this insignificant globe, and the stellar universe itself is but a moment in the endless evolution of Being.

Under the impression of thoughts like these who can justify his folly in thinking his life, to his fellow-pilgrims in the wilderness of this world, of sufficient importance to be recorded? The justification may lie in the fact that men need amusement on the way to annihilation or hell, as the case may be. Besides, the perspective for man is in things human, which strikes normal persons as much more real, and grander far than the sidereal universe. We invert the glass, look at things non-human, and see them vastly reduced in size and dignity; and we see our human world magnified, filled with beauty, and all possible splendor. This sacred hallucination, if such it be, cannot be broken for any length of time. Human things for human beings must continue to be supreme. We men find it next to impossible to believe that mind is only an incident in the history of a bit of highly organized matter; mind finally asserts itself, not as a function of the body, but as a great responsible master, as indeed transcendent in meaning, and the sole ultimate reality. Then, too, since warriors we all are, soldiers in the liberation of humanity, the memories of those who have fought bravely, in other times, private and petty officer, no less than great commander, may serve to cheer and inspire as they are recalled round the camp-fire of to-day.

Three things are necessary to give moment and interest to the record of any man's life. The first is that the universal experiences of life should have meant much to the writer; the second essential is that experiences of more than

ordinary range should have been his; the third essential is
that the truth and nothing but the truth should be told.
The Scottish judge who divided witnesses into three classes,
liars, damned liars, and experts, might have said, instead
of experts, autobiographers. These three tests I venture
to believe I may perhaps meet fairly well. Almost all the
experiences, similar to those of other men, that I have
passed through, have been deeply significant to me; and
some of my experiences have been somewhat exceptional,
and I claim to be an honest man. I shall therefore endeavor to record some of the things that my eyes have seen
and my heart has felt in the changing environments in
which I have lived.

After all, how little any man can tell of himself! The
sources of his being are in the Infinite Mystery; the relations of his life to his cosmic and human environments are
established by an invisible hand; the tides of decrease and
increase are an ebb and flow from a sea eternally screened;
the original fountains of our existence, our nurture, our
psychic force, and our fortune, are past finding out. It is a
superficial tale that we relate; the deep things are with
God. Perhaps the story may conduct, like a mountain
path, to an occasional outlook other than and infinitely
greater than itself; such a path was that which, a generation ago, led from Zermatt and the brawling Visp, first
through the woods to the Riffel Alp, and then upward to
the Gorner Grat. The path, its toil and its terminal, were
lost in the transcendent outlook; there was the supreme
thing, the solitude, the majesty, the incomparable sub-
limity of the Everlasting. Any truly human life, simply
told, will bring writer and reader alike to the verge of

fathomless abysses of being and to the vision of Infinite
heights. Whittier sings,

> 'Alas for him who never sees
> The stars shine through his cypress trees.'

Whether it be cypress tree or rosebush, it is the splendor
of the Everlasting that glorifies it; whether it be the great
human experience or the ordinary, its meaning lies in the
Infinite.

II

I was born on the estate of Pitodrie, in the parish of Oyne,
Aberdeenshire, Scotland, January 2, 1853. The estate of
Pitodrie rests on the side of Bennachie, a very shapely
mountain less than two thousand feet in height, but much
more impressive than many greater elevations, owing to
its central pyramidal form and its black appearance. It is
seen over a wide stretch of territory; it has served as the
meeting-place for the eyes of parted lovers, and I recall
walking with my mother three miles when I was seven
years old, and she twenty-nine, that from a position of advantage she might see the summit of the lovely mountain
within sight of which her rarely happy girlhood was passed.
I cannot forget the tender memories that she recalled that
afternoon nor the sight of the tears that filled her large,
beautiful eyes. Bennachie is the immemorial sentinel of
East Aberdeenshire; itself the survivor, it has become the
symbol of the waste and havoc of time. Uncounted generations have passed in review before its searching eyes; the
character that has gone into the well-cultivated soil from
the age-long procession of toilers and the character that has
been won in the struggle, it has witnessed. It stands the

great Recorder of all these silent generations, the solemn memorial of their achievement, their bequest, their forgotten love and grief. As one born beneath its shadow looks toward it, one feels the wonder, the pathos, and the character of a vanished humanity.

My father whose name I bear was the grieve or overseer of the estate of Pitodrie. He was born in the neighboring parish of Insch, and descended from the Gordons of Huntly, but beyond three or four generations back nothing is known of the family tree. Mist and cloud, impenetrable to the keenest antiquarian eyes, cover the far-off lives that lay behind his. The race of the Gordons has a history in Aberdeenshire of eight hundred years; nothing remains, however, but this general appeal to imagination. Here in the fruitful county of Aberdeen the blood that flowed in my father's veins descended from the far past of the Gordon clan; all definite knowledge has been swept away by the flood of the years.

George Gordon, of Pitodrie, my father, was one of the most remarkable men whom I have known. He was one of ten children, eight sons and two daughters, born to William Gordon, Largie, Insch, and his wife, Ellen Roger Gordon. My grandfather was farmer and schoolmaster, a man of amazing industry, upright in all his dealings, proud and independent, an Elder in the Established Church, universally respected for his worth, a God-fearing man, as the saying went, and thereby made free from all other fear. When his ten children successively reached the age of twenty-one, they received from this most honorable father sixty pounds or three hundred dollars each; a great sum considering the time, the place, and the scale of in-

BENNACHIE

comes. He reserved a sum sufficient as he thought to carry his wife and him to the end of their days with frugal comfort. When he attained the age of eighty-one, this small reserve was almost spent. His youngest son, who had returned with a modest fortune from New Zealand, offered his father thirty pounds or one hundred and fifty dollars a year. The old man declined the offer, saying that he and his wife could live comfortably on seventy-five dollars a year, that his wife had twelve hundred and fifty dollars of her own still untouched. If worse came to worst, the old stoic added, they had decided to begin on his wife's reserve fund. This would save him from the one humiliation he could not brook, of becoming a burden upon his children.

Two years before his death a son was accidentally killed in New Zealand. His fortune — for so it was then called, of fifteen thousand dollars — went to his father, whose pride was now saved and his independence secured, although he added not a penny to his usual expenses. After his death at the age of nearly eighty-four, this money was equally divided among the nine surviving children.

These eight sons and two daughters were carefully educated and unalterably fixed in the faith of John Calvin. Calvinism was the perfect philosophy of the Old and New Testament, the last word about God and the meaning of man's life. Prayers were offered morning and evening, a chapter read from the Bible, and a Psalm sung; the last exercise was both pious and humorous in the highest degree since there was not a singer, natural or trained, in the whole family. I suppose it was assumed, and rightly, I think, that the Deity of John Calvin was without the sense of humor, or that he possessed it only in the way of scorn; 'He that sitteth in the heaven shall laugh; the Lord shall have them in derision.'

Since these eight sons and two daughters were splendid specimens of physical humanity, play, pranks, and often the heartiest fun were irrepressible and abundant. Halloween in particular was a great night. Cheese and bread and a glass of spirits were allowed each, and sometimes a little more was taken. The broom and gorse had been gathered in vast quantities from the hill behind the farm beforehand, and two armfuls of precious straw were allowed to each of the sons, and the old man turned his back when the young men stole two more. Sperm oil in quarts was poured upon the heaped-up material, and then a spark from the flint touched off the paper filled with saltpeter, and dried, and the bonfire went into glory. More cheese and bread and light refreshments followed; this went on till morning when the call came to worship and work.

Yuletide, then held on January 5th, was another alleviation of the stress of John Calvin. Here was a veritable feast, barley broth, boiled beef, plum pudding and cakes, and a conservative allowance of whiskey, the good mother adding a little to the allowance when she thought the father had been a little too strict with the lads. Two or three fairs were added during the year, at which there might be some sparring, and now and again a genuine fight, as well as the transaction of honest business, and if his sons concerned came off victorious no questions were asked by the sedate and dignified father; but if any one came home with a black eye, or other signs of an ominous character, there followed from the High Priest of the family the plainest words to the victim that he was headed for the ill pairt — hell, in our rougher speech.

No one of these sons became a drunkard; no more industrious men ever lived; all became men of mark in the several communities in which they lived; all became rich or well off for their time and condition, except my father; all were sincerely religious men, and to most of them religion, although it never became inconsistent with toddy or economic concerns, in four of the eight sons, and in the two daughters, was turned into victorious joy: this is the victory that overcometh the world, even our faith.

I made one visit that I clearly recall to my paternal grandfather and grandmother. My grandmother received me, a boy of nearly twelve, with tender and beautiful affection. She was a handsome old lady, and she and I had a world of happy conversation while my grandfather was outside. The discipline of bringing up a family of ten children had given her some of the best things in life, grace of spirit, ready sympathy, tenderness, fullness of heart, eager and loving solicitude for the highest good of all her kith and kin. Her serene sadness, her beauty in old age, and her goodness have remained with me a pathetic and influential memory, and I can see her now in that far past, among the swift-gathering shadows of evening, her children long gone from her, her work almost done, with wonder and the sense of the sorrowful mystery of life in her sad sweet eyes. We knew each other at once and forever as friends.

My grandfather, I could plainly see, had little use for me. For one thing I talked too much, and I expected too much from this world, which seemed to me then, and still

more now, so great with wonder. Brilliancy my grandfather detested as a sure sign that the person so endowed
was not to be trusted, as indeed one better fitted to be a
servant of the Devil than of the Lord. Solid worth in
mind and character he alone respected. My father was
infinitely the most brilliant of his children, but he was not
equally distinguished for self-control, and consequently
his father, although always kind, had little real regard for
him, and no confidence in him. I fell to praising my father
to the old man, and at the same time expressing my surprise that he should apparently have forgotten his promise
to meet me at my grandfather's at a certain hour. The
austere old man listened to me mute as a block of granite,
and when I paused for want of breath, he replied sarcastically, 'Your father's nae to ride the water on,' the image
here being that of an unreliable horse fording a river. My
father came only an hour late, and as I thought to the utter confutation of his grim critic. Their conversation, free,
abundant, informing, external, exact, I clearly recall, and
I remember how formal and wanting in affection it seemed.

One item in this visit is of special interest. My grandfather, after bidding me welcome, asked me how much my
fare on the train cost me. I had walked six miles to the
train; I had ridden by train ten miles, and I had walked
four more from the station to my grandfather's farm, all
of which had to be done again that day on returning home.
My fare was eighteen cents. My grandfather brought me a
shilling, twenty-five cents, from his slender store, put it
in my hand, saying that he wanted no one to be at any
expense coming to see him. This extreme independence
makes credible the story of the two Highlanders lost in

THE AUTHOR'S BIRTHPLACE, PITODRIE, ABERDEENSHIRE

their small boat in a fog off the west coast of Scotland.
One watched, at the same time steering the boat, while the
other prayed thus: 'O Lord, bring us to land and we will be
greatly beholden to you' — 'Stop, Donald,' cried his
friend, 'I see the land, let us not be beholden to anybody.'

That visit was so depressing, and I was so happy when
it was over and done, that I failed then to see, what I afterwards came to recognize, the moral dignity, the clean
honor, the great human worth of my grandfather Gordon.
He was a terror to children because he believed they were
all of them either evil-doers, or what was worse, silly; but
he was an honest man outside and inside; he dealt justly,
and for all his sternness he loved kindness, and walked
humbly with his God. Such a career is in its own small
sphere a kind of grand epic.

The parting between my father and his aged father and
mother I have described elsewhere; here let it be added
that the scene was real as the inmost heart of life. For the
first time I saw in my father the filial depth of his nature,
his deferential manner, his deep respect and his clear, gen-
tle answers to his mother's pleadings for family unity after
she and her husband had gone. On the side of the two old
people the scene was beautiful in its silent, inexpressible
tenderness, in its dignity and composure against the dark
background of mystery, in its high religious solicitude, and
in its complete rest in the Infinite Will. My grandmother
was the speaker at this farewell; the trembling tones of
her voice I can still hear; she looked sorrowful, ineffable
tenderness. My grandfather stood mute, and his look of
approval and reverence while my grandmother was speaking is unforgettable. The scene hangs framed in my imag-

ination like some picture on the walls of a room in a humble cottage, whose deep human meaning no one knows save the venerable owner of the cottage. So fade from sight things of infinite moment, like the stars at sunrise, as the glare of the present takes possession of the life of man.

My father was born June 12, 1818. He received an excellent common-school education, which he extended to the end of his life. He was a man of understanding, of clear, strong intellect, without any corresponding endowment of imagination. He was everywhere regarded as brilliant; this judgment I consider had its origin in his clearness of mind, his passionate force, and his unusual efficiency. He was a scientific farmer. Everything he did on the farm was admirably done, and the quantity of his work was equal to its high quality. He had æsthetic perception and feeling, mainly expressed in two ways. His work on the farm was done to satisfy two tests, utility and beauty. In ploughing, the furrow must be of a certain depth and width; it must be straight and it must be turned so as to result in an angle, the edge of equal height with the edges of other furrows, and the whole furrow, being not crushed and broken, but standing solid and entire. This is a characteristic of the best Scottish farming. My father's specialty was in stack-building. The grain when cut is bound in sheaves; when ripened by the sun, the sheaves are brought to the stack-yard, and are built into forms which at their best are extremely handsome. The stack is built on a stone or wooden foundation, in circular form to about ten feet in height; upon this an 'eason' or fringe is extended in one round of sheaves; upon this is built as perfect a cone as can be made. The cone is thatched carefully and the thatch is bound down by ropes made of straw and applied so that the spaces between are square in shape and exact in regularity. The top is in the shape of the rose comb of the Spanish cock; the shank of the stack is shorn into even, smooth circularity. All this is first to protect grain and straw against the weather, and in the second place to satisfy æsthetic feeling. A yard with twenty stacks built to perfection after this manner is a sight worth seeing. In this sphere my father was a consummate master; indeed, he had no rival.

My father's sense of beauty in nature was strangely limited. To him the sea was a wild enemy of man and he had no praise for it. Mountains had no place in his esteem. I recall a remark of his on one occasion when we had climbed together to the summit of the mountain on whose side I was born. He turned toward the wide expanse of cultivated fields, rich with ripening grain, bordered with green meadows, with herds of cattle quietly feeding in them, and set in the centers, the peaceful farm buildings, the abodes of human beings, and he said, 'A bonnie howe (valley) that.' Then, turning toward the west with the higher Grampians in the distance, with the snow lying in their black arms, in midsummer, he called out — 'A cauld cruel place yon.'

To my father, as to many another hard-pressed man, Nature was beautiful only on the side friendly to human beings. The farmer's stern fight with Nature, his scorn of the worthless rich, and his noble independence are well described by Burns:

> 'Think ye that sic as you and I,
> Wha drudge and drive through wet and dry,

Wi' never-ceasing toil;
Think ye; are we less blessed than they
Wha scarcely tent us in their way,
As hardly worth their while?'

There is a vast popular misunderstanding about the majority of the Scottish people and drinking. Almost every one drank whiskey, at times, in my boyhood; a few times a year it could be said of most people that they had been fu'. Feasts were rare, but real when they did take place; then the eating and drinking were in the grand style. The farmers went to the house of the proprietor of the estate; the feast was spread by him, and the clergy were always represented, as were likewise the professions of law and medicine. It was quite the thing to take a drappie o'er muckle on such occasions, and resulted in no disgrace to the person or persons concerned. Often has my father told me of harnessing the 'shalt' or pony to take from a Pitodrie feast a more than half-intoxicated minister or two, and of helping them, with all respect and kindness, into the manse. In his 'Lines on meeting with Lord Daer,' Burns is not ribald, but a faithful historian of what occasionally would happen pretty much all round Scottish society:

'I've been at drucken writers' feasts,
Nay, been bitch-fou 'mang godly priests,
Wi' reverence be it spoken!'

It may have been a poor way in which to find cheer, and doubtless, though years have brought enlightenment and improvement here, still it should be said that habitual drinking was non-existent. The country people were among the hardest and best workmen in the world; fitness for work and the use of alcohol are incompatible; and, as work was the main business, the chief interest and function of the farmer and his servants, drinking, except on occasion, was simply ruled out.

Some of the finest human touches his sons would have missed had they not seen our father when he had taken a dram; intoxicated they never saw him. No one ever heard him utter a boastful word except when he had taken a dram. Then the contrast to his uniform dignity and reserve was highly amusing. On one such occasion we were taking a walk together when I was seventeen, and he was telling me that he was about to annex the calling of an auctioneer, in which he had no experience, and that of land-measuring in which he was an expert, and I stopped him with the question, 'Could you do it?' 'If I couldna' who could?' was the freezing but amusing rejoinder. He was in the habit of driving, at one time, an old gentleman with a weak heart, who carried with him in the carriage a small flask of brandy, too strong to be taken till weakened by water. Driving one day the attack came on, and my father had to take the dose of brandy to a near-by spring of pure water to be weakened. The spring was out of sight, and my father seemed to be staying too long. The voice of affectionate expostulation reached him from the carriage. 'Come awa', George man, the brandy is weak enough now, man.' Father would himself tell this tale with the keenest merriment.

My father's abilities as a land-measurer were unusual and gave him wide repute. In early manhood he seemed fitted for the highest service in his line. He held many excellent situations, was extremely popular with the great because of his prompt efficient service and also because of his respectful and obliging manners. One thing he could not endure, the feudalistic sense of the rich man's superiority, and the brutal ways in which he expressed, when out of temper, that superiority. My father's nature was essentially and profoundly noble, but it was undisciplined. His great fault was his lack of self-control. His temper under insult and outrage was a hurricane of wrath that spared not the persons of the great, and that counted no cost either to himself or his family. He threw up position after position till he found himself out in the cold. He had to return to the life of farm-overseer, in which the work of his head had to be combined with the work of his hands. This break in a highly successful and promising career took place when he was eight and thirty years of age. Henceforth to his death at the age of sixty-three his existence was on the level from which he had so brilliantly risen. The bright morning had gone to wreck by noon, and for the rest of the day there met him only sleet and rain and stormy winds. Here, however, is the chief inspiration of his life. He did not lose heart, nor become bitter; he did not complain in working with men and for men immeasurably inferior to him in mental power and worth; he rose into heroic manhood, served with amazing diligence, improved his mind, took to the Bible with the greatest avidity, went onward through the stern years with an increasing sense of moral dignity, won an honorable living for his family, secured his independence, commanded the respect of the whole neighborhood, and in all times of distress and neglect gave this as his comfort: 'I have a mind above the world.' His life was an economic failure compared with

what it might have been; in this economic failure it became
a human success that, as I recall it against the perspective
of the past, fills me with wonder and admiration. He lost
the prospect of a fortune; he won a conscious place in the
kingdom of man.

III

My mother was Catherine Hutcheson, one of eight children born to David and Catherine Fraser Hutcheson.
David Hutcheson was for forty years working overseer of
two farms on Donside, Wester Fintray and Kincail, four
and eight miles south of the charming village of Inverurie.
He did not possess the moral dignity, the high intellectual
power, or the religious passion of my father's father, but
he was far more interesting on account of his wit, humor,
capacity for all sorts of rough but clean mirth, and still
more engaging to his children and grandchildren because
of his great athletic abilities. Three of his four sons were
remarkable for strength and agility, yet their father at
fifty could easily beat them at every athletic event. At
forty-five he could do from eighteen to twenty feet at the
long leap, and he was equally good at the high leap. He
was on the field at five o'clock in the morning, during the
summer months, and, except for one hour in the middle of
the day, there till six or seven, or even later, in the evening,
with powers of endurance and efficiency that were unmatched. David Hutcheson's name was famous in Aberdeenshire, and everywhere regarded with the deepest respect. One of his best feats was walking, between six
o'clock in the morning and twelve o'clock in the evening,
seventy-two miles. In his day there were no railroads, and

he used to drive a pair of horses, harnessed to the farmer's cart from Stonehaven to Inverness, and from Inverness to Strome Ferry, a lonely road and infested with highwaymen. He went wholly unarmed, except for his fists, which were the largest and the hardest that I have ever seen. Swift as an arrow shot from a bow and in force like the kick of a horse were his blows, and many an adventurous highwayman did he surprise and leave a helpless heap of bruises by the roadside. In a short time he became famous among that class of human beings, and had little trouble afterwards.

On one of these visits to Strome Ferry he crossed to the Isle of Skye, where he met at Portree Catherine Fraser to whom he was married in 1820. She was the most amazing compound of kindness and temper that I have ever known. Her tongue took the skin off wherever it struck, like a cat's, and her kindness would immediately nurse and heal the wound. I knew her well and, in my boyhood, loved her beyond any human being except my mother. Her sarcastic speech was poetry to me, and her wide power of characterization was of the nature of the finest caricature; it depicted the truth always, but in exaggerated and amusingly distorted forms. Her sons-in-law, for whom she would have given her life, were the habitual targets of this weapon. The husband of her youngest daughter, Mary, genial, mirthful, thick-set, and over-talkative, was the 'Paddy' Simpson, although he was Scottish to the core. My father, owing to his dignity and reserve, was 'My Lord!'

Never angel came to any door to receive a warmer welcome than this rarest union of overflowing affection and caustic remark found in the homes of all her kin. She was, indeed, the dearest and the most amusing of old ladies, and her hands were always full of gifts for her grandchildren, and of help for all; especially did she pity, house, and feed the mendicant and vagrant, nor would she turn empty from the door the most worthless of suffering human beings. She died in 1864, her husband in 1876, she seventy, and he eighty-six, and they sleep side by side in the little graveyard, made weirdly impressive by the ruin of the medieval house of worship still standing in it, just behind the building in which they lived many of their happiest years.

Her mother was a MacDonald, I was told, a native of the Isle of Skye, a woman of a far higher type of intellect than her daughter, of great energy of character, and of pluck without limit. Early left a widow, she brought up her four children with pious care and wisdom. With her two sons she went to South Carolina some time in the late twenties of the last century, and remained there till the late forties; during this time her sons had made a modest fortune. She was eighty years old when she returned and she lived to the age of ninety, a sovereign influence to the end, a spark of celestial fire always, a pure and steady flame of love when I knew her. I saw her for the last time when she was ninety and I was five years of age. She and I were exactly the same height. She received my mother and me with a Celtic storm of endearment, kissed my mother and then me many times, much to my sorrow, and then ran for the whiskey bottle and the teapot. Her end, which came soon after, was in a way weird. She informed her daughter, Mrs. Hutcheson, who was visiting her, that she was to die that afternoon at four o'clock. She took her bath with the serenity of Socrates before he drank the hemlock, called for the white graveclothes that had long been in readiness, dressed herself in them, took to her bed at two o'clock, and at four quietly and tenderly breathed her last. Among the sacred memories of my childhood is that of listening from behind a half-open door to a recital of this strange and affecting scene, by Mrs. Hutcheson to my mother. The story was told in tones only a little above a whisper, in a voice full of the sense of the pathos and sanctity of life.

On account of what she was in herself and also because of her influence over me, my mother deserves a notice somewhat extended. She was born in September, 1831, and married to my father who was more than thirteen years older than she, May 1, 1846, four months under fifteen. Her schooling was quite imperfect, but she had a wonderful memory for wise maxims and for ballad poetry, and as she saw a good deal of persons better educated than she had been, she absorbed much of real culture, and in maturity became a wise and diligent reader. She was considered through life as much inferior in intellect to her husband, but this was true only of the logical understanding. In imagination she was greatly his superior; in insight, in speculative faculty, in sympathy, and in another grace of mind, seldom found in her sphere, refined, and moving expression, especially after a profound and permanently influential religious experience following the deaths, within two months of each other, of her oldest daughter and her youngest child, a son. These two she seemed to love above all others among the thirteen children born to her, seven daughters and six sons. I asked one of her sons, while fighting in the Soudan, and engaged in the inhuman and hardening practice of war, if he ever got a letter from his mother, in the wild and bloody desert, that he was able to read through without tears. His answer was never. Although she would have thought we were mocking her had she heard us say it of her, she had style in her entire self-expression. She wrote seldom, for she found it difficult to say what she wanted, and as she wanted. She would spend a whole evening putting her thoughts together, then arranging them, and then waiting for the best, the winged word, to come. The result was a sacred writing, one worthy to be added to the most cherished wisdom of one's life. One such letter I will subjoin, her last to me, and in response to the cablegram I sent her on my wedding day, carried by me in my card-case these five and thirty years since she left the world, brief, but a gleam of light from a soul that was a fountain of light:

MY DEAR SON:
I would like to send a few words of thanks, for all your great kindness to me, especially for the cablegram. I knew by that, that you smiled on me. In the light of thy countenance is life!
Ever your loving mother,
CATHERINE GORDON

Comrade of her children she was lots of fun. It was long before the older sons could beat her at running even with a baby in her arms. She could tell in abundance the best of ghost stories, and the wonder-working power of these tales came largely from the fact that she believed them. The long winter Scottish evenings were filled with the beauty and terror of these preternatural experiences. I greatly enjoyed them, but very early came to regard them as wholly fictitious, and in my mind God's orderly world was in no wise darkened by this witch's dance, at once so thrilling and terrible.

My mother had no servant, except for the first six years of her married life, the period of my father's good fortune. She cooked and kept house for us all, aided, of course, by all, and she made all the clothing for her children till they were able to go into service and earn their own living. She was excellent at every kind of work, ready with a resourceful mind and skillful hands for every emergency, of perfect health, of a serene, sunny, and hopeful disposition, and with all this labor sang, in the most melodious way, the best of Scottish songs, or recited some moving bit of ballad poetry. Our darkest days were bright with her presence.

I had the unspeakable privilege of the closest fellowship with her mind in my childhood and boyhood, and when I went away to earn my own living, it was my chief joy to bring home to her part of my wages, to ease a little the burden that pressed upon her shoulders. After her death in 1891, due to falling from the top of a stage-coach, I saw on my visit to Scotland the shawl that I had given her in 1866, when I was a boy of thirteen, still sound and good, with the newness hardly gone from it, symbol of a relation and an experience too deep, too sacred for words. Thus did poverty, toil, and hardship bind us together in dearest and happiest friendship.

She was a widow for the last ten years of her life, and during that time she was my sole and sacred care. Five times I crossed the ocean to see her, and to spend the summer vacation under her roof. She was in the highest degree happy, loved extravagantly as she was by all her children, of whom several lived with her. Her only incurable sorrow came from her depth of heart, and the intensity of her love for the members of her family. Our partings were almost too much for her to bear, almost canceled the joy of the summer companionship, and nothing that I could say in the way of humor or hope could avail very much in lessening the darkness of the hour. Her own method of recovery was seclusion for days, spent with her Bible and in prayer. Then she would come forth all the more exalted and beautiful because of conquered grief and triumphant faith. My last look at her on parting in 1889 was from the street, before entering the cab to drive away to the station. There she stood at the window, her figure framed by the large pane of glass, her face wrought into an expression of love and woe indescribable; the tears were few, but the sense of bereavement and deathless love was unutterable and unforgettable. How many mothers whose sons and daughters have gone to the ends of the earth never to return she represented in their 'childless, voiceless woe.'

IV

DARWIN tells us that the stream of descent from one generation to another is controlled by two tendencies; first, the tendency of the parent to repeat his character in his offspring, and second, the tendency of the offspring to vary in character from that of the parent. These two tendencies, repetition and indefinite variation, according to Darwin, are the guiding forces in the stream of descent.

Heredity is general and specific. Every child that comes into the world has behind him the whole biological movement of this planet, human and sub-human; he has, further, behind him the physical and spiritual character of the universe; he has behind him the being and the character of God; so vast, so majestic, so mysterious is the background against which every individual human being stands. There is the house on the hillside; it stands out against morning, noon, and evening, against the glory of day and the gloom of night, it stands out against the Universe. So the individuality of man stands out against an immeasurable, incalculable, infinite background.

Less of what is poor and more of what is good get into certain races than into others, and the races in whose inheritance are found less of what is poor and more of what is good are the great races. The Egyptians, the Persian people, the Hebrews, the Greeks and Romans, in ancient times; and in the modern world, the French, German, English, including both Scotch and Irish, and our American polyglot edition, are the great races. Our American race is still in the making; out of the great amalgamation now going on we may expect a new, an extraordinary type of human being.

I recall spending two summers with Admiral Porter, of the United States Navy, who fought for four years as a Commander in that Navy. He told me that the racial greatness of the sailors behind the guns was something passing all possible praise. Among my parishioners in Maine was a veteran of the War of 1812, who was with Lieutenant — afterwards Commodore — Perry in the victorious battle against the British on Lake Champlain. One could not imagine a finer specimen of racial vigor than he. One incident from the battle of Jutland is significant here.

In the heat and heart of that battle, when every other five minutes a battleship or cruiser was going down with a thousand or fifteen hundred men, two stokers came up to get a breath of fresh air; all that the journalist was able to catch of the debate between those two men, carried on in as calm a fashion as if they had been sitting on the piazza of a summer hotel, was this: 'I say, Tom, he ought to have married her.' There is racial power.

When one comes to specific heredity, there are two things to be avoided in any discussion of the subject. The first is, losing the essential in the incidental. There is such a thing as conventional aristocracy, a mere name; there is such a thing as biological aristocracy, the real thing. The poet Burns, and our own Lincoln, are examples of biological aristocracy minus the conventional. Washington is an example of the concurrence of the two, the conventional and the biological. Let us never forget this distinction which goes to the very heart of life.

> 'The rank is but the guinea's stamp,
> The man's the gowd for a' that.'

In looking into heredity, we must not be misled by conventionality; we must look into the color of the biological stream.

The next thing to be avoided is such overemphasis of the excellent qualities of our own ancestors as to bring upon us the proverbial rebuke that we are like potatoes, the better part of us being underground. 'Daddy,' asked a small boy, 'what is an ancestor?' 'My boy,' replied the father, 'an ancestor is one who goes before; I went before you, so I am your ancestor, and your grandfather is another ancestor; do you see?' 'Yes, I see; but if that is what it means, Daddy, why do people brag about it?'

Locality has a great influence upon specific heredity, given a certain length of time. Conceivably one might have been born in China or Japan or Ireland, or among the Turks or the Hottentots, but if one were born of the same parents the difference would not be very great unless one remained a very long time in that locality. It is very difficult to tell what country one belongs to if he is born *in transitu*. I heard of a man who was born of Scottish parents while they were on a visit in Canada. He said he was not a Canadian, he was a Scot. The retort was, 'But you were born in Canada, therefore you are a Canadian.' The contention finally so worked upon the poor man's nerves that he yelled, 'If a cat had kittens in an oven, would they be buskits?'

Heredity stands clear and high of localities. Gladstone says that he was conscious of the presence in him of his Highland Scottish mother and his Lowland Scottish father, like two currents in a channel of the same river, flowing side by side. There was the Celtic fire in his blood and there was the Saxon wariness of judgment, and the two together made the background of the individual man. I could say the same of myself. All through my life I have been conscious of these two forces — the clear, logical, strong, commanding father, and the profoundly meditative, profoundly imaginative and great-hearted mother. I find a poem which will abbreviate this discussion, by Thomas Bailey Aldrich:

> 'A soldier of the Cromwell stamp,
> With sword and psalm-book by his side,
> At home alike in church and camp:
> Austere he lived, and smileless died.

'But she, a creature soft and fine —
From Spain, some say, some say from France;
Within her veins leapt blood like wine —
She led her Roundhead lord a dance!

'In Grantham church they lie asleep;
Just where, the verger may not know.
Strange that two hundred years should keep
The old ancestral fires aglow!

'In me these two have met again;
To each my nature owes a part:
To one, the cool and reasoning brain;
To one, the quick, unreasoning heart.'

The subject of heredity has been brought to our attention in an extremely interesting way by Lytton Strachey's faithful and brilliant book on Queen Victoria. It will be interesting to look into the matter with the help of the pedigree of Queen Victoria. She was about a year younger than my father, and a little more than twelve years older than my mother. She was Royal born, according to convention; they were peasant born. Let us see which had the better chance in life.

Queen Victoria's father was the Duke of Kent, the fourth of the seven sons of King George III. King George III was a fool most of his life, a lunatic by spells. The final spell continued for eight years and till his death. Strachey tells us that all those seven brothers were nasty old men, unreportably filthy, immoral, sunk in debt incurred through gambling, useful to nobody, nuisances to everybody. The Duke of Wellington has a word on the subject. It is well known that the Duke would swear on occasion, but he seldom swore except to good purpose. He called

the father of Queen Victoria the 'Corporal.' When there
was an attempt to get, through Parliament, some money
for the Duke of Kent and the Duke of Clarence in their
matrimonial enterprises, the Government was defeated in
the House of Commons. At this the Duke of Wellington
was not surprised. 'By God!' he said, 'there is a great
deal to be said about that. They are the damnedest mill-
stones about the neck of any Government that can be
imagined. They have insulted — personally insulted —
two-thirds of the gentlemen of England, and how can it be
wondered at that they take their revenge upon them in
the House of Commons? It is their only opportunity, and
I think, by God! they are quite right to use it.'

Here is a glimpse into the heredity of Queen Victoria on
her father's side; but there is more and worse to be said.
When for political reasons he was told that he must marry,
he said it was going to be the great sacrifice of his life and
that he ought to be paid for it, that he ought to get at least
twenty-five thousand pounds a year. That is, he was
mated with the woman who became his wife exactly as one
animal is mated with another animal.

The mother of Queen Victoria was better than the father.
She was a substantial German princess; not intellectual,
but with a faculty for contentment; and I believe she was
fat. There was nothing striking about her in any way.
She could not have loved the Duke of Kent; there was
nothing in him to love; she married him for ambition and
for nothing else. Again, she mated herself with that man
exactly as one animal is mated with another. There is the
specific heredity of Queen Victoria. What an illustrious
person she must have been, with that horrible handicap,

to achieve what she achieved and to conduct herself as she conducted herself throughout life! Royal blood, aristocracy! Such expressions are biological blasphemy. If Queen Victoria had only been blessed with such a father and mother as I had, how much happier, and how much greater she would have been!

One reason why I have dwelt on this subject at such length is that I have in truth been depicting the origins of the people of New England. My antecedents are the antecedents of most New England men. They may be rich to-day, wear fine clothes, and occupy fine houses. Go back two or three generations and you will find their ancestors in exactly the conditions that I have described. Take, for example, the most famous family in New England, the Adams family; they all came from John Adams, the Quincy farmer, who was the fourth in descent from Henry, a Devonshire farmer. From him came the characteristics in John Adams, President, and John Quincy Adams, President, Charles Francis Adams, Minister to England, and in the Charles Francis Adams that I knew; in Henry Adams and Brooks Adams; they all go back to the Quincy farmer; there is the biological fountain of worth. And this is precisely the case generally in our New England life. One, in getting back to those origins, is impressed with the incomparable dignity of the men and women; there the women were ladies, the men were gentlemen, in the best sense. Self-respect and sympathy, these are the marks of the lady and of the gentleman. Self-respect and sympathy were nearly universal in old New England; they were widespread in Scotland.

Let us conclude with a word from Kipling:

'Truly ye come of The Blood; slower to bless than to ban;
Little used to lie down at the bidding of any man.
Flesh of the flesh that I bred, bone of the bone that I bare;
Stark as your sons shall be — stern as your fathers were.
Deeper than speech our love, stronger than life our tether,
But we do not fall on the neck nor kiss when we come together.

  .   .   .   .

'Look, I have made ye a place and opened wide the doors,
That ye may talk together, your Barons and Councillors —
Wards of the Outer March, Lords of the Lower Seas,
Ay, talk to your grey mother that bore you on her knees!—
That ye may talk together, brother to brother's face —
Thus for the good of your peoples — thus for the Pride of the Race.

'Also, we will make promise. So long as The Blood endures
I shall know that your good is mine; ye shall feel that my strength is
    yours:
In the day of Armageddon, at the last great fight of all,
That Our House stand together and the pillars do not fall.
Draw now the threefold knot firm on the ninefold bands,
And the Law that ye make shall be law after the rule of your lands.

'This for the waxen Heath, and that for the Wattle-bloom,
This for the Maple-leaf, and that for the southern Broom.
The Law that ye make shall be law and I do not press my will,
Because ye are Sons of The Blood and call me Mother still.
Now must ye speak to your kinsmen and they must speak to you,
After the use of the English, in straight-flung words and few.
Go to your work and be strong, halting not in your ways,
Baulking the end half-won for an instant dole of praise.
Stand to your work and be wise — certain of sword and pen,
Who are neither children nor God, but men in a world of men!'

One great fault I found in my ancestors, looking at them from the point of view of my boyhood, they were all of them too fond of work and too religious. Work was for them the romance of existence and religion was a continuous and passionate joy. At that period of my life Kingsley's question and answer were counsels of perfection: Your favorite occupation? Doing nothing. To what sins are you most lenient? To all except lying. I am sorry to have lost so much of my original fondness for doing nothing, but thankful that I have kept all my scorn for liars, and made additions to it with the years.

CHAPTER III

MEMORIES OF MY FOURTH SUMMER

THE scene of the memories I am to describe was the early home of my mother, to which she and I were on a visit, my grandfather and grandmother being still alive, and living on this same farm. Kincail was the name of the farm, situated on the banks of the Don, about two miles from the picturesque and important borough of Inverurie, and comprising many acres of richly productive land. My grandfather was grieve or overseer of this and an adjoining farm, the tenant of both farms being a Mr. Partridge; the landlord was the Earl of Kintore, whose ancient and stately mansion of one hundred rooms was a place of splendor to a small boy whose days had been spent in a very humble cottage.

The time of the visit was summer, as it mellowed toward harvest, probably August and September of the year 1856. It must have been a glorious summer because it lives in my memory mainly as a series of splendid days, touched indeed everywhere with the sense of mystery and pain, disturbed with awakening thought, startled in the presence of unexpected things, amazed by the confusions that so often clouded the shining sun. A few wet days I remember, the misery of having nothing to do and no one to play with, and the impatience of my ever-venerated grandmother with my complaints. On one of these wet days — Scottish wet, be it noted, which means something like a flood — I broke out of doors, found my way to the 'Old House,' where an uncle had his study, who was making his final preparations to go to India as a Wesleyan missionary. As I had just begun to read, the missionary's books appalled me; the labor and the pain that they represented made me sick at heart. I pitied profoundly any son of Adam whose fate it was, out of the sunshine, and away from the beauty of God's world, to dig there, as among dead men's bones. This benign uncle received me kindly, spoke words of primitive religion to my poor little soul, in a manner truly winning, although without avail; I at that time having no fondness for suffering with the people of God, and being extremely eager to enjoy the pleasures of the sinful world for a season. When this benign uncle told me that he was going to preach to the heathen who dwelt on the other side of the globe, I was ready to weep to think that so good a man should be wasted on the heathen. The forlorn, old thatched cottage where he studied, the mud floor of the room in which he lived, the small window through which so little of the glorious sunshine could win its way, the peat fire, the piles of ashes and the 'reek' or smoke, I recall with the vividness of yesterday. It seemed to me the picture of gloom, the image of misery, the naked form of tragedy; and yet the young preacher, with his benign manner and radiant face, as of one who had seen God, and who knew that his life was set in the everlasting, victorious order, brought to the scene a higher meaning, and as I can now see, set in relief in my poor heart, the kindness of humanity as against the cruelty of Nature, and man's lot as a child of Nature.

Well do I recall the day when this uncle left for his mission in India. The morning was bright, but the clouds were heavy on my mother's face, still heavier on the face of the dear old grandmother. The morning wore on to noon, the midday meal was eaten in silence. The missionary's father bade his son good-bye, as one who long ago had made his peace with fate, who, having given up hope for this world, had nothing to fear. This old Spartan in modern uniform shook his son's hand, spoke his blessing as a face of flint might speak, then looked his farewell in calm, stony silence. Not so the sister and the mother. They convoyed the young preacher about a half-mile, while I ran close behind watching the tragedy. The parting came, and it seemed the end of the world. Dignity there was everywhere, the restraining sense of the errand for God on which the young preacher was going, but inside that circle of high demeanor such silent tears and woe as I have witnessed again only once or twice in my life. The walk back to the half-empty house was broken by repeated turnings and hand-wavings; at length each vanished from the other, and the rough world of work came, cancelling sorrow in the imperative mood of the present. There was no time to weep; there was time only for work; the sore heart thus grew calm and confided its unutterable secret to the Infinite Compassion.

Personally I regarded this sorrowful business as an unfortunate interruption to my happiness. One immense advantage came with it, however; I was left as never before to my own devices. I had found the most precious things in this world, freedom, and clear individuality in freedom. In this new Paradise a few mishaps overtook me which I cannot forget. The mill on the farm was run by water from a dam in the dark woods near by; the big water-wheel was said to be the pride of farmers in the whole region. I conceived the idea of getting into this wheel, on the inside, expecting that when the water struck the wheel I should get a glorious merry-go-round. When the water struck the wheel I started the sound of woe; I was rescued by my grandfather with considerable difficulty, and with a litany of indignation that became a lasting warning. My mother, too, added her blessing in the way usual then, in such circumstances, and not, I believe, even now altogether unusual.

Another feat was to fall into a ditch from which I was fished in infinite disgrace; and, owing to the limited extent of my wardrobe, there was nothing to do but to take a bath and go to bed till the damaged clothing could be got ready for a fresh adventure in the kingdom of freedom and growing individuality.

About this time I saw my first funeral. I had seen death in the family, but knew not what it meant. A little sister, under two years of age, had died, and I had seen her in death as one asleep, and could not understand my dear mother's grief. The man who closed the lid of the coffin, screwed it down tight, and who carried away the little body for burial, I blamed as the cause of all our woe. Here, however, was a funeral on the road along which I had wandered, a Scottish funeral, with a hearse whose plumes were enough to darken the day, big and terrible with gloom, and walking behind were men, and men only, all dressed in black, and looking blacker than their dress. This pageant struck terror into me; I ran at full speed to the house, got in before the hearse entered the graveyard, which was at the back of my grandfather's house, made more dismal by the ruin of a chapel of the fourteenth century that stood on its edge; I hid till the calamity was overpast. Next morning I crawled into the graveyard to look at the new-made grave, sick at heart for

'The poor inhabitant below.'

Near by was the finest granite headstone in the graveyard. It told of the early death of the wife of the tenant, Mrs. Partridge, whose good deeds and sweet soul had made her one of the religious memories of the neighborhood.

In experiences such as I have described, I have always held, is to be found the source of the Scottish imagination, interwoven as it is with hope and melancholy, splendor and gloom. There is first of all in the Scottish people the deep sense of humanity, the presence of precious affections, the feeling that life has through love an infinite treasure. In the second place, there is the clear view that this human treasure is under constant menace, is in fact the child of hard and troubled days, and at last falls under the black empire of death. The cold sky, the wet weather, the sunless hours, the short sad days of winter, the gloom of the moors, and the blackness of the unfeeling hills form symbols of the Scottish imagination of singular fitness. The brightness of life often seems

'Like the rainbow's lovely form
Evanishing amid the storm.'

The loyal, loving friend often seems, as in Carlyle's exquisite tribute to his wife: 'she was the rainbow to my poor dripping day.' Depth and tenderness of human feeling are surely Scottish traits; so, too, is the sense of the dark tragedy of man's life on this earth. This experience would

be insupportable were it not for another Scottish characteristic, unshakable faith in man's soul and in the Soul of
the universe.

I recall two experiences of that wonderful summer that
exhibit, in childish forms, the substance of which the Scottish imagination is made. A cousin came one morning,
from the village of Inverurie, to visit our grandmother.
She was six years old and I was three and a half. She was
tall for her age, and slight, overflowing with vivacity and
affection, and her lovely hair fell in ringlets to her shoulders. She appeared the prettiest and the most affectionate
creature I had ever seen, and her faculty seemed to me endless for devising ways and means of entertainment. We
fished in the brook, caught minnows, put them into a tin
pail, and spent the long hours in heavenly happiness. This
experience of sunbeams is vivid because of its absolute
singularity, a fortunate circumstance, and fortunate will it
be, for my young readers, if such experiences are rare in
their lives, till the time is ripe, and Destiny in the glory
of the new day truly arrives. Here was the world, rolling
forward in a morning without clouds, and earth looked as
fair as Eden when as yet there was no serpent and no break
between the soul of man and the Soul of the universe. How
could one repress the desire to live in a world of such elevation and charm?

I have said that behind my grandfather's house there
was the country graveyard. From the window of the room
occupied by my mother and me, she could point to the
grave of her youngest brother who died at the age of five
years; to another grave, that of her oldest sister, who left
behind her a motherless infant, a cousin whom I loved and

pitied. Here was the other picture, the rain and tempest in which the day went to wreck, the abysses of bereavement and desolation into which the fair worlds of home and love and kindred were finally plunged. How often I sat at that lonely, sad little window, watching the long, wild grass waving wearily over those dear graves, and always the dark mystery of it all would cloud my poor heart. Had it not been for the certain sense of heaven, the divine capacity for laughter as well as tears, the hope that I might, for a while, at least, continue to evade my doom, and enjoy things, I should have been melancholy indeed. The elasticity of childhood, its susceptibility to variety of emotions, and the transfusion of all the sad and bright in feeling, by the prevailing instinct of life, and later by the magic of imagination, are the wonderful appointed ways of escape from premature seriousness. Here again is the world in which especially the Scottish imagination is born; it rises up in dark hues and bright; it is clothed with radiant tenderness and dull leaden grief; religious faith works upon this compound that the darkness may pass, and the light alone remain. The victory, however, is seldom complete; the star of hope twinkles and trembles in the wild and infinite night.

I now ask my young readers to endeavor to recall their first impressions of Nature. To me, as it appeared in my fourth summer, it was a wonder, a splendor and a terror. I was puzzled by the horizon line; I could not be convinced that I could not touch the sky where it rested on the earth, were I only there. The same puzzle confronted me about the mountains. The sunset clouds, all purple and gold, overhung the summits of the hills, and I was sure that if I then could have stood on the hilltop, I might have thrust my hand into the blaze of glory. No amount of instruction or ridicule could move me from these convictions. I have often reflected since of the sway of erroneous notions and pure superstitions, when firmly fixed in the mind; in all spheres of intellectual interest great is the obstructive force of ignorance; it has the might but not the fruits of genius.

The mountains and hills themselves were to my childish mind anything but attractive. They were somber, solitary, unsympathetic, with no capacity in them for friendship, remote, stern even in the sunshine, centers of dismal gloom, the first to invade the perfection of the day, the last to consent to its restoration; barren, unlovely, save for a few weeks in autumn when the heather was in bloom, symbols of want, obstruction, and woe. My later joy in mountain scenery stands in utter contradiction to my earliest feelings.

Another aspect of Nature that impressed me greatly was the cruel might of the wind. It kept me indoors; it blew the sea into terror and sent hundreds of poor sailors to their doom. It tore through the forests, uprooting the finest trees; where it was incapable of killing or maiming the trees, it gave them no peace. The leaves and the boughs were tossed ceaselessly all day long as by an invisible fury. So, too, the poor helpless grass, and the fields of hay and oats. They were all tormented by the same cruel foe. The sight of them writhing in helpless agony filled me with pity, filled me, too, with the feeling of the wild pitilessness of the boundless world.

The wild flowers did not greatly appeal to me, the glorious yellow flower of the broom and the whin, because associated, the first, with toil gathering the ripe broom for kindling, the second, with lacerated bare feet. The field daisy was sweet, but I was told that it indicated polluted or even poor soil, and not till much later when I read Burns's poem, 'To a Daisy,' did I begin to love that flower. The primrose I did dearly love looking up so pure and wan in countenance, in the lonely woodland. The honeysuckle flower I hated, and I have never been able to get over the early offensiveness of its rank odor, the nearest to that of a muskrat or a polecat that I know among flowers. Lilies and roses were seldom seen; they belonged to the rich; so, too, the flora in the gardens of the great. But in my grandfather's garden there were the cultivated daisies, crimson and white, the boxwood and other modest beauties; and, more interesting, the gooseberry, blackberry, raspberry, and red currant bushes, and the fine apple tree, standing against the southern wall of the house, with its arms spread out and nailed to the mortar.

The things in Nature that I loved most were the trees, streams, and sunshine. The rowan tree or mountain ash was wonderfully beautiful; it was large, abundant in foliage, crowded with great clusters of red berries. How many happy hours that summer I spent with my mother among the rowan trees! How I admired the beauty of these trees, and how deep was my disappointment at the bitter taste of the lovely berry; part of the disenchantment of life, the beautiful appearance concealing the cruel acids of reality! The river near my grandfather's house was a fearful enchantment. It was fearful because it had drowned many men and boys; it was an enchantment because it carried in its murmur the voices of all my dead kindred for nearly a thousand years. The sunshine was a glorious birth, a never-ending delight; so it has remained. 'Truly the light is sweet, and a pleasant thing it is for the eyes to behold the sun.' 'Thou makest the outgoings of the morning and the evening to rejoice' — and man's little day falls between splendor and splendor.

Of living things in Nature I recall few perceptions belonging to this period. There were, of course, the domestic animals, sheep, oxen, horses; these existed for use and took little hold upon imagination. I recall making acquaintance with the skylark, and the mavis, an afternoon, and not a morning singer, as in the popular song:

> 'I have heard the mavis singing
> His love song to the morn.'

The mavis eats in the morning and sings after his noon dinner and nap. Best of all I recall a mighty Newfoundland dog with whom companionship was a delight. He had infinite frolic in him, patience, affection, although his love-making often knocked me down. 'Gardie,' for that was his name, has a permanent place in a grateful and dear memory. It seems cruel to think that so much intelligence, affection, mirth, frolic, and serious worth should be lost to the universe. Perhaps 'Gardie' still lives somewhere. If so, may I meet again his massive and tender soul.

So far my memories imply no specially human perception, no hint at moral education, no sign of any religious instinct. There was my mother's great nature, the best thing I then knew, and one of the few supremely good things I have met in life. I was truly sorry to be compelled to believe that the depth of my mother's heart was no safe guide to the heart of God. There was my grandfather's stern honor; of that, and the judgment of that, I had an

awe that was completely reasonable, all things considered.
I recall him at worship always just before bedtime. He
read from the Bible, an awful Book, utterly unintelligible
except to ministers and wise men. There were the impressive prayers of the grand old farmer; my chief admiration,
however, was over the mysterious fact that the worshiper
knew what to say to the Almighty; I knew not then that
the full heart craves such free, abundant utterance. There
was the dear old grandmother, infinitely loving and for-
giving, and at the same time finding fault with everything
and every one, the Lord included. Endless affection went
to her and utter indifference to the mere surface fret and
worry of her existence. All these influences were good, and
did me good, I suppose, but as they were taken for granted,
belonged to me by right, as it were, they did not create an
epoch in my plastic little soul as was done by the hero of
that glorious summer.

Sandy Barnet was his name. He had been a soldier, had
served with his regiment through the Crimean War, and he
had been honorably discharged after the war, and was
now one of my grandfather's servants. He it was who
showed me one of the most awe-inspiring objects of my life,
the trunk or box of a certain sergeant who had been killed
at the battle of Balaclava. His name was printed on the
box; his feathered hat and his tunic and other sacred relics
had been sent home, as the only outward comfort to his
sorrowing parents. Awe-ful and woe-ful was this relic,
speaking of man's inhumanity to man; many a time my
heart was filled with tears as I looked at this box that had
gone all the way to the Crimea with its brave owner, and
that had come home, with infinite melancholy, alone.

Sandy Barnet stands as the finest and most fascinating man in the whole field of my childhood. His courage, his achievements, his vast experience overcame me with admiration; his silence about the war and his part in it, except now and then a word, and his modesty, were mysteriously great to a wondering child. These were not, however, the qualities in him that won my limitless and grateful devotion. That glorious quality was his perfect kindness to a restless, inquiring, and bothersome child. During 'the leading' — the bringing of the sheaves of oats from the field to the stack-yard — against the stern admonition of my grandfather and the rest, I was out every morning at seven o'clock, hunting for Sandy Barnet. I watched him till his load was unloaded, waylaid him on the way to the field, was lifted kindly into the cart, lifted into the field while the cart was loaded, and lifted again on top of the cart, there to hang on till we made the stack-yard; and just before entering, the horse was stopped and I was lifted down to earth. This process continued day after day till dark, Sandy sharing his meals with me, so that I should not be trapped at home at meal-time. One day I confided to Sandy my fears of my grandfather; I was told to scramble into the cart before the horse was hitched to it; to lie down, and all would be well. Sandy and I kept our compact so well that we were never caught, and I had the uttermost kindness from this old soldier, and the uttermost joy of my whole early life. One night I got home at ten o'clock; my grandfather was reading the Bible; I was three years and eight months old, and I received the most solemn warning that if this deed of darkness were repeated I should never again see the light of the sun. I trembled at the terrible warning, but in my heart I vowed that, even if I had to die for it, nothing should part me from the glorious companionship of Sandy Barnet. The next morning a more skillful raid was made by me, and, with new caution, I was completely successful. I had my delight, and got home, without the execution of the sentence of doom.

Kindness is the *summum bonum* for the childhood of the world; it is for children, at least, the excellence that sets life and the universe in eternal radiance. Nothing better, deeper, more enduring than companionship with the rich and tender heart of this old soldier did I meet in that early world; nothing so influential over feeling, purpose, and hope. I believe that the example of this man of high courage, inexhaustible patience, boundless sympathy, this friend of the heart of a child, has been of immeasurable influence over my whole life. He was kind to everybody and every living thing, to flocks and herds, to his fellow-servants, to his master; he was especially polite to women, all in the quietest, finest way; and to me he was and still is a king.

Sandy Barnet fell heir to an estate, enjoyed it two or three years, lost it through further litigation, returned to humble life, died quietly and bravely, was buried with all honor, and rests, 'after life's fitful fever,' in a soldier's grave. A hundred times since, I have passed the farm where he toiled, looked at the fields where we had our delight, listened to the sigh of the noble river still flowing by, now as then, and never could I resist the feeling that the soft, sweet music of its current was a perpetual requiem for the repose of the soul of my dear, illustrious friend. Kindness he lifted before me as the greatest of all human excellences; as I grew older and came to wonder as to what might be the ultimate character of this wild, mysterious universe in which we live, Sandy Barnet's compassion seemed an index finger pointing the way to the supreme thing in Jesus, the Ideal Man, indicating the path to the sovereign attribute in the being of the Eternal.

CHAPTER IV
THE INFLUENCE OF NATURE

THE influence of Nature is coeval with our existence; it is something deep, mystic, unfathomable, and absolutely past finding out in the totality of its power. In the first place, Nature is an unconscious admixture with our being; in the second place, by reflection, by thought, it becomes a conscious, continuous, ineffable admixture with our existence. Byron's familiar lines are an excellent example of what was first in his instincts, and second in his thought:

'There is a pleasure in the pathless woods,
There is a rapture on the lonely shore,
There is society where none intrudes,
By the deep Sea, and music in its roar,
I love not man the less, but Nature more,
From these our interviews, in which I steal
From all I may be, or have been before,
To mingle with the Universe, and feel
What I can ne'er express, yet cannot all conceal.'

I wish it to be understood that it is my conviction that the influence of Nature upon the human mind defies all exhaustive analysis; it seems to be hopelessly impossible to trace it in its entirety. We drew our first breath in communion, in ineffable communion, with Nature, and we draw our last breath in the same mystic fellowship.

Nature as an educational influence has affected me mainly in three ways.

First, there is Nature in herself. Nature is something in

herself; exactly what she is in herself, it is perhaps impossible to say. We know Nature only in her association with our minds, in fellowship with humanity. How, then, can we know what she is abstracted from humanity? Yet we all are sure by instinct, plain people and philosophers alike, that Nature is; that she was here before we arrived, that she will be here after we are gone, and that she has a character of her own. This is the assumption on which we do business, pursue scientific investigations, think sanely. Nature appears in our life as an economic wonder, an æsthetic wonder, a scientific wonder, a philosophic wonder, as a whole with meaning, and as a religious wonder, as referring back to a primeval, aboriginal source.

Passing all that over, I should like to say that Nature in herself — if I may use the expression — affects different persons in different ways. Although this aspect of Nature has been touched upon in the last chapter, a somewhat more extended notice of it may not be amiss here. Nature filled me as a child with pity and fear. There was the river flowing through the valley near where I was born; it was to me an object of mournful sympathy; it ran on and on and on, never had a holiday, had no companions, nobody to play with; it was forever running, restless, weary, and it never came back. It really was a painful thing for me to look upon. There were the trees — it is almost always windy in Scotland; if it is not windy, it is raining, and sometimes it is both, as in the fine song:

> 'But sic' a day o' wind and rain,
> Oh, wae's me for Prince Charlie!'

The trees would be blown about with such savage power, tossed upwards, tossed downwards, bent over, boughs broken, sometimes uprooted. What a life; struggle and pain! I pitied the poor trees. Then there was the innocent grass, so lovely, so velvety; yet those tiny spears were all bent over by the same cruel power. And the field daisies, trying to lift their unassuming heads, shared the same fate. There was the sea, about eight miles away, eternally groaning as if it were sick, sending forth the most mournful sound, as if doom were coming. And the mountains; they were the loneliest, dreariest things that one could look upon; they had to leave the earth in order to be, and then they were so far apart that they could not have any companions, the valleys were between them; and when they got up where they were, how far they were from everything above them! Last of all there were the stars, bright and beautiful, but I soon learned that they were immeasurable distances apart, lonely, God-forsaken lamps blinking about in infinite space.

My first feeling toward Nature, therefore — that is, Nature in herself — was one of pity; and when night came on, it was an inexpressible comfort to get into the house and see father and mother, brothers and sisters, and in talk, fun, and frolic forget this awful ghost of a thing outside.

This feeling, I can now see, was a revolt from Nature to humanity; and what lay in the instinct of the child has been one of the principal doctrines that I have preached during my ministry. One revolts from mere vastness, one must return to humanity. The God that Nature gives us is not the God that we need. The Christian religion is God through man, God through the best human beings, God through the ideal man; there is Christianity. The instinct of the child revolting from bare, stark, unfeeling, unloving Nature, and returning to humanity, aflame with intelligence and love, was in reality opening life to the Christian religion.

The first comet that I saw was in the winter of 1862. It seemed to me to be a portent, and my father's jaunty way of chatting about it did not at all ease my feelings. It was approaching the earth, so I was told, at an incalculable speed, and as it had apparently broken loose from all restraint, it seemed to me that our world was under certain doom. As there was nothing visible to stop this celestial vagrant, or head it off, we thought of praying about it. This resolve was blasted by a remark of our mother, that the prayers of the wicked were an offense to God, that they would probably make things worse for us, and that it would be better for us to mind our business and trust God to mind his. Austere, perhaps, a bit unsympathetic, but not bad advice for imaginative and wildly vigorous boys. Too many sweets are bad for children, physically and metaphysically; let them face the specters of the mind and lay them.

The second influential aspect of Nature is the superstitious aspect; Nature as the abode of ghosts, witches, demons, the big Devil himself — more enlightened human beings must not judge the rest of the world by their superiority. Nature has been from time immemorial identified with these unearthly and supernatural beings, and the point that I am to make here is that a great part of education is in the triumph over superstition thrown into one's face by Nature; that was my experience. The things that I am about to relate I never did believe; I fought them;

suffered from them — was scared almost to death by them; yet I finally as a boy obtained victory over them.

An adversary would seem to be necessary in order that any young man should get a good education. If one has never had an adversary, one has not gained the intellectual muscle that one should have gained. The Devil has played a great rôle in the advance of civilized man; old Martin Luther and his inkstand are a precious symbol of the adversary that all men meet, and the adversary put to flight.

When we boys came home at about ten o'clock at night from a visit to the village where we had had a jolly time, as we were passing a barn we would stop and listen, and each would say to the others, 'Do you hear the flails going?' The flails were the instruments by which the grain was threshed in the generation ahead of mine and a long way back into time. The idea was that if on the farm there had been a murder or some cruel misdeed fifty, a hundred, two hundred, or five hundred years ago, at night when everything was still one could hear the flails plying in the barn. We never stopped to listen that we did not hear the flails. In company with others, or alone, I have listened and tried to imagine that I did not hear them, but they were always there; and there were always two at it; there was the rhythm, flip flop, flip flop, right through the dark and terrible night. Here was the world of darkness, of principalities and powers, demonstrating its ghastly reality. Two or three of us would go together and open the barn door, and then the noise would cease; but when we closed the door, we could hear flails going again. That superstition was a weird antagonist and teacher.

Another belief was that if on one's way home in the dark

one should meet a funeral procession, it meant a death in the family or among friends in the neighborhood. I never met one of those funeral processions, but I was told that they existed, and I must declare that I was always on the lookout for one of them. There was the Scottish hearse — if one ever saw a Scottish hearse, one knows what it means — black and big and with the most awful plumes; then there were the black horses, also plumed; but there was no noise; horses and hearse moving, but no noise; and the procession behind, of men all dressed in black broadcloth, all with silk hats, the whole line sometimes a quarter of a mile in length, moving, but making no noise. Fancy meeting that on your way home, in a sequestered place, with woods on both sides! There is a rousing experience, a hair-raising possibility.

There were the graveyard experiences. From Plato downwards, there is the belief that unhappy spirits come back and sit on the tombs where their bodies repose; that is, I suppose, an immemorial superstition and a very real one. There was current in my boyhood the story of the minister's wife who had died and was buried too soon. The gravedigger noticed that on her finger was a gold ring, and he resolved to come unseen and take it. He came that very night, dug open the grave, unsealed the casket, but could not get the ring off the finger. He was not to be beaten; he took his penknife and began to cut off the finger, in order to get the ring. The dead woman, who was only in a swoon, gave a cry of pain, sat up in her white graveclothes — Scottish people always clothed their dead in white — the horrified gravedigger fled and the woman went home, was recognized by her husband, and lived with him for twenty years afterwards. We boys read the inscription on her tombstone, or thought we did, 'Twice dead and twice buried,' and then passed it in the pitch dark, fearing that she might rise again.

My oldest brother, four years my senior, who grew up to be a courageous, useful, and honored man — he is no longer living — was easily frightened when he was about twelve years old and living on a farm about a half-mile away from our home, and used to get me, when he had made an evening call, to go with him to the top of the hill and shout to him till he got out of the valley on to the road, and the last cry from him would be, 'I'm all right now!' How about my condition? I had to work my way back to the house, not over two hundred yards, but in pitch dark; in the house there was only a wick-lamp, which did not shed a great deal of light; it was in the front of the house and I was at the back. Again and again in going back I felt almost every second something taking hold of me. To fight, to conquer what I inwardly knew was simply a superstition, stimulated intelligence, judgment, rational power, until finally the whole base thing was trodden underfoot. I regard that as a great step taken in education, the conquering of a superstition that had been imposed upon the mind by a false view of Nature and of Nature peopled with ghastly products of imagination.

Burns's most striking poem, 'Tam O'Shanter,' is true to the popular belief of his time, and with certain modifications the poem was a faithful version of popular belief in my boyhood. Tam's ride is a symbolic ride:

'By this time he was cross the ford,
Where in the snaw the chapman smoor'd;

> And past the birks and meikle stane,
> Where drunken Charlie brak's neck-bane;
> And thro' the whins, and by the cairn,
> Where hunters fand the murder'd bairn;
> And near the thorn, aboon the well,
> Where Mungo's mither hang'd hersel.'

At all these places terrible sights were likely, and fearful to flesh and blood was the endeavor, in the black night, to dash past them. Yet these were nothing to the grewsome horrors that met Tam's sight, in the old Kirk-Alloway:

> Coffins stood round, like open presses,
> That shaw'd the dead in their last dresses:
> And by some devilish cantraip sleight
> Each in its cauld hand held a light,
> By which heroic Tam was able
> To note upon the haly table
> A murderer's banes in gibbet-airns;
> Twa span-lang, wee, unchristen'd bairns;
> A thief new-cutted frae the rape —
> Wi' his last gasp his gab did gape;
> Five tomahawks, wi' blude red rusted;
> Five scymitars, wi' murder crusted;
> A garter, which a babe had strangled;
> A knife, a father's throat had mangled,
> Whom his ain son o' life bereft —
> The gray hairs yet stack to the heft;
> Wi' mair of horrible and awfu',
> Which even to name wad be unlawfu'.'

Let me remind my reader that superstition dies in one form to come to life in another. It is a man's duty to separate the wheat from the chaff, to resist superstition in politics, in science, in medicine, in religion; superstition is to-day what it has always been, an insult to God and man. I had my lessons in the ghosts and witches of my youth;

you, my reader, have yours in the ghosts and witches of to-day. Face them like a man; and while people say that this is true, and that is true, and the other is true, try the spirits for yourself and see whether they are real or products of a wild imagination.

Nature is greatest as an educator when she is invested with humanity. This aspect of Nature has had very great influence over my mind. I began to love Nature as the home of lovely people, of kinsmen and kinswomen whose souls looked out with sympathy and pity upon my little struggling life; their homes rose up into loveliness. There is Portree in the Isle of Skye, where an unconquerable and wonderful little great-grandmother was born, who, at the age of sixty, crossed the ocean with her sons, in a sailing vessel taking three months for the trip, toiled with them in South Carolina for twenty years, returned to Scotland and lived like a princess for ten years or more before she died. There is the valley in which my ancestors cultivated the soil for hundreds of years, in which they gained character, displayed industry, won independence, faith in God, great human quality, and where Nature became beautiful to them and to me. Mountains, rivers, plains, the seas, the whole Scottish peninsula, became to me a symbol of a great race of men and women who loved, toiled, suffered, believed in God, died, and left behind them a mantle of humanity thrown over the whole. Burns sings in one of his finest songs,

'I see her in the dewy flowers —
    I see her sweet and fair.
I hear her in the tunefu' birds —
    I hear her charm the air.

> There's not a bonnie flower that springs
> By fountain, shaw, or green,
> There's not a bonnie bird that sings,
> But minds me o' my Jean.'

Universalize that sentiment, and Nature stands forever invested with humanity. Carlyle is typical as he goes to Haddington, an old man, and desolate, that he may look at the window at which he first saw the face of Jane Welsh Carlyle; deep-hearted old men know many such homes where they that looked out of the windows be darkened.

This I take to be the wonder of Egypt; it is a land hallowed by an immemorial humanity. One visits Greece and what does one find?

> 'The isles of Greece! The isles of Greece!
> Where burning Sappho loved and sung,
> Where grew the arts of war and peace,
> Where Delos rose, and Phoebus sprung!
> Eternal summer gilds them yet,
> But all, except their sun, is set.'

There is Palestine, and its everlasting charm. The mountains of Moab in the east, the great sea on the west, the desert in the south, Lebanon in the north, the plain of Sharon, the plain of Esdraelon, the mountains round about Jerusalem, the fields of Galilee with their wild flowers, are touched with majesty, and are in everlasting glory because the mightiest religious race in history lived there, and because He was there who is the crown of our humanity.

Horace Bushnell, in a remarkable sermon on 'The Dissolving of Doubts,' preached to Yale students, says: 'There is a story lodged in a little bedroom of one of these dormitories, which I pray God, his recording Angel may note, allowing it never to be lost.' Many centuries before Bushnell, there lived one of whom we read that he dismissed his company and tarried at a certain place all night, and there wrestled a man with him, and when he had won his new name and his great moral victory, he called the name of that place Peniel, for, he said, 'I have seen God face to face, and my life is preserved.'

The traveler in Palestine as he looks eastward sees there a mountain forever associated with the greatest of all the Hebrews; he looks at the mountain and he thinks of Israel's deliverer and lawgiver. In a single example there is Nature invested with humanity. And this world of ours wears the garment of God through that investiture; humanity comes to us with every sunrise and every sunset, out of every star visible in the heavens, in every blade of grass that comes up out of the earth in the spring, and in the beauty of summer; all the great eyes that have ever looked upon the world have shed their truth, their tenderness, their beauty, and their humanity into Nature for all succeeding generations of thoughtful men.

This great and dear land, the United States of America, land of Hope and Glory, is under the mightiest of all invasions. Pilgrim and Puritan have made a beginning; colonial character and achievement continued the noble tradition; the war of the Revolution and the winning of Independence sent a fresh wave of glory over the face of Nature; the establishment of the Government, the adoption of the Constitution, its interpretation and defense, added new ideas and sentiments to the Nation; the Civil War, its tragedy and its issue in freedom for all Americans, reflected in the countenance of our country a new and more moving beauty; the ever-increasing development of the national resources, the wise hospitality of these shores to all worthy human beings are swelling to a flood the original invasion. Think what this continental land will mean when genius in art, in science, in letters, in wisdom of the highest kind, and character of the noblest sort, expressed in every relation of life, in all business and in all public service, shall have shed for a thousand years their glory and pathos over river and lake, over mountain and plain, and when the stars in their brightest array appear as the myriad eyes of American lovers and heroes! Americans of that far-off time will not be slow in counting among the greatest educational forces the face of Nature transfigured by the humanity of man.

CHAPTER V

FIRST LESSONS IN METAPHYSICS AND LOGIC

THE great science of metaphysics, the science of ultimate reality in our human world and in the universe, a Scot has perversely described or defined as follows: 'When the perty that listens doesna ken what the perty that's speakin' means, and when the perty that's speakin' doesna ken himsel' what he means, that is metaphysics.' Humor is always particularly amusing when it is a travesty upon the truth.

In the same way, logic is perversely misrepresented as the art by which one gains an advantage, wins a victory, over his adversary, whether the truth is on his side or not; if the truth is on the adversary's side, and he wins a victory over him, by so much is he the better logician. This is pure perversity; logic is not the art by which one man gains advantage over another by some trick, some device; it is the process by which we discover, whether by induction or deduction, the sacred and beautiful face of truth.

This disreputable definition of logic accords with the practice that sometimes obtained in Athenian courts of law four hundred years before Christ. Here is a case brought into court; a teacher wants to compel a pupil to pay the fee he promised to pay. The pupil says, 'Teacher, what did you teach me?' 'The art of persuading any one you please.' The pupil answers, 'Then I persuade you to remit your fee; if you do not, you have not taught me the art of persuasion, and in that case I owe you no fee; if I succeed, of course you will remit the fee, because I have persuaded you.' The teacher replies, 'If you persuade me to remit the fee, I have taught you the art, and you pay your fee; if you fail, you still owe me the fee.' And what did the Court say to this? Let me quote the Greek, and then I will translate: 'κακοῦ κόρακος κακὸν ᾠόν.' The whole process is the bad egg of a bad crow; the sick egg of a sick crow. Four hundred years before Christ the modern perversity was in full swing, and even then, it was probably a recent version of a custom vastly more ancient.   I recall a maxim which prevailed in my own home, that on Sunday morning the boy who did not eat his porridge and milk could get no tea, and the boy who did eat his porridge and milk needed no tea. That was the same sort of sophistry; but it did not convince, it did not prevail.

My first introduction to metaphysics — to take up the science first named — was when I was seven years of age. I had been taught that God had neither beginning nor end; that He was an Eternal Being. I remember the sense of mystery that this statement brought to me, and my incapacity to deal with it. Everything that I knew had a beginning, everything that I knew had or would have an end. How approach this Being who had neither beginning nor end? How long I was occupied in the meditation of this subject I do not know; it seemed to me then, it seems to me now, a long time, but probably it was not more than a few hours. This is the way I proceeded — the process may interest those who teach children; it may recall to others some of their own early experiences on the same profound and ultimate mystery — I began to think away everything that I could; I thought out of existence the sun, moon, stars, seas, streams, hills, mountains, fields, all animal life that I knew, and the whole human race. I got down to a little piece of desert; everything was gone but that piece of desert, and that was vanishing. But there was a bush in the desert, a small bit of a bush that persisted, would not disappear, and I noticed a fire in it and eyes, terrible eyes looking out of the fire at me. Of course I had been reading the story of Moses and the Burning Bush; I could easily get rid of everything except that patch of desert and that bush with the fire and the terrible eyes in it, and I concluded that this was God, and it filled me not only with awe but terror. This will recall 'Alice in Wonderland' and the cat with a grin, and finally the remark that a cat without a grin had often been seen, but a grin without a cat — who ever saw that? Here was one last entity, one faint glimmer of reality left; that was the ultimate thing; that was God. Symbolic this must be called of the deeper and more serious side of the mind of our children.

The same season I had a dream which is as vivid to me to-day as when I had it sixty-three years ago. A great deal was said in those days about the Judgment; it was a momentous, a tremendous thought, that of the final Judgment, the wind-up of affairs in this world and the settlement of destiny to all eternity for every human being. I dreamed that the great Judgment Day had come, and that I found myself exactly where I had expected to be, on the wrong side, on the left hand, among the goats; and after waiting in awful suspense, my turn came; I was in a group, and we heard the terrible words, 'Depart, ye accursed.' I have often thought of the influence of that sentence upon a young mind. We went away — not weeping as a child would; the despair was absolute, the woe was altogether too deep for tears; we went on our way, and finally we came to hell, and I remember the trapdoor was opened and I was dropped in, and the surprise of my life was to find that it was all concreted inside, well ventilated, and a chair was waiting for me. I was vastly encouraged; it was all infinitely better than I had expected, and I recall exclaiming with a sigh of grateful relief, 'If this is hell, I can easily endure it to all eternity.' I think this early discovery of the groundless and infamous accusation against God went into the depths of my life.

Not long after this I had, as every boy has sooner or later, a bout with the doctrine of Predestination. Any one who knows Mrs. Stowe's beautiful book, 'The Minister's Wooing,' will have seen for himself the picture of the New England of that time and the indescribable suffering of sensitive human beings over the doctrine of Predestination. It does not trouble people to-day; I wish it did trouble them a little. Some one went to President Sparks, of Harvard College, and told him that in his town the people were greatly troubled over the 'Perseverance of the Saints,' whereupon President Sparks said, 'We have no such trouble in Harvard College; our trouble is over the perseverance of the sinners.'

I remember well putting this question to my earliest and best teacher, my pious, beautiful mother, 'If I should try all my life to be good, do you think that I should get into heaven?' 'No; not if Predestination is against you; many are called, but few are chosen.' I put the question again, 'If I should try with all my might, all my life, to do my duty in the love of God, do you think that I should get into heaven?' 'No; many are called, but few are chosen; unless you are elected, there is no hope.' 'Then,' I said, 'I am done with religion. I am not going to throw away both worlds. I am going to have a good time here and take what comes to me there.' Calvinism was the reigning religion, accepted as the final truth of things; God was not on the side of all; he elected some for heaven, and the rest he consigned to hell, all for his own glory. And for the next ten years of my life I was destitute of religion, and all on account of that metaphysical horror.

Burns is not a caricaturist, but a faithful expositor of Scottish belief, when he gives us Holy Willie's prayer:

> 'O Thou that in the heavens does dwell,
>   Wha, as it pleases best thysel',
> Sends ane to heaven and ten to hell,
>   A' for thy glory,
> And no for ony guid or ill
>   They've done before thee!'

We come now to the first lessons in logic. My earliest and best teacher had a vast store of songs and ballads with which she used to entertain her children. One especially, the ballad of Sir James the Rose, caught our fancy as boys. He was a warrior, a knight in spirit, and he was in love, and the lady with whom he had fallen in love was an ideal creature. She had another suitor, and when she chose Sir James the Rose, the other suitor, mean and utterly inferior, with his clansmen, plotted against the life of his successful rival, and at last treacherously killed him while he was defending himself against twenty men. The close of the ballad was heartrending to a boy. There was the dying hero, leaving his farewell for his betrothed, and she comes to him and, with frantic hand drawing his sword from his left side, cries, 'I come, Sir James the Rose, I come to follow you,' and the hilt of the sword she leaned against the ground and bared her snowy breast,

> 'And fell upon her lover's face,
> And sank to endless rest.'

My mother's eloquence had reduced me to tears. 'Mother, did she go to heaven?' I asked. No; no one who takes his own life can ever go to heaven.' 'Then the last two lines are a lie; they say, "she fell upon her lover's face and sank to endless rest." ' And the discomfited teacher turned her back and walked away in unbroken silence.

I had a brother three and a half years younger than I, very dear, but a great nuisance when I wanted to go off with older boys. It was a maxim in our household — an irrational maxim — that if a younger brother used bad words he must have learned them from his older brother; the younger brother was warned against the influence of the older brother, and the older brother was flogged. One afternoon our father was building a stack in the stack-yard. I had a 'call from the wild'; three or four boys of my own age wanted me to go off with them, and this younger brother wanted to go with us. He knew the rule. He said, 'If you run, I will call out "Devil." ' I ran, and he called, 'Devil, devil, devil!' Father shouted that, if we did not take care, he would come down and settle our dispute for us. Then this little fellow said, 'If you run again, I will call "Devil" louder.' I was chained, I was completely defeated by the logic of this young renegade.

Consider the logical reasoning here; look at the syllogism. When a small boy uses bad words, his older brother is blamed for teaching him to do so. This is the major premise. I am about to say bad words and my older brother will be blamed. Therefore, I shall be warned against his influence, but he will be flogged. It has always been amazing to me that a boy not unusually bright should actually have constructed a perfect syllogism; it was a wicked one, but the form of it was all right. Here is a possible insight for those who are teachers, an example of what goes on in the minds of children. They all are working on ultimate problems; they all are working on the sciences of metaphysics and logic.

Literary criticism used to abound in our family. There would be read at school some piece of poetry which would fascinate us and we would discuss it at home and call into distinction the line or stanza that seemed to us best. We condescendingly admitted our mother to the interview. Of course, we knew much more than she and had far better taste than she. That, I believe, is still the general feeling among young people. In the case in mind it was 'Lord Ullin's Daughter' that was the subject of debate. There were three or four different opinions. One said the opening lines were the best. '. . . I'll give thee a silver pound to row us o'er the ferry!' These surely were words of a generous and knightly fellow. Another said that the old boatman's words were better, 'Now, who be ye, would cross Lochgyle this dark and stormy water?' and another had a still different choice. And just for courtesy's sake, not expecting any contribution, we referred it to our mother, who gave her judgment with ease and finality, 'The lines that I think the best are these:

"One lovely hand she stretch'd for aid,
And one was round her lover."'

Our discomfiture was complete; not another word was spoken.

This is a glimpse into a Scottish home of sixty years ago; there should be noted in it the activity of mind, the reciprocity, and a noble mother's decisive influence as teacher in concerns of taste. We never went to our father with these difficulties; a few plain words would have settled the whole nonsensical process with him. A patient, brooding, sympathetic, prophetic mother, what an immense influence! I have never known a man or woman of exceptional consequence to be given to the world by a frivolous, flashy, good-for-nothing mother. I have known many a son and daughter of consequence with a poor stick for a father, but I have never in my life known an exceptional son or daughter as the issue of an unserious, superficial, worldly mother. It is a sovereign thing to be a good mother, to run one's mind into the life of children, and without any sort of consciousness on their part to guide, approve, disapprove, stimulate, and lead them on in the epoch of education, which is perhaps the most important, the first ten years of their existence in this world.

Ultimate reality is the quest of every serious mind, and this quest begins in childhood in all normal homes. Looking back over a long life of strenuous and continuous study, I can see that the metaphysical and logical impulses of boyhood were intimations of what followed. Technical metaphysics and logic are for experts, and for the professional side of the minister's life, solely for himself. But then disciplines may be employed, as Plato employed them, in a free and imaginative style, and in this way the work of the expert is related to the universal interests of thinking men and women. Technique is indispensable, but it should be supplemented by literature as the universal expression of the deepest intellectual interests of human beings. Nothing takes so vast a hold upon the serious mind as clear discussions upon ultimate reality when related by the imagination to feeling and to courses of human experiences. All thoughtful men and women are essentially metaphysicians and logicians; let this statement be tested by reading Washington Gladden's fine poem, entitled 'Ultima Veritas,' which follows.

'In the bitter waves of woe,
    Beaten and tossed about
By the sullen winds that blow
    From the desolate shores of doubt,

'While the anchors that faith had cast
    Are dragging in the gale,
I am quietly holding fast
    To the things that cannot fail.

'I know that right is right;
    That it is not good to lie;
That love is better than spite
    And a neighbor than a spy;

'I know that passion needs
    The leash of a sober mind;
I know that generous deeds
    Some sure reward will find;

'That the rulers must obey;
    That the givers shall increase;
That Duty lights the way
    For the beautiful feet of Peace; —

'In the darkest night of the year,
    When the stars have all gone out,

That courage is better than fear,
That faith is truer than doubt.

'And fierce though the fiends may fight,
And long though the angels hide,
I know that Truth and Right
Have the Universe on their side;

'And that somewhere beyond the stars
Is a Love that is better than Fate;
When the night unlocks her bars
I shall see Him, and I will wait.'

CHAPTER VI

THE SCOTTISH PUBLIC SCHOOLS SIXTY YEARS AGO

ABOUT three or four years after I left my native country, in 1871, for the United States of America, the public school system of Scotland underwent entire regeneration; not that it had been bad before, but a new impulse seized the leading men simultaneously to make it better, to regenerate the whole system. They recalled the dream of John Knox in the Reformation, that the church and the school should stand side by side in every city, every town, every village, every county, every parish, from Maidenkirk to John O' Groats. Grants from Parliament were so large that the teaching profession became the best-paid profession in Scotland; the salary was larger than that in the ministry, larger than the average doctor could command or the average lawyer. The very best men went into teaching, not as formerly, as a temporary vocation, but as a permanent profession. And besides this large and inviting fixed salary there was a grant from the Government to the principal in each school for every scholar that he was able to raise above the grade of seventy-five per cent of the maximum of one hundred. The examination was conducted by the Government once or twice a year, and the ambitions of the principal and his subordinates were naturally increased; the result was a united and enthusiastic endeavor to raise the grade of scholarship to the highest pitch. The system was well organized, well conducted, and many splendid new buildings were erected.

Nothing since I knew anything about Scotland has ever
made so great a change upon the people as this has done.
Its effect reached everywhere, and education became the
aspiration of even the humblest people, and thereafter one
would find in the colleges in far greater numbers the
brightest boys from these humble homes.

This change in education made the people of Scotland in
two decades one of the best-educated peoples in Europe;
and I believe that Scotland to-day, in its system of popular
education, has no superior in any part of the world.

The teacher himself, in this great movement, was held in
the highest esteem. That has always been so, but there
was a new accession of esteem and respect for the teacher
and his calling, and he found an open door to the best social life. I was taught as a boy to lift my hat to three persons in the community, the minister who took care of our
souls, the doctor who took care of our bodies, and the
schoolmaster who took care of our minds. I have always
thought it a singularly good condition of the public mind
that these three professions, whose excellence is so essential to the welfare of the community, should be held in universal popular esteem. There is hope surely for the people
among whom it can be said, 'The teacher shall shine as the
brightness of the firmament,' and none for those among
whom he is disregarded.

The time of which I am writing lies immediately back
of this renaissance. The teaching then was not, of course,
up to the level of that which I have just described, yet it
was excellent. The school hours were from nine to three, or
from ten to four, with a half-hour intermission in which to
eat our lunch — which, however, was usually eaten on the

way to school. The vacation period was six weeks in the whole year. The school exercises opened with a short passage of Scripture, the singing of a Psalm — a rather weird performance unaccompanied as it was by any instrumental music — and a brief prayer by the master. These religious exercises were sincere, clear, and impressive; yet we boys observed that they had no influence whatever over the temper of the teacher and held out no mercy whatsoever to the boy who had failed to learn his lesson.

This reminds me of a tale that Professor Park used to tell about Samuel Taylor, Principal for many years of Phillips Academy, Andover. A friend of Professor Park had sent his boy to Phillips Academy, and, thinking the boy might feel a little strange and lonely, asked the Professor to look after him a bit. Professor Park promised that he would, and he did, but in an unfortunate way, for he invited the boy to dinner when he had at the same time invited the senior class in Andover Seminary, men of about twenty-five. The little boy's chin just came up above the table; he was lonely and out of place. The Professor thought he would try to make things easy for the boy by asking him to tell how Principal Taylor opened his school in the morning. The little fellow answered, without looking up at all, 'First he calls the roll, then he reads a passage of Scripture, then he gives us a blowing up, and then he prays.' I have told that tale to many of Dr. Taylor's pupils, and they all testify that it was true to the letter.

The schoolhouse in my day in Scotland was a modest but completely wholesome building, well ventilated, and well heated in the winter. The walls of the schoolroom were covered with excellent maps of England, Scotland, Ireland, the British Dominions overseas, the chief countries of Europe reaching as far as Russia; and one fine map on which I used to gaze with wonder and delight was the map of North and South America.

Geography was a chief study. This is not the order in which it was put, but let me say here that it was a very popular study, and I think it engaged all the brighter boys very much indeed. We had to bound all the countries, tell the great rivers of the continents and of the world. I always supposed that the Amazon was the greatest until I came to America, when I found a dispute as to the Mississippi, and I supposed that the Nile was the longest until I met my fellow-citizen here. We had to learn the population of the greater cities. In my time that of London was two million five hundred thousand, whereas it is now about seven million. Scotland had a population of two million and a half, and now it has about five million. Everything about geography was immensely interesting except one thing, which was torture; we had not only to learn where a river took its rise, but also to describe the direction of its course — southwest, northeast, west, etc. — and tell where it found its fall or end. It is a very difficult thing for a child to hold the points of compass, and apply them to the windings of a river. This discipline was painful and useless, as every one failed in it, and it spoiled an exceptionally interesting subject of study.

The subjects taught were the usual ones, reading, writing, and arithmetic, a thorough discipline. The latter was not well taught; the teacher was too severe and Friday was the dark day in the week when we all were called to judgment. Geography, as I have said, was a principal additional study; a bit of history, Latin for the boys who were fitted for it and looking forward to college; literature, some for every grade, and in the higher grades the English classics; music, not instrumental but vocal; the Bible, and the Shorter Catechism; these were important additions.

Let me say a word about the last two. The Bible was the first exercise every morning. Usually the passages were from the first five Books of the Old Testament with due omissions, and one of the Gospels. I think I went over the Pentateuch five times in the public school, and the first Gospel, which was usually chosen, also many times. We found it extremely interesting reading, and that part of the morning was generally a happy part, but the effect of the Gospels was not visible on the temper and kindliness of the teacher nor that of his own prayer.

The Catechism was a different proposition. The Shorter Catechism consisted of a hundred and three — or seven, I forget which — answers to as many questions. The answers were elaborate definitions, constituting, when taken together, an outline of the Calvinistic system of theology. For boys who had a poor memory Catechism day was an awful day; those of us who had a good memory got through it nicely. The only time I ever got ahead of my older brother was in this extraordinary test. At one time I was able to repeat every question and every answer in the Catechism. It was a sheer feat of memory; I understood nothing whatever of the meaning of Pardon, Justification, Sanctification, Adoption, Effectual Calling, Redemption, and all the rest. I sympathize with the position of one of the characters in 'Bunty Pulls the Strings,' who said, 'But, Father, I don't understand the Catechism,' and received the stern reply, 'Wha said you were to understand it? Learn it!' To me it was a feat of pure memory, and I recall with what pleasure I was sent to the top of the class — I did not stay there long — passing my brother four years older than I who was an admirable scholar. As it was the only time I ever did it, the event was of course memorable.

I had but two women teachers. One taught me my letters. She had a terrible voice; it was like a siren whistle; one can hear such a whistle when the steamboat wants to have the drawbridge pulled back. I was sure that she had murdered scores of children and I thought she was after our lives. 'O X, ox; A S S, ass,' as if she were describing our characters, miserable wretches that we were.

The reverse of the first woman teacher was the second; she was of great personal beauty, rarest refinement, and gentlest influence. I was then six years old and I had an affection for her that still remains unspent. She had an infirmity, one leg being much shorter than the other, and she bobbed up and down in a very interesting way. Until the instance I am to relate I stood very high in her esteem, but I fell, like Lucifer, never to rise again. At play one day I thought I would entertain the girls and boys with a piece of acting. I said, 'Would you like to see me "take off" our teacher when she walks?' which I did, and a Judas Iscariot of a girl went and told. I have never forgotten, never will forget, the reproof that this teacher gave me; — 'I never should have thought that *you* would have done that.' I never got back into her esteem; I felt ever afterwards like an excommunicated soul.

The men teachers were of the first order; they all were university men and generally *in transitu* for the ministry;

graduated from the university, they took two or three years, perhaps four or five, at teaching before they qualified as ministers. I never knew how good an early training I had until I sent a child of my own to school in the enlightened city of Boston. The subjects taught here were more numerous and the points of contact with modern knowledge were richer, but there was no parallel to the university teacher with his inflexible standards, his severity, his thoroughness, his absolute refusal to accept anything but the best that a pupil could do. Weeping parents in those days there were none; the parents sided with the teachers every time; the boys never went home to borrow sympathy.

These teachers were greatly overworked. In many instances a teacher would have to instruct from eighty to one hundred boys without help of any kind. His life was the life of a slave; and this accounts for the fact that he was always as cross as a bear. He went about the whole day with a cane and a leather strap, and almost every minute some poor victim was getting a thrashing. I recall one of our best teachers, a second cousin of my mother, Mr. Dunn, a handsome man, and considerate, for a Scottish schoolmaster, and inclined to be just, from our point of view. My oldest brother was eleven and I was seven, and when we were dispatched to the school, father handed a letter for my brother to give to the master. We wondered what was inside that letter, and my brother proposed that we open and read it, and I assented. The letter read: 'Dear Mr. Dunn, I am sending my boys to your excellent school. They are very wild boys. Will you be especially severe with them?' My brother made the suggestion, to which again I assented, that we take a stone out of the fence on the turnpike road and put the letter in there and then place the stone back again, which we did. Father never got any answer to his letter. That was in 1860. That same brother and I, in 1884, hired a machine and went up that road and hunted many hours trying to find that letter. I fear that twenty-four terrible Scottish winters had soaked through the sand and gravel and destroyed it; at any rate, we could find no trace of it. Boys even in those days knew how to protect themselves against austerities of parents and schoolmasters. To this day I think the action of my brother, and my assent, just; self-preservation is, if not the first, one great law of life.

The best public teacher that I ever had in my boyhood was one Lewis Beaton, who afterwards became a prominent minister. He was the fiercest character that I ever knew. He was always thrashing, from morning till night, and yet we all admired him as a scholar and as an instructor. We fancied that perhaps we could change his practice a little if we showed our appreciation of him, so we clubbed together and bought him a watch, as he had none, and we selected Friday morning to present it, as Friday was arithmetic day and he was always fiercest on that black day. After the sober and ominous prayer, one of the older scholars asked the teacher's permission to make a few remarks. Beaton stood like a Rhadamanthus listening to a sinner's plea; the address of the pupil was excellent, full of respect, and ended by begging our teacher to accept a watch from the scholars in token of their admiration for his ability and his patience! Beaton was utterly overwhelmed; he had regarded us all as enemies, his feeling had been that we would shoot him if it were not that we knew we should be hanged for it — and he was not far wrong in that suspicion. He took the watch, and for that whole day he went through the exercises, though carrying the strap, without thrashing anybody. But the next Monday morning he was on the job again with all the old fervor.

Playing truant — I suppose there is no such thing in this country — was the gravest crime in my childhood. It was not the thing itself that was so bad; it was the lie that always accompanied it. The public sentiment of the school was that a boy was a simpleton if he confessed his act. It was expected that he would lie and in that way get out of his difficulty, and it was considered no crime to lie, any more than in military procedure. Here is the German line, let us say; make a feint of attacking here as if you meant to conquer here; then attack over there. That is a deception justified by the fact that you are contending against the enemy. The lying that I am speaking of was an exercise of the same sort. I played truant only once, and I did not really lie, I simply did not tell the whole truth. When I was asked to explain my absence from school for three days, I said that I was helping my father to get in hay. Another Judas Iscariot got up and said that he met me in the woods six miles away from home, which was the part of the truth that I had suppressed. From a leather strap as long as one's arm and with five fingers to it I got two heavy blows for the truancy and six for lying. I concluded that I could never hope to make a successful liar, and that telling the truth in a straight and fearless way was far simpler, and, all things considered, safer.

As a general thing, boys go through this phase of experience whether their mothers know it or not. 'My boy never told a lie in his life' is a remark which we sometimes hear from serenely sentimental and ignorant mothers; it reminds me of the story of the minister who came upon five or six boys on a Sunday afternoon, and asked them what they were doing. 'We are playing a game. We have a knife here to give to the one who can tell the biggest lie.' 'Oh,' said the minister, 'when I was a boy I never engaged in any such game as that.' 'Give him the knife!' shouted the boys.

What did I learn in school? I was taught well how to read and write; I got discipline in arithmetic, I learnt a good deal about the surface of the globe; I learnt to love certain fellow-students whom I have never seen since and whose images have been with me all through the years with a kindly influence upon feeling to this day, and constituting a sort of pathetic human reminiscence. Once when I was on a steamer in the middle of the ocean I heard about several of them. I sat beside a gentleman with whom I conversed, and he told me of the fate of three of my schoolfellows, thirty years after those school days; it was extremely interesting. And the other day at Bishop Slattery's Consecration, the rector of a church in Massachusetts came to me and asked, 'Did you go to the public school in Insch?' I said that I did. 'Who was your schoolmaster?' 'John Wilson.' Then he replied, 'John Wilson was my uncle.' For a few moments that scene of fifty-four years ago came back in a strangely vivid and moving way; it is indeed strange how any hour a wizard's wand may be waved and bring back to us, significant and tender, worlds that we thought had long since utterly vanished.

In addition to the things mentioned, I learnt to fight. No boy, unless he was a coward, ever went through a Scottish school without learning to fight; a certain measure of pugnacity was absolutely essential to peace and to self-respect. It was not necessary to be the aggressor; it was necessary to be ready for the foe when he came. I have been trying to recall my history in this matter. There was one drawn battle which I remember well, and there were others that I engaged in with boys of my own age which turned out favorably for me. After a half-dozen good fights a boy would be molested no more; he had the respect of his fellow-students and went on all right. These struggles were not perilous, they were good healthy sport. Once in a while the result was a black eye. Mother would say, 'You will end your days on the gallows.' It did not look to me as if I should, considering the black eye; it looked more as if the other fellow might. Father said nothing at all at such times, but when we were alone he would ask if I licked him, and if I could answer 'Yes,' I felt that the stars in their courses were on my side.

In the Scotland of my time it was necessary for a boy to learn how to defend himself, how to give battle when he was challenged and fight it out to victory if he could, and if not, then to be brave and unhumiliated in defeat. I do not think that sort of thing is without influence upon after life. Never begin a fight, is a good rule; never be aggressive, but never run away. Respect every one, treat all fairly, and allow no one to treat you with disrespect, is a maxim that makes life smooth and prosperous. The reason why the Irish and the Scottish get on so well together, in Glasgow, for example, is that both are good fighters and they know it. It makes for peace; no one wants to attack a good fighter.

Above all, I learnt to love good literature. I heard the upper classes reading Shakespeare and Milton; I heard the master's comments on Shakespeare, Milton, Dante, Bacon. These mighty names were away beyond me, but I resolved that if I lived I would know something about them and their writings. It was an amazing influence that these upper classes, with their sympathetic, imaginative teacher, wielded upon the listening boys. The joy, the ecstasy of those hours! The wonderful ballad poetry caught us. The one which had the greatest fascination for me was 'Chevy-Chace,' studied by a class two or three grades above me. As I listened I was spellbound, and when intermission came I stole — or 'hooked' — a book from the upper class and stayed in three or four days in succession till I got that ballad by heart. The first collision, how thrilling:

> 'Our English archers bent their bows,
>   Their hearts were good and true;
> At the first flight of arrows sent,
>   Full fourscore Scots they slew.'

That looked bad for my side. But the next stanza came on with this:

> 'Yet bides Earl Douglas on the bent,
>   As chieftain stout and good;
> As valiant captain all unmoved
>   The shock he firmly stood.'

And this:

> 'His host he parted had in three,
>   As leader ware and try'd;
> And soon his spearmen on their foes
>   Bore down on every side.'

The criticism that one is compelled to pass upon the Scottish public school of my time was its undue severity, its want of sympathy with young life, its imposition upon boys of the standards of devotion proper only to those much older, and the utter absence of anything like affection in the fellowship of teacher and student. The fear of hell reigned largely as a motive in Calvinistic theology, and fear was the dominant motive to which the teacher appealed. Had love been added to stern justice, had the teacher been our friend and comrade, had he spoken to the higher side of our nature and called forth enthusiasm as we went to our tasks; above all, had he given us the sense that it was our inmost nature to be honest and not dishonest, noblemen and not knaves, how much more those able and devoted masters might have done for us, how much more they might have induced us to do for ourselves.

This criticism which in justice must be made does not in the least cancel my reverence and gratitude for what I received. I still say thanks to the old schoolhouse standing against the sunshine and against the bleak, weird sky; thanks to the accomplished and stern old schoolmaster; he taught the love of learning; he exalted thoroughness of work; he frightened the shirk out of nearly every boy that came under his influence; he gave a sense of the wealth and beauty that men of genius have created all through time; he prepared for college, and something better, he prepared for a life devoted to the improvement of mind and character on to life's last hour; he prepared for the greatest of all universities, the University of the World.

CHAPTER VII
FEUDALISM AND DEMOCRACY

I

AS a description of feudalism, the following paragraph from Sir Walter Scott's 'Waverley' is interesting. At the trial of Vich Ian Vohr for high treason in the war of 1715, Evan, his vassal, is making his plea:

'I was only ganging to say, my lord,' said Evan, in what he meant to be an insinuating manner, 'that if your excellent honor, and the honorable Court, would let Vich Ian Vohr go free just this once, and let him gae back to France, and no to trouble King George's Government again, that ony six o' the very best of his clan will be willing to be justified in his stead; and if you'll just let me gae down to Glennaquoich, I'll fetch them up to ye mysell, to head or hang, and you may begin wi' me the very first man.'

Notwithstanding the solemnity of the occasion, a sort of laugh was heard in the court at the extraordinary nature of the proposal. The Judge checked this indecency, and Evan, looking sternly around, when the murmur abated, 'If the Saxon gentlemen are laughing,' he said, 'because a poor man, such as me, thinks my life, or the life of six of my degree, is worth that of Vich Ian Vohr, it's like enough they may be very right; but if they laugh because they think I would not keep my word, and come back to redeem him, I can tell them they ken neither the heart of a Hielandman, nor the honor of a gentleman.'

Here is feudalism at its best, and at its worst; at its best because of its magnificent loyalty, the loyalty on the part of the vassal to his chief; at its worst, because the chief was not worthy of any such sacrifice. No man is worth any such sacrifice from his fellowmen.

Feudalism, as all know, was a good in its time. The

General Government in Continental kingdoms and empires, and also in a little country like Scotland, was not strong enough to defend the people against invading clans and tribes who destroyed life and property. We must recall the absence of roads, the extreme difficulty of moving from place to place in the country so recently as one hundred years ago. Even a small country like Scotland, two hundred and eighty-eight miles in length, and in breadth varying from thirty to sixty miles, could not be covered at all adequately by the representatives of the General Government. There came into existence, therefore, within the general kingdom a multitude of little kingdoms, simply for the protection of life and property. The lord, or the chieftain of the clan, as it might be, gave protection to life and property within his realm, and as a return he claimed the services of all those who lived within his domain and the complete command of their lives; they promised him unlimited service for his defense of their lives and the few things that they owned. One can see at once that in an unstable condition of society this was a good, and that where the chief was a nobleman in mind and in character, the relation between him and his vassals was like that of a great and noble father to his children.

There are many aspects, therefore, of feudalism which are enchanting and many more that are delightful to contemplate. But feudalism was only a temporary form of human society. It could not last, for one great reason; it made too much of the one and altogether too little of the many. There is the fundamental defect of feudalism. Too much power, too many resources were given to the one, and too little account was made of the many.

Sir Walter Scott, it is well known, is the great delineator and idealizer of feudalism in Scotland. He has done his work with genius and with splendor, and his productions are a permanent contribution to the literature of his race. But there is nothing in his writings, so far as I know, to show that he had any sense of the degrading force of feudalism, any sense that it was an indignity to man's nature. He is far behind his older contemporary, Robert Burns, in this respect. Scott is the delineator and idealizer of a temporary phase of social arrangement and constitution, something bound to pass away; Burns is the prophet of the coming, the final, form of human society, the sovereignty of the kingdom of man. There is no sort of equality between these two men of genius or between their respective contributions to human thought. Scott will take us into a feudalistic world, entertain and charm us there; but he tells us nothing of remedies for the evils of that state of the world, he holds out to us no hopes of anything better to come. The moment we make the acquaintance of Burns, we feel upon our spirit the breath of a coming world; our best hopes for human beings find in him a mighty prophet, our best endeavors a great and steady inspiration.

II

WHEN I first began my acquaintance with this old world, Scotland was still in the grasp of feudalism. I speak wholly of life in the country. A farmer had his farm and his family. For example, my paternal grandfather, who had ten children — eight boys and two girls — had his farm. These boys could not all live on the farm. They were obliged, in the first place, when they became of age, to go out with the gift of money which their father had made them on that date in their history, to serve on other farms, to be 'farm servants' to other farmers, till such time as they had accumulated enough to lease a farm on their own account. All of these sons except one became farmers in due time, and continued farmers to the end of their lives; and the two daughters married farmers. The whole process in a large family was, as I have described, to leave home in succession and go to other farms to serve there till independent power arrived.

The hours of labor in my time were ten hours a day all the year round and eleven in harvest. The servant was hired for six months, and he was not paid his wages till the end of the six months, the farmer getting the interest on the wages, which made a considerable deduction — or would have made, if the wages had amounted to anything. The most that I ever got was fifty dollars in six months.

The farmer, if he were vicious — and I regret to add that he usually was — could discharge a servant after two, three, or even four months of service without giving the servant any wages for what he had done; the expense of law, and the uncertainty of it, were such that very often servants were thus discharged and were unable to recover anything for their work. There was a custom according to which a farmer could not discharge a servant within six weeks of the close of his contract without giving him full pay and board wages, and I think this custom was usually regarded.

About work and weather; Scotland is not famous for its soft climate, especially in winter; and this will explain why all the servants on the farms, in my time, were young men.

A man over thirty was rarely to be found among them unless he belonged to the establishment. All were young men, because none but vigorous young men could endure what these servants endured.

The ploughing was done in the late autumn and in the winter, in rain, in sleet, in snow. The only mitigation was when the weather was too bad for the horses; they were valuable property and their lives were precious in the farmer's sight; then, indeed, there would be an exception to the rule. However, the farmer usually found something for the men to do outside after the horses were put inside. There was the pulling of the turnips. The staple food for cattle in Scotland is the turnip, white, yellow, and the Swedish turnip. These are pulled out of the ground in the winter-time. It is a very, very lovely task on a wild winter day, for example, to go out and with your hand scrape the snow off the top of the turnip and pull it out and clean it, three hours of this in the forenoon and three in the afternoon. We had woolen mittens, but the trouble with them is that they get wet, and when they are half-frozen they do not warm one's hands very much. There was no mercy shown for the servants in this sort of weather. Ploughing, driving, getting food for the cattle from the field was the programme; one day was just about as good as another — or as bad; and this explains, as I have said, the absence from the farms of all but young men, men in their vigor, who could stand anything, who could get wet to the skin three times a day and have their clothes dry on their backs.

There was abundance of food, but it was of very uninviting quality. The keynote of it was oatmeal and milk, in various concoctions, one about as unsavory as another.

President Eliot tells a story about my first visit to his home in Northeast Harbor. He offered me oatmeal at breakfast, and I refused it, 'because,' I said, 'I had very little else during the first eighteen years of my life, and I wanted no more.' Of course, there were vegetables, such as we have here, cabbage, kale, and good turnips, such as one never sees here, really good ones. Here one meets an ancient fallacy; it has been said that this food has turned out a splendid race of men. That is pure humbug; I was glad to see an eminent medical authority stand up for my point of view the other day. The race was a good one in the beginning, it had a good start, and the race and the climate go on in spite of the diet. An oatmeal diet for all but those who do manual work out of doors is bad food; for children at school it is highly indigestible, and stupefying.

The lodgings were the very worst. From four to six men would sleep in a loft, usually over a horse-stable, with no heat except the heat coming up from the horses. In severe winter weather one's shoes would be frozen hard every night, and they were thawed out by the heat of one's feet in the morning. The music of kicking one's feet into one's boots in the morning was something delicious; the boots were hard as rocks.

As to the bed, when I was a boy, often in the winter I stood looking at the sheet with the frost dancing on it like diamonds — not so valuable but just as brilliant — and wondered whether I had courage enough to make the plunge. What a yell would come from the boys when their warm skin touched this brilliant surface.

There was one washbowl for all these men, and a towel, renewed, according to the farmer's wife's ideas of sanitation, once a week or once a fortnight. Here was a clear outrage upon cleanliness, upon decency, upon humanity.

Sometimes a servant would live in a cottage and have a little garden of his own and plant and cultivate vegetables. If a rabbit or a hare were to eat his vegetables, he could not set a trap and he was not allowed to shoot. If he did, in the case of a rabbit the fine would be more than he could earn in two months, and in the case of a hare, as much as he could earn in three months, and more still in the case of a partridge or pheasant. Yet we had — if I may borrow one of Theodore Roosevelt's classic phrases — 'a bully time' poaching; I do not think I ever enjoyed anything more in my life. The adventure of it, the risk of it, and the joy of getting off. About midnight, when the moon was full and the stars were out, we started with guns, dog, and ferret; usually we brought home a fine bag of game by four in the morning.

All this is a window through which one may look into the remnant of feudalistic world still existing in my time. It was a world of utter disregard for human well-being, and an atrocious condition of life. It is the habit of certain people to speak of the 'good old times.' For whom were they good? They were good economically for the few; they were bad for them, humanly speaking, because these good old days made them tyrants, made them brutal. These days were, for the vast majority of human beings, a burden and a curse; they took out of the human heart the desire to live; they filled it with bitterness toward wealth and power, and with scorn for the Christian Church that had no other gospel than

'To come in an' 'ands up an' be still,
An' honestly work for my bread,

My livin' in that state of life
To which it shall please God to call me!'

Lord Bryce, in his book on 'Democracy,' has some hard words about this form of government. I do not find in his writings any adequate sense of the abomination that democracy has abolished. Here is the great defect of writers like Bryce. He moved up into the aristocratic fold and looked upon the world from that point of view. The eonian woe of human beings disregarded, their lives afflicted and shamefully treated, should be recalled and considered when one looks at the defects of democracy. The farm servant in my time had no standing; he was no part of the State. The only right he had was the right to toil. He had to accept such treatment as his employer gave him, and his life was that of a beast of burden and nothing but a beast of burden. That was feudalism; that was one of the good old times. Reader, would not you like to go back and live in it, see it, and feel it, not with the few for whom it was economically profitable, but with the many for whom it was a crushing and an infamous burden?

III

HERE it would appear to be fitting to consider face to face the character and hopes of democracy. I shall do this by presenting two witnesses from classic Greece, one in favor and one against democracy. The first witness is Pericles, the greatest of Greek statesmen as Thucydides the greatest historian of the ancient world presents him:

Our form of government does not enter into rivalry with the institutions of others. We do not copy our neighbors, but are an example to them. It is true that we are called a democracy, for the administration is in the hands of the many and not of the few. But while the law secures equal justice to all alike in their private disputes, the claim of excellence is also recognized; and when a citizen is in any way distinguished he is preferred to the public service, not as a matter of privilege, but as the reward of merit. Neither is poverty a bar, but a man may benefit his country whatever be the obscurity of his condition. There is no exclusiveness in our public life, and in our private intercourse we are not suspicious of one another, nor angry with our neighbor if he does what he likes; we do not put on sour looks at him which, though harmless, are not pleasant. While we are thus unconstrained in our private intercourse, a spirit of reverence pervades our public acts; we are prevented from doing wrong by respect for authority and for the laws, having an especial regard to those which are ordained for the protection of the injured as well as to those unwritten laws which bring upon the transgressor of them the reprobation of the general sentiment.

Plato is our witness against democracy, and nearly everything said against this form of government since his time will be found, in one form or another, in his grand indictment. Let us first get Plato's ideal before us — an ideal which, I think, all Americans will heartily accept:

Unless, said I, either philosophers shall become kings in states, or those who are now called kings and potentates shall become philosophers, genuinely and adequately, and these meet in the same person, political power and philosophy, and the greater part of those who now proceed separately to each (that is, the pure politician and the dabbler in philosophy) shall be absolutely excluded from the one and the other; there is no surcease of ills, my dear Glaucon, to states, and I think not even to the human race, nor will this constitution which we have described till then ever grow up into possibility and see the light of the sun.

There is Plato's ideal; now for his criticism of democracy; let us get the whole case before us and then attempt an answer.

First, Plato sees democracy as founded upon excess of

freedom. Every man does what he likes, does what seems good in his own eyes. There is no unity in democracy, no homogeneity, no order. Democracy presents a multitude of separate units with nothing to bind them together. Plato says that the mind of a democracy is like a bazaar. Those who have seen a Turkish bazaar must admit that Plato's simile is full of wit and humor. Democracy is a vast bazaar of governments, all varieties, highly colored, gaudy, cheap, intolerable.

Second: In a democracy Plato holds that there is no obligation for a man to hold office, even when he is conspicuously and preëminently fit; and there is no way of keeping the unfit out of office, provided they are pleasing to the people.

Third: In a democracy the administration of justice is lax. Men, Plato says, are convicted here in Athens of crimes for which the punishment is banishment or death, and in two or three days after they are supposed to have been sentenced and executed, one will find them walking about among their fellow-citizens perfectly self-possessed, and nobody paying the slightest regard to them; and that is to be expected in this order of society.

Fourth: In a democracy there is great neglect of education, especially the education of rulers — high intelligence, a large share of the best wisdom of the past, upright character, a wise programme for the public good — all these are not necessary; all that is necessary is that a man shall blow with all his might for the people.

Further, Plato says that in a democracy all the people are equal in all respects, which he adds is manifest folly; and the inference is made from this premise that all thoughts are equally right, and all desires equally good, and that everything in a man has its right to be heard, to be expressed, to be experienced, to be lived. Plato sums up his criticism by declaring that democracy is government gone on a drunk with the wine of freedom.

The passage that I am summarizing is, indeed, a magnificent piece of writing, serious, full of humor, and splendor. The democratic cup-bearers pour out the wine of freedom and hand it round, he says, in two big drafts, and all the people get drunk together.

What shall we say to these things, we who believe in democracy? In the first place, let us accept with the utmost heartiness Plato's ideal, which never was expressed more clearly or more magnificently. Until the highest wisdom and the supreme political authority unite in the same men, until the best in intellect and the best in character become our rulers, there is no surcease of ills for states, nor for the human race; nor is there any hope that our ideals for mankind will ever grow up into possibility, or see the light of the sun.

That is undeniably true, and we accept it as our ideal. An ignorant ruler is indeed a calamity; when you have an ignorant and a perverse master, and put him on a ship, he will land you on the rocks; put him on the ship of state, and what will the issue be? We accept, then, Plato's ideal, and we ask how shall we gain our goal, how shall this ideal be realized? There are only two ways conceivable, as far as I can see, either our rulers must rule on the hereditary principle, or they must rule as chosen — and as chosen by the people. The hereditary principle has broken down. Look at the kings of England, the kings of France, the kings of

Germany; listen to them as they talk of ruling by the grace of God. If that is true, the grace of God has made some monstrous mistakes. The German Kaiser ruled by divine right, and by the grace of God! That is blasphemy if anything can be; but let us reason on this point, all feeling apart; if the Kaiser ruled by divine right, the Power that made him has a great deal to answer for.

The other method is choice, and let me say that twice within seventy-five years the American people chose as their supreme ruler in each case the best man then living. Washington might well stand for Plato's ideal embodied, the man in whom wisdom and political power of the highest type met. And again Lincoln, and our people throughout our history — if one shall read the history apart from passionate feeling, and after men have forgotten that their candidates were defeated — our people have chosen their rulers remarkably well. It is on the whole a cheering piece of history that we present to the world.

Let me now attempt an answer to Plato's arraignment. And first, with all due respect to Plato, he is not criticizing democracy, he is criticizing anarchy. Our democracy is ordered freedom, freedom governed by law, reasonable, and with large regard in it for the rights of the other man. Our democracy hates two things equally, and fights them — despotism, which means slavery, anarchy, which means dissolution of all society. Plato's first criticism is aimed, not at democracy as we know it, but at anarchy.

Second: there is no way in democracy of compelling good men to hold office, or keeping bad men from getting into office. Is that true? There is public opinion. Again and again in the history of the American Republic, in times of great crisis, public opinion, enlightened, conscientious, tremendous, has drawn the best men into the field, and driven inferior men off the field in defeat. This is what we want more and more of, an enlightened, compelling public opinion, so that every man shall vote, and the public opinion be so intense that good men who do not want the odium of public life shall yet offer themselves a living sacrifice. That process is going on, and if one shall analyze the situation, one will be amazed to find how much there is on the right side, and the instances that loom large as defeats of democracy are, after all, not so many.

The third criticism refers to the lax administration of justice. Well, let me give two cases of the administration of justice in one of the best monarchies of the world — Great Britain — within eighty-five years. A boy of fourteen broke into a candy store on Fleet Street, stole a handful of candy, and was hanged for it. Of how much more value was candy then in London than the life of a boy? In Scotland, in the public square in Aberdeen, where the statue of the last Duke of Gordon stands, a boy of fifteen was hanged for stealing a sheep belonging to his grace. Democracy has humanized law, put justice into law, refused to execute law that simply was an outrage. Think of such things, when you hear democracy attacked for its lax administration of justice. We admit that we are lax, that is, compared with the ideal; but we are infinitely better than Europe was a hundred years ago. It is not necessary to hang everybody who is accused of having done wrong. It is one thing to accuse and indict, and another thing to prove guilt; and still another thing to match and not overmatch the misdeed with punishment. It is a great thing to have the State set human life above everything except the destruction of other human life.

The criticism as to our neglect of education is simply not true. American democracy was preëminently free from illiteracy till the vast influx of illiterates from the monarchies of Europe lowered our standing. There is the trouble; when monarchists throw this in our face we throw it back; 'our illiterates came from your shores, and your community, not from ours.' The American democracy pure and simple, I say it again, was preëminently free from illiteracy; it was grounded in good sense and sound knowledge.

Further, in no country since history began, within the same length of time, has so much been done for education, scientific and every other kind. The money given by our wealthy citizens to this end is simply without parallel, and there is no reason why, if the monarchies that produce illiteracy should put an embargo upon their illiteracy, we should not, within a generation, return to our original state of a universally educated community.

Mr. Gladstone said in a great campaign, I think it was in 1879–80 when the Beaconsfield Government went to smash under his assault, that the Tory Party in England was founded upon distrust of the people, and that the Liberal Party was founded upon trust in the people. There is the great cleavage in the history of government, and I ask, how long can one hope for it to last if one's business is run upon the principle of distrust in the people? The American Republic is built upon popular confidence and trust. Again Lincoln's homely phrase expresses our faith: 'You can fool all the people some of the time, and some of the people all of the time, but you cannot fool all of the people all of the time.' One recalls here Daniel Webster's closing words in his great speech in reply to John C. Calhoun; if all argument should come to nothing, and all other appeals should prove of no avail, he said he would still, with a voice feeble, perhaps, but earnest as ever issued from human lips, call upon the people to come to the rescue.

Our review would be incomplete if we did not look at the religious basis of democracy; and here let Whittier be our witness. Whittier's addition to our insight is this, that he sees that Jesus is the original democrat in human history, that His teaching that all men are the sons of God and brothers one of another, is the only adequate basis for democracy. Plato and Aristotle — everlasting lights of mankind as they are, thinkers for whom I have the greatest reverence, companions of my whole life — had this fundamental defect, neither had any conception of humanity. All the privileges of life were for the elect; for the poor slaves, for the multitude of the illiterate, and for all barbarians beyond, they had nothing but scorn. Jesus, with His teaching of universal sonhood to God, universal brotherhood, was the first great creative democrat in the history of mankind; and Whittier bases his belief in democracy thus:

'Not from the shallow, babbling fount
  Of vain philosophy thou art;
He who of old on Syria's mount,
  Thrilled, warmed, by turns, the listener's heart.

'In holy words which cannot die,
  In thoughts which angels leaned to know,
Proclaimed thy message from on high,
  Thy mission to a world of woe.

'That voice's echo hath not died!
From the blue lake of Galilee;
And Tabor's lonely mountain-side,
It calls a struggling world to thee.

'Thy name and watchword o'er this land
I hear in every breeze that stirs,
And round a thousand altars stand
Thy banded party worshippers.

'Not to these altars of a day,
At party's call my gift I bring;
But on thy olden shrine I lay
A freeman's dearest offering:

'The voiceless utterance of his will,
His pledge to Freedom and to Truth,
That manhood's heart remembers still
The homage of his generous youth.'

What does democracy at its best mean? The Christian organization of human society, the Christian structure and administration of government under the Christian conception of human life, and under the Christian conception of the universe.

IV

DEMOCRACY was coming in my boyhood. A man who paid a rental of fifty pounds had a vote. That was beginning to tell. A decade later, this was reduced to ten pounds, then to five, then to thirty shillings. Then the humanity of the nation asserted itself; the people by their votes broke into Parliament — I am still thinking of rural Scotland; suddenly reform swept the country from end to end. Farm servants must have a place for sleep apart from the animals; in cold weather they must have a fire; each man must be provided with a chair in the sleeping-apartment, and proper means for washing, and the bed linen must be clean. Something like a revolution came because the people broke into Parliament. The game laws were modified. A man might shoot anything that touched his garden; rabbit, hare, pheasant, whatever it might be; the produce of your garden or farm belongs to you. The statute book underwent swift revision when the people obtained power and a whole lot of unjust laws went suddenly to the dust-heap.

Democracy has made many mistakes and has committed not a few crimes. Here let me repeat that, so far as I know, it has never yet been guilty of hanging boys of twelve and fourteen, one for stealing a sheep and another for stealing candy; it has yet to live up to that. Democracy has chosen many very queer rulers and leaders. Has it ever chosen one to equal George III or William IV? Look over the list of English kings. One will find a few good ones, a few great ones; as to the 'divine right of kings,' I am unable to see any meaning in that theory; kings in general I should rather say were appointed by the Devil and that they served their master well. Look over the list of the Roman emperors and note how few of them were good, worthy men, and how many were other than imperial blackguards.

Feudalism is not coming back in any form. Democracy is here to stay. What we all want to do is to educate the people. Educate the people so that they shall know the difference between essential good and seeming good, the genuine leader and the demagogue, the man whose purpose is by trickery to prey upon them and the man who wants to help, to uplift, and to lead them into ampler life and greater good. Education is the religion of democracy, it is absolutely essential to its existence and to its high function. Many mistakes democracy has made, and many more it will make, because it is a form of government in the hands of imperfect human beings. But when one grows pessimistic, let him think of what democracy has superseded, let him think of the worlds of woe and blackness that it has abolished, of the substantial good that it has brought into being, that it supports, that it gives reasonable hopes of increasing more and more. Democracy does not disparage worth; it often makes mistakes as to who are worthy, but the people have an instinct for reality, and whenever they find a real man, a man of intellect, character, especially courageous character, they not unfrequently go with him with the power of the tide.

How poor is feudalism, even when glorified by the genius of a Sir Walter Scott; how poor it is in comparison with the following prophetic utterance of an infinitely greater genius:

'Is there for honest poverty
    That hings his head, an' a' that?
The coward slave, we pass him by —
    We dare be poor for a' that!
For a' that, an' a' that,
    Our toils obscure, an' a' that,
The rank is but the guinea's stamp,
    The man's the gowd for a' that.

'What though on hamely fare we dine,
    Wear hoddin grey, an' a' that?
Gie fools their silks, and knaves their wine —
    A man's a man for a' that.
For a' that, an' a' that,
    Their tinsel show, an' a' that,
The honest man, tho' e'er sae poor,
    Is king o' men for a' that.

'Ye see yon birkie ca'd' a lord,
    Wha struts, an' stares, an' a' that?
Tho' hundreds worship at his word,
    He's but a coof for a' that.
For a' that, an' a' that,
    His riband, star, an' a' that,
The man o' independent mind,
    He looks an' laughs at a' that.

'A prince can mak a belted knight,
    A marquis, duke, an' a' that;
But an honest man's aboon his might —
    Guid faith, he mauna fa' that!
For a' that, an' a' that,
    Their dignities, an' a' that,
The pith o' sense an' pride o' worth
    Are higher rank than a' that.

'Then let us pray that come it may
    (As come it will for a' that)
That a sense and worth o'er a' the earth,
    Shall bear the gree an' a' that!
For a' that, an' a' that,
    It's comin' yet for a' that,
That man to man the world o'er
    Shall brithers be for a' that.'

CHAPTER VIII
KEEPING THE SABBATH

SLANDEROUS tongues have said that 'the Scot keeps the Sabbath and everything else he can lay his hands upon.' This idea of the acquisitiveness, and also of the thriftiness, ascribed to my race is very old. A friend who always cherishes stories on these points and hands them to me when I meet him has told me of a case where a physician was called in and said, 'Sandy, you will not live till morning.' His wife heard it, and after the doctor left she said, 'Now I am very weary, having taken care of you all these days and nights, and I am going to take some rest, and I will leave the candle burning by your bedside, and before you draw your last breath, please mind and blow out the candle.'

The people of Scotland are really divided into two classes, the thrifty and the spendthrifts. We have them both in the opening lines of one of Burns's poems:

'It's hardly in a body's pow'r,
    To keep, at times, frae being sour,
        To see how things are shar'd;
How best o' chiels are whyles in want,
While coofs on countless thousands rant,
        And ken na how to ware't.'

The origin of Scottish thrift, since this has been wittily and with malice aforethought associated with 'the keeping of the Sabbath,' I cannot pass without an incidental remark; Scottish thrift has its origin in the passion for independence. No man can be independent who has not an economic basis for it, no man is independent who is a beggar, who lives upon another or whose physical subsistence depends upon the bounty of another. Scotland is naturally poor in resources; it has been made rich by the industry, the character, and the thrift of its people. Having won an economic basis for independence, the people do not care to part with it. Again Burns discloses this motive:

> 'To catch Dame Fortune's golden smile,
>   Assiduous wait upon her;
> And gather gear by ev'ry wile
>   That's justified by honour:
> Not for to hide it in a hedge,
>   Nor for a train attendant;
> But for the glorious privilege
>   Of being independent.'

There is no nation on the face of the earth that needs a lecture on thrift more than our own American Nation.

To return to our subject, how did Scotland keep the Sabbath? The Sabbath was kept as if it had been the seventh day of the week and not the first; it was kept as if it had been the religious day of the Jews; it was not kept as the sacred day of the Christian religion. The Lord's Day was the day of resurrection, the day of triumph, the day of freedom and of joy. All that was outside Scottish notions of the Sabbath. No one ever heard sung in Scottish assemblies the hymn: 'O day of rest and gladness, O day of joy and light.' Never in Jerusalem nor in New England nor anywhere else was the Sabbath day more austerely and tremendously kept than in the Scotland of my time.

It was a duty to penalize one's self, one's family, one's friends; it was a duty to be intolerant and even censorious in regard to all who might differ in opinion as to how the

Sabbath ought to be kept. The familiar tale is true to life of the dear old lady who having administered a sharp rebuke to a young man who had broken the letter of the law as to Sabbath-keeping, and who defended himself thus, 'The Lord allowed his disciples, in going through the cornfields, to rub the ears of corn in their hands and to eat them on the Sabbath'; the reply to which was, 'Aye, I ken that, and to tell ye the truth, I never thought any the better of the dear Lord for his behavior on that day.'

Let us now consider some of the things that were done, and endured, on the old-fashioned Sabbath. First, work of all kinds was reduced to a minimum, and with it, of course, all exercise, all entertainment, and all pleasure, outside of religion. In the country, the animals were fed and cared for, the horses and cattle; beyond that nothing was done. In the stricter homes everything had been prepared in advance; only works of necessity and mercy were allowed on that solemn day. Physically it was a day of idleness. For young people with abounding energy, it was a day of repression and of inward protest.

In the second place, church-going was an obligation. There was one exception, one excuse, shabby clothes or a mishap to the Sunday suit. The Scottish people are proud; they do not like to go abroad in poor clothes, nor do their friends wish to see them among other people poorly dressed. Either of these conditions, shabby clothes or an accident to the Sunday suit, constituted a valid excuse. Here was one of the uncovenanted mercies of God that came with extraordinary frequency in the case of the hardened unregenerate sinner.

The church, in the country, was usually from one to

three miles distant; sometimes it was two miles; often, however, it was six, so that going to church meant a walk of twelve miles. The church was not heated; in winter it was cold outside and inside. The seats were about eight or nine inches wide; there were no cushions, and the backs were exceedingly straight; there could be no lounging — everybody had to sit up.

In the country, in my time, there were scholars among the ministers, but there were no preachers who had any power to interest young people. The sermons usually were on abstract subjects, the abstract treatment of Calvinism usually, the doctrine of Predestination, for example. The discourse would be, let us say, on 'Supralapsarianism,' or again, on 'Sublapsarianism,' and I never learnt the meaning of either of these words till I studied for the ministry. The first means that God's eternal decree determined the order of the world from the beginning, including everything; Adam's fall was a mere incident and flowed from the decree like all the other events. The sublapsarian doctrine was that things went pretty much their own way till Adam fell and that then the Divine Purpose stepped in and took charge of the world. These were very fine metaphysical points to discuss before boys, and they were not ably or luminously discussed.

The sermon might be on 'Limited Election.' God had a right, like the rest of us, to choose his friends and to turn down those whom he did not like. It might be on 'Limited Atonement.' Jesus Christ did not die for the whole world, although the New Testament says that He did; to set aside the plain teaching of the New Testament required subtle reasoning and some sleight of hand. Then there was the subject of 'Irresistible Grace.' To those whom He chose God gave the spirit in large measure; they had to go to heaven; but one could not get there, no matter how hard one tried, if one did not have the irresistible grace. The subject might be the 'Perseverance of the Saints.' The elect might appear to fall away, they might be unable to give a very good account of themselves, they might not be thought very well of by their neighbors; all the same, through persevering grace they would arrive, one way or another. Lastly there was the 'Everlasting Punishment' of the wicked. To us boys this was the only vital part of the sermon; here the preacher was dealing with the class to which we belonged.

The sermon lasted usually from an hour and a quarter to an hour and a half. It was generally divided into four heads, with four subdivisions under each head, and a 'finally' added. Four times four are sixteen and four make twenty; and four more, twenty-four. It was a serious intellectual feat to keep all these heads distinct and to know from moment to moment where we were in the programme. Many times we had a gleam of hope, in our wonder as to how much longer our punishment was to last, when the preacher said 'Finally,' and we would look for the end; but the hope would speedily be blown out when he changed his voice and went back to 'Secondly.' We were all at sea then; there was nothing to do but stupidly to wait for the end, whenever that might come, of the irrelevant and stupid performance.

Sermons were usually argumentative in quality, in tone, in method, and in all sermons things were argued which we boys thought should have been taken for granted, which, at the same time, would have helped in getting up a little speed. 'Hence' and 'therefore' were favorite words and were so repeatedly used that I came to hate those two words; I wanted to say 'Hence!' to the whole thing.

Carlyle, in his 'Reminiscences,' gives a good description of a sermon which he and one of his friends went to hear by Robert Hall, one of the greatest English preachers in the early part of the nineteenth century, on the text, 'God that cannot lie.' The sermon was an attempted demonstration of the fact that God cannot lie. Carlyle's friend said, 'No need of proving that; one might as well prove that God never fought a duel.' This excess of argumentation added to the dullness and unprofitableness, especially in men of small ability, of the discourse; a wearisome business was made more wearisome.

Boys were not altogether without resources under this incomprehensible discipline. I recall one minister, greatly honored by my father and mother, who was nevertheless to us an intolerable bore. He really could not speak; we never saw the color of his eyes; he had the habit while preaching of touching his nose with the little finger of his right hand and giving a kind of grunt every time he did it. We boys would wager something before we went into church as to how many times the preacher would touch his nose with his finger and as to whether there would always be the grunt with the touch or whether once in a while they would be separate. Then we would sit up, watch, and count, to see who would win. No human person, least of all a human Deity, could grudge us this relief, considering our long affliction. I must add that with three exceptions I never heard in my boyhood or youth from a Scottish preacher a word that had the least meaning or interest for me. Scottish preachers embrace some of the best that have ever lived, and some of the worst, and I happened to be brought up among country ministers who had no gift of public speech, no juice in mind or heart.

The singing, on the other hand, affected me greatly. It was simple in the last degree, weird, but it had something grand in it. There was the bleak old kirk, and the people, hard-featured, heroic, looking as if they had had a tough struggle with the world, which was indeed the truth. Outside — let us say in winter — was the wild, stormy universe beating against the bleak old building. There was no organ, no piano, no instrumental music of any kind. The congregation, perhaps crowding the building, rose and sang with sincerity heart melodies that told of their faith in God, their purpose to be men, their sense of the pathos of life, and their willingness to accept whatever God might ordain. Weird and moving were those heart melodies rolled out against the wintry sky. Burns, in 'The Cotter's Saturday Night,' gives an exact picture of what occurred in church:

> 'Perhaps Dundee's wild warbling measures rise,
>   Or plaintive Martyrs, worthy of the name;
>   Or noble Elgin beets the heaven-ward flame,
> The sweetest far of Scotia's holy lays:
>   Compar'd with these, Italian trills are tame;
>   The tickl'd ears no heartfelt raptures raise;
>   Nae unison hae they with our Creator's praise.'

There were no hymns — the Hebrew Psalms in metre were our songs — and once in a while a great burst of poetry would come, and with it a volume of music from those sincere men and women, music that would pierce one's heart with a sense of God and the grandeur of human life. For example, this passage from Psalm one hundred and seven:

> 'The storm is changed into a calm
> At His command and will,
> So that the waves that raged before
> Now quiet are and still.
> Then are they glad because at rest,
> And quiet now they be;
> So to the Haven He them brings
> Which they desired to see.'

Magnificent words, receiving up into themselves the sternly resolute life of heroic men and women, 'sorrowful, yet always rejoicing, . . . poor, yet making many rich, . . . having nothing, and yet possessing all things.'

What took place after we came home from church? The afternoon was spent in Bible-reading, committing Psalms to memory, a toilsome afternoon; in the evening there was the Catechism, a mournful hour; and the day ended with family prayer; and at the last exercise the exhausted boys and girls would fall asleep, and get punished for it.

Some of these evening scenes were not only touchingly pious, but also overwhelmingly humorous. Our good father would gather us in a circle, round him and our mother, weary as we were with the religious toil of the day. He would select a chapter unmerciful in its length, and he would skip nothing. By the end of the chapter we were nearly all asleep. When the reading was done we knelt in prayer, and those prayers of our father were the spoken burden of parental anxiety and hope, rich in tender feeling, and impressive in the highest degree, had we not been already done up. While this exercise was going on, a brother considerably younger than I succumbed, fell over on the tea-kettle, the water in it being supposed to be boiling hot, but which had become quite cold. This youngster overturned the kettle and when the water struck him he yelled, 'I am burnt!' This was too much for me; I burst into a loud laugh, nearly the unpardonable sin at such a time. My father paused in his prayer, rectified the kettle, struck my brother a smart blow, struck me a heavier blow, knelt again and went on with his devotions.

There are two things that abide with me in the keeping of the Sabbath; first the immense number who went to church. I believe this custom still reigns. At the hour of service the beautiful city of Aberdeen, on Union Street, a noble street running a mile and a quarter through the city, not a vehicle of any kind is to be seen; there go the multitudes blackening the street, tens of thousands, dressed in their Sunday clothes, on their way to the House of God. In Edinburgh, on Princes Street, not a vehicle anywhere is in sight, but human beings filling the street from sidewalk to sidewalk, all bent on the same high errand. The Scotch are a church-going people, especially in the cities, and they are a Sabbath-revering people; no games, no fishing, no shooting, no play of any kind. Why? They believe and revere; the religion of the nation must be respected; the immemorial habit of the people must be regarded; the unbeliever must conform; conformation is a tribute due from the individual to the community, to the nation.

The second impression that remains with me is that of the fortitude of the people under disappointing circumstances. No matter how dull the sermon might be, they were not discouraged; they did not go to church primarily to hear a minister; there was the House of God, the Bible, the songs of Zion. They went to worship God; that was the primary object. If the sermon was interesting, all the better; if it was not, they could endure it.

I recall an instance, when I was much older, of going to a church that seated seventeen hundred, and the church was packed to the doors. The sermon was a little critical essay on Galatians and very poor at that, with no more reference to human life than the quack of a duck in the milldam. I looked round to see how the people were taking it. There was perfect equanimity, nobody was disturbed, nobody was impatient. The sermon was three-quarters of an hour long, the services were two hours long. I myself was so disturbed by the whole thing that when I went out I walked behind three or four constant worshipers that I might catch the comment, and I got this: 'Dry to-day, wasn't he?' 'Aye.' 'Drier than usual?' 'Aye.' Up piped another, 'Na, na; just about his usual.' But the seventeen hundred would be back the next Sunday. There is something fine and high in this, that the people are not going to be chased away from the House of God by a poor or a dull preacher, that they are not going to allow their relation to God to be disturbed by the incompetence of the minister, or their worship marred.

I must add that the country people did not take to a preacher who was brilliant. 'He's a gude shop-window'; that is, he puts all his goods where they may be seen; if you should go into the store, you would find the rest of it empty. A man that they could not understand was often very highly regarded. 'Wasna that a grand sermon?' 'Aye, but did you understand it?' 'Understand it? I wou'dna hae the presumption.'

On another occasion I went with my oldest brother, an elder in the Established Church, and a man of marked ability, to hear a certain preacher. Again the church was crowded. The sermon was on Paul, a man with a thousand points of contact with our modern world; no one of these points was made; what we got was a quiet little essay upon a man who lived nineteen centuries ago. I asked my brother what he thought of the sermon; his answer was, 'It was a good sermon for Paul, and I am sorry he was not there to hear it.'

My father had heard the mighty Chalmers once or twice, and always rose into the language of eulogy when he spoke of him. He had frequently heard Thomas Guthrie, and was greatly moved by his oratory and his humanity. We were told that in the great cities there were preachers of extraordinary power, and that where one could hear such divines and prophets church-going was not an obligation but a privilege. For myself it never rose to the plane of privilege; it stood, like the sun at Joshua's command, on the level of painful obligation.

The religion of my boyhood and youth was austere and unlovely, viewed in itself; it appeared grand and heroic in my father, and in one or two others of my kinsmen; in my mother, especially after her great religious experience in the mid-forties, it appeared absolutely real and supremely beautiful. This was because she was a Wesleyan by descent, and because her religion exalted and sweetened her whole great endowment as a human being. The current religion was under the shadow of John Calvin and his Scottish followers; and to me it was meager, blasted, unlovely and indeed inhuman. The version of the national faith that I saw and pondered was likely enough a poor version; it was not the sublime figure of Christ upon the cathedral of life, but a gargoyle. Often did I resolve to have nothing to do with it, preferring life in its integrity and abundance to an emaciated and fantastic ghost of it.

This reaction was largely that of boyhood and youth, abundant in the joy of living, or rich in the sense of life's tenderness and struggle, against the religion of mature men and women for whom the world was essentially an illusion. I can now see that those men and women had gone through great experiences, that life had proved itself a thing of many disappointments and sorrows, and that having found existence a stern affair they had matched it with a stern faith. What was austere and unlovely to a boy becomes impressive and moving in its somber strength as I view it over the expanse of the years. The sense of God was great in it, and this even then was visibly its transfiguring soul, as after a wild and stormy day in Scotland I have seen the setting sun disclose the glory that had all through the dark hours been behind the thick clouds, and before he disappeared set on fire the whole lurid heavens. If in the religion of my native land there was too much of the flint of the rocks, in its season there would surely appear the bloom of the heather. In my judgment a Christianity that should combine the passion for righteousness and compassion for poor human beings, rigorous ethical idealism and sympathy, the consciousness of the perfect God through the sense of humanity, the flint of the rock with the heather over it in perpetual bloom, would be a close approximation to the religion of Jesus, the sovereign prophet of man and of the Most High.

CHAPTER IX

PRE–MORAL RELIGION: ATHLETICS

HAPPENING to be in Scotland in 1901 when the great Highland Gathering in Aberdeen took place, I invited one of my sisters, a good companion, sympathetic usually, to go with me. I found that she admired things that did not appeal to me and that she overlooked almost all the things that did appeal to me. While I was looking upon the magnificent forms, the strength, symmetry, agility of the great athletes, she was looking at the representatives of the great families present, Duke this and Duchess that, Marquis this and Marchioness that, Lord and Lady this and that; and while I was watching the records that were made, she was diverting my attention to something else; the only things she was really interested in were the dancing competition and the beautiful costumes worn by the dancers; then, too, there was the tent for afternoon tea, into which the nobility and the ordinary people were gathered. The fact is, this good sister, in the idiom of Sir Harry Lauder, 'made me sick'; and when thinking of possible readers of this chapter, and that I might have many hundreds of sisters to entertain, I am unable to see how I ever selected the subject of Scottish Athletics. The only way out of it that I can imagine, with any sort of satisfaction, is to ask my feminine readers to think of their brothers, their sons or young men friends between the ages of sixteen and twenty-five, and read and reflect for them on the bearing of athletics upon the life of youth. The question is urgent and difficult to answer, during the years of peril and promise, how to conserve the strength of the body, and all the finer instincts that come into being with normally born and normally trained young men, how to conserve this unwasted through a very dangerous period and before there is any distinct moral purpose in the individual, any high personal aim; and even in the case of a youth of a decided Christian purpose, the subject that I am to consider means an immense auxiliary force.

Objection is sometimes raised to athletics on account of the strain and the injury resulting to health by over-exertion. That is a real peril. The Greeks had a motto which should never be forgotten here, 'Nothing too much.' Everywhere that motto is applicable, and nowhere more than in athletics. The objection is serious, but may be easily surmounted by reasonable minds and by their advisers. There is another objection, and this time of a moral nature, that athletics are competitive, and that the competitive spirit is harmful. I admit that the highest form of human fellowship is coöperation; coöperation of mind, of will, of sympathy. But even in religion rivalry is allowed. One will find that idea in the New Testament, and surely no harm can come to society from each one of us trying to excel, to go beyond his neighbor in doing good to the community, in becoming a nobler benefactor to mind and body. For myself, I am quite convinced that the principle of competition is absolutely indispensable to the life of the world as it is to-day. Let me give an example. When I began to cross the ocean, the Cunard Line, the oldest and in many ways the most magnificent of all the lines, had poor little tubs of boats, twenty-two hundred tons burden, the poorest kind of service for saloon passengers, to say nothing about the steerage or the intermediate. The saloon was in between staterooms, running from midships to the screw, unwholesome, indeed unsanitary; but the appeals for better boats, better accommodations, and better services were unheeded and contemptuously turned down. The captain was a boor, the officers were not gentlemen, the servants on the ship were all half-contemptuous toward the passengers. What brought about the change? Competing lines. Line after line came in with better boats, better service, better accommodations, more civility, higher spirit, bidding for the travel. The old Cunard Line bethought itself, and we got, instead of boats of twenty-two hundred tons, boats of five thousand, then seven, eight, thirteen, thirty thousand, and upward, and everything to match; speed, comfort, civility; all issuing from the operation of the competitive principle; we should not have had a single improvement but for competition. Wherever you withdraw competition, you have a monopoly. If that monopoly is bad, it is a tyranny; if it is a good monopoly, it is good because it is continually threatened by the appearance of a competitor. Let us not fool ourselves. This world as we find it to-day cannot be run in the fair interest of the consumer, in the just interest of the community, without the force of competition. And in athletics there need be no bad blood. There may be genial rivalry and manly contention, and such there were in athletics as I observed them in my youth.

What do I mean by pre-moral religion? Any interest powerful enough to keep the mind against low temptation, against the appeals of vice; any interest powerful enough to keep a man's life clean. There are many such interests. There are those with whom friendship is a religion; there are those with whom music is such; young men know that if they are to excel in music they must look out for the body, the health, and the character, in order to appeal to and to win the suffrage and the attention of the better classes in the community. They may have no interest in goodness itself, but their desire for excellence in their art wields a conservative influence upon their feeling and behavior; besides, music becomes an absorbing passion lessening the strength of other passions. This is true of manly sport of any kind, of travel, and of many other interests. Wherever we find an interest powerful enough to lift a man above base appeal, powerful enough to keep his life clean, even if it may not be regarded as a moral or spiritual interest, it may be defined as a sort of pre-moral religion.

I remember well the hour in college when the thought came to me that any motive that keeps a young man or young woman out of the power of evil and in the maintenance of a clean life is a good motive. All motives should be looked upon as good that operate upon boys and girls, upon young men and women in their immaturity, to raise them above the base appeals in their environment and to keep them eager and able to maintain a clean life.

A serious question with the Scottish people — I refer now to the masses of the people, farm servants and tradespeople of all sorts — is this: what to do with their time during the long evenings of the loveliest summer on the face of the earth — except when there is an occasional wet or bad summer, which occurs only when Americans in too great numbers go there. Scotland has about the worst

climate in winter, but the best that I know of in summer —
that is, from May to October. The men knock off work at
six o'clock, eat a hurried supper, and are out at half-after six,
and the question is, What shall they do with their time and
their surplus energy for the next three hours? Shall they
go into the public houses and drink and there absolutely
spoil life? Or shall they go to the village green or the field
and engage in manly sports that keep them in the wholesome air, in the sunshine, and that send them afterwards
back to their beds to sleep soundly and to get up in the
morning fit and well for the work of the day?

Scottish athletics are divisible into three grades of competition. There are the Annual Games in almost every
parish in Scotland, and the preparation for these from May
till July or August is the great interest of all athletically
inclined young people, and in that preparation all take
part, the good, the fairly good, and the not at all good; it
being no disgrace to fall behind. Here is a delightful exercise and a stimulating rivalry; the performers are, in
turn, performers and spectators; the practice includes
throwing the hammer, heavy and light, the twenty-two-
pound and the sixteen-pound; putting the shot, also heavy
and light, twenty-two and sixteen-pound; tossing the caber,
one of the most engaging exercises, the turning of a tree
end over end, the tree being accommodated to the size of
the individual tosser, in weight running all the way from
fifty to seventy-five pounds, and up to three hundred
pounds, and in length from a dozen to twenty-one or
twenty-two feet; wrestling of all kinds; running of various
distances; leaping, long leap and high leap, and hop, step,
and leap; dancing, and other features.

This goes on generally throughout the parish. The finest men go to the Parish Games and compete; the best men among the competitors win, and they are encouraged by public sentiment to go to the next grade of competition, the Inter-Parish Games, a larger affair. Here a number of parishes unite and send their select athletes to compete on this higher level; these athletes, having been victorious in their several localities, try their fortune on a larger scale. The events are the same; from these contests we have a new body of victorious athletes who are known as stars within a radius of eight or ten parishes. All this is still local and informal; athletics have not yet reached the stage of national importance.

When we come to the third stage, we are really in the athletics of Scotland. From these Inter-Parish contests the best men are again encouraged to go to the great Highland Gatherings that are patronized by the highest families in the nation; subscriptions are made to them by the wealthy, the noblemen are on the committees that arrange for them and that administer judgment.

The final form of the athletic contest is a social event as well as an exhibition of strength, agility and skill; it is a National Festival. It involves the character of the people, aristocratic and democratic; all classes meet together in a common interest in the development of physical power. There are many of these Highland Gatherings; a few of the greater of them are Inverness; Balmoral, in her time, always patronized by Queen Victoria; she would be there punctually to witness the whole function, and rarely would she leave before the last competition was concluded. The Prince of Wales, later Edward VII, gave a famous prize

for a hurdle race of three hundred yards and the crossing
of the River Dee at the end; the depth varies from two to
five feet, and the struggle to get to the other side was very
interesting for the spectators, not always so interesting for
the competitor, the current being swift; then there are
Aboyne, Aberdeen, Dundee, Edinburgh, Glasgow, Bridge
of Allan, Oban. These were open to all comers from all
parts of the world, and each event was reported fully and
in detail by the leading newspapers of the country — who
were present, and whether any records were broken.

This was with me, I confess, an absorbing interest, and a
source of vast happiness. I could now name the leading
athletes of Scotland, in all branches of athletic contest, and
their best performances, over a period of more than sixty
years. In running and in leaping there are no records in
Scotland equal to those done in the United States; there is
something here, not only in the training, but also and still
more in the air, that make possible unequaled achievements especially in the high leap. Nothing over six feet and
one inch was ever done in Scotland, although that height
has been frequently attained. Taking into consideration
the conditions of competition, in the heavy events, the
feats performed by the best Scottish athletes would compare favorably with anything that has ever been done in
the same style, in America. The American amateur competitor works under the most favoring conditions, and he is
usually confined to one event. Ralph Rose did fifty-one
feet at the Olympic Games in Sweden, but the fatigue of
travel so affected him that the best he could do in Germany
was forty-seven feet with sixteen-pound shot. Had he
gone the round of the Highland Games in Scotland, and

shared with other athletes the fatigue of travel, the uncertain weather and the poor opportunities for food suitable to an athlete, he would have found himself down to forty-four or forty-five feet with the same weight. In judging of performances conditions must be considered, and whether the athlete is a one-event man or an all-round performer.

It should be said that it was the person and the performances of a great Scottish athlete that started the United States on its splendid career in track athletics. Donald Dinnie, the greatest of all Scottish athletes, visited the United States in 1870, in 1872, and again in 1882. He did here in America what he did in Scotland, he glorified the sport, and created among vigorous young men the passion to excel in it. He could do forty-nine feet six inches with a shot over sixteen pounds in weight, thirty-nine feet nine inches with the twenty-two-pound shot; his performances in throwing the hammer, heavy and light, were amazing, and as a caber tosser he has been regarded by experts as the greatest ever seen; while weighing from two hundred and ten to two hundred and twenty pounds he could clear six feet one inch at the high leap; he was also a good runner. At wrestling Scotland never had anything like him. He kept his form till he was well over fifty, and in length as well as in excellence his athletic career stands unique.

I have tried to present a picture of one great method by which the surplus energy and time of a people physically great are profitably and pleasantly occupied; I close with two or three remarks as to the character of this interest and enjoyment.

First, as to the wholesomeness of the recreation. I look back upon it with delight. Could there be a better thing than two hours spent in the summer air, with companions younger and older, in friendly rivalry, plenty of laughter, fun galore, no bad blood at any time, the defeated laughing at himself as heartily as any one, the champion always modest — if he were not, he would be made so before that crowd got through with him? I cannot think of a healthier recreation for the body and for the mind of those who have no aspirations after literature or science or intellectual glory in any sphere.

The second remark that I have to make is, that young men discover very quickly that excellence in any kind of athletics demands temperance and a clean life. We saw athlete after athlete formerly full of promise knocked out by doing things that were disgraceful and wrong. The ambitious lads quickly caught on to the idea that to excel in any feat of strength or skill or speed required a certain kind of morality that must be observed. There is the beginning of character, and it is a fine beginning; it is to be recognized as such, and laid to heart. This matter is understood well to-day by our college athletes; there must be no intemperance, no dissipation; the men must be guarded if the team is to do its best, or the individual his best.

The third thing to be noted is hero-worship; here surely is one of the delights of life; it is one of those interests that take a youth out of himself. You say that what we have here is a low grade of hero-worship, and I grant at once that it is not the highest. But a strong man has always made a vast appeal to a boy; a finely developed physique, a man who can do extraordinary feats, simply captivates a boy. I have in mind such an athlete, one whom I have just described — Donald Dinnie — who was king everywhere. As a boy, as a lad, I would rather have been like that man than like George Washington, or Hannibal, or Napoleon; and I believe this represents the real heart of the boy everywhere. This man was a superb human being. I have a picture of him wearing one hundred and fifty medals, slung round his chest and back, and he had twice as many more; in fact, it was said that no man could stand up under the amount of silver and gold that he had won. To meet that human being sent a thrill through a boy's life. Even such hero-worship induces wholesome moods; it means self-forgetfulness, admiration of consummate physical ability kept in consummate condition. Hero-worship, along any line of excellence, is a great thing for a boy, a great thing for a youth. Although I did not know it at the time, I can now see here a fresh beginning in my life. I moved on to greater heroes, to heroes in the intellectual realm, in all spheres of the intellectual and religious realm; those beginnings of hero-worship were revised, indeed, yet were they continued, developed, and glorified by what came after.

It will, I trust, be understood from this discussion, what I mean by athletics as a pre-moral religion; any wholesome and absorbing interest that your boy has before he cares anything for your prayer meeting, before the sermons that you think are wonderful mean anything other than an endurance test for him, before God is other than a name, and when goodness is somehow without form or fire. Here is an interest to hold him, to give him glow, enthusiasm, to open to him the necessity of self-control and manliness, to teach him that, if he is to excel, he must be clean, to open up his heart into admiration of those who are bigger than he, who can do things that he cannot do, that tell him about a super-world for which he may, indeed, be a candidate, but which is altogether above him. This, I think, is something that parents, teachers, and all religious people should consider seriously and devoutly; for there is a period in life when such motives are indispensable, when the higher motives are unavailing.

If I were asked which I would rather have done, when I was a lad of fifteen, go to a Highland Gathering or go to church, I would say the Highland Gathering every time. All lads are of the same stuff. Have faith in them, work for them; by and by you will get them responsive to the highest motives, those that move, exalt, enrich, purify, and greaten the many-sided soul of man.

CHAPTER X
THE DISCIPLINE OF IMMIGRATION

IMMIGRATION, in the first place, is the beginning of a new epoch in the life of the immigrant. There is the romance of it, the adventure, a voyage at sea, crossing the mighty ocean, landing in a new country, in a new continent, a mystic land lying in the sunset. There are the crowding and multitudinous impressions of a new land, and the awakening of the mind by a stimulus and appeal not experienced before. And the queer people one sees when one comes to these shores; for every immigrant brings a standard of perfection with him from the country that he left behind. The Italian, German, Frenchman, the Irish, Scottish, English, all feel what a queer lot of people live here; their Declaration of Independence, their Constitution, their Republic; and their poetry, music, painting, and all the rest, how indescribable; and themselves, all so funny. Americans think the immigrant is funny, but he thinks Americans are funny, and there is a good deal to be said for his view. The romance is everything at the beginning; in contemplation the immigrant's feeling is that of Byron's 'Corsair':

'O'er the glad waters of the dark blue sea,
Our thoughts as boundless, and our souls as free,
Far as the breeze can bear, the billows foam,
Survey our empire, and behold our home!'

The second experience is of hard fact. There is the terrible experience of farewell for deep-hearted young men and women, farewell to father and mother, to brothers and sisters, to kindred, to those who have been friends from life's beginning, to the total environment, to the earth and sky in all their mystic and wondrous moods by which they attach every normal human being to the place where he was born.

> 'Breathes there the man, with soul so dead,
> Who never to himself hath said,
> This is my own, my native land! '

John Stuart Blackie, famous Professor, for many years in Edinburgh University, wrote a lyric on the immigrant, true to life.

> 'As I came wandering down Glen Spean,
> Where the braes are green and grassy,
> With my light step I overtook
> A weary-footed lassie.

> ' She had one bundle on her back,
> Another in her hand,
> And she walk'd as one who was full loath
> To travel from the land.
> . . . .

> ' " I'm fresh and strong, and stoutly shod,
> And thou art burden'd so;
> March lightly now, and let me bear
> The bundles as we go."

> ' " No, no! " she said, "that may not be,
> What's mine is mine to bear;
> Of good or ill, as God may will
> I take my portion'd share."
> . . . .

> ' " Belike it is some present rare
> From friend in parting hour;
> Perhaps, as prudent maidens wont,
> Thou tak'st with thee thy dower."

'She droop'd her head, and with her hand
She gave a mournful wave;
"Oh, do not jest, dear sir!—it is
Turf from my mother's grave!"'

Consider the actual sea voyage. Fifty years ago a jail sentence of two weeks was nothing in comparison with it. The steerage passenger was treated to food absolutely disgusting, unfit to be set before human beings or even pigs. I was perfectly well all the way over, and in the fourteen days I lost just fourteen pounds; I was almost starved. There was one meal a day, oatmeal, which they could not spoil, but all the rest — the odor of them was enough. The quarters where we slept were simply scandalous. On my side of the ship there were five beds below, over them another tier of five, and then an upper tier, and in each bed there was about fifteen inches of canvas to sleep on. We paid £6 10s. for the passage, and it was reported that the company cleared more on each steerage passenger than was made on a first-class passenger. What changed all that? Competition, to which I referred in my last chapter. Many years after this I went into the steerage quarters of the new steamers and I found them better than the first-class quarters of fifty-four years ago. Our ship, the Corinthian of the Allan Line, was eighteen hundred tons burden; she jumped on the sea like a catboat. The last steamer on which I crossed the Atlantic was twenty-five thousand tons, and we know that there are steamers in service to-day of more than twice that tonnage. I resolved that I never would cross the ocean again if I had to go back the way I came. Once is enough of that experience. The treatment of human beings by the company was heartless, inhuman, devilish.

The sail up the Gulf of St. Lawrence, and on the great river, was a new experience; so was the landing in Quebec and the sight of the quaint and wonderful old city. We started from Quebec about nine o'clock in the evening, July 12th; it was hot as Tophet, and I watched from the window sparks of fire in the grass. We were told that the country was full of snakes, and I thought these were snakes' eyes winking. I found later they were only fireflies. The carriages in which we rode were immigrant carriages; trucks for cattle they appeared to me to be. We got to Richmond, Canada, and were there changed to the Grand Trunk Railway, and here the carriages were so good, so beautiful, that my sister and I did not dare to go into them, they were such a violent contrast to what we had been in. Finally I said to my sister, 'They cannot do more than order us out; let us go in anyway'; and we did. I inquired of the conductor, 'Does this train go to Portland and Boston; are we in the right car?' and he said, 'Yes.' What a relief; what joy to step from hell to heaven! The train stopped somewhere, I know not where, that we poor immigrants might breakfast. I there got a cup of tea which I thought was poisoned; the taste was sickening and indeed alarming. I learnt afterwards that this horrible drink was simply Oolong tea and that American ladies were fond of it. After a long hot and dusty ride we arrived in Boston at half-past six o'clock on the evening of July 13, 1871.

A farmer's son is grounded in sensitive self-respect. At home he does not have to go out and look for a job; half a dozen persons compete with one another to hire him; he is in demand. It is a new experience for this kind of a youth, when he comes to a city and has no trade, to go and beg for work. The pain, the humiliation, of going to see person after person, asking to be allowed to work, has not escaped the eye of Burns:

> 'See yonder poor, o'erlabor'd wight,
>   So abject, mean, and vile,
> Who begs a brother of the earth
>   To give him leave to toil.'

Of my own experiences with fellow-workmen I have a very happy memory. The place where I found work was a safe-factory; from farm to safe-factory, what a rise! After the Civil War burglary had become a profession and burglar proof safes were in great demand, and I went into this business. I have never heard that any safe that I helped to build was ever burst open by a burglar — nor have I ever heard that it was not. This place, which is a horror to me still, was a subterranean region on the corner of Green and Pitts Streets. The men went in by a dark door, down a dark stairway, into a place that their eyes had to get familiar with before they could see anything. There for ten hours in the day we hammered and hammered the cold steel. There were thirty men, and twenty of them were Irish. How good and kind the Irishmen were to this young Scot of eighteen, alien and 'greenhorn'! They were bound that he should have fair play; sympathetic they all were, not a word was spoken that was unkind or ungenerous or unfriendly; I have a happy memory of these men, all vanished now into the Unseen.

There was a German in this assemblage, a powerful man; not at all a bad man, but a little 'fresh.' He had been in the factory a good while longer than I, and he wanted to make fun of this poor youth, when we knocked off work in the evening, by forcing him to wrestle. I had taken a vow to keep out of all 'scrapping' of every kind if I possibly could. I remembered the apostolic injunction, to live as far as possible peaceably with all men. The apostle knew life well, as his qualification, if possible, shows. I felt that my stock was going down, had indeed gone down fifty per cent; I was losing the respect of my fellow-workers; this man was forcing wrestling and I was refusing. I accepted his challenge on the fourth evening. It was not at all new business for me, but I did not in the least expect to throw so powerful a man — he weighed about two hundred and twenty-five and I about one hundred and seventy-five pounds. It should be added that a youth of eighteen, well built, vigorous, well trained, has endless endurance; he could wrestle all day. I let my friend force the issue, and I waited till he began to puff, and, without the least expectation that it would have any effect, I gave him a twist and he went down like a thousand bricks. 'Mere accident,' I thought; 'he will be up on his feet again and I shall have to meet a tougher trial.' Instead of that, he rose and ran for the door as fast as he could. I then learnt that skill, endurance, and courage are more than a match for mere brute strength. Another thing I laid to heart; while doing all that one can to avoid trouble, when it is here, inevitably here, there is only one thing to do, and that is to meet it like a man.

I had one experience in this factory which opened my eyes to the ignoble side of life. I was able to save a fellow-workman from being crushed to death by a heavy steel door which fell, or would have fallen, on him if I had not caught it. It was too heavy for me to hold long; I could only hold it till he got from under it; then it fell on my finger; it did not amputate the finger because it was soft ground into which my finger was pressed; but I received a severe and an ugly wound. At 9.30 in the morning I went to the Massachusetts General Hospital, and I was there a daily visitor for five weeks. When my finger got well, I returned for my pay, and I got my pay up to 9.30 of that morning, and this notwithstanding the fact that I had saved a human life.

In those days there were many employers who would take every possible advantage of an ignorant, inexperienced immigrant. I recall working for a German — I had a good deal to do with Germans in those days — for six weeks. I was promised pay every Saturday night, but the pay was deferred, for one reason or another. Finally I demanded my pay, and I was discharged, and got nothing for the six weeks. I had my satisfaction. That gentleman ran into a locomotive when it was going the other way and he was half-killed, and he got no damages. I have never been able to regret this experience of my German friend; it seemed to me then and it seems to me now something that he richly deserved; an act of God, let us call it.

I must allude briefly to one heroic day in my life as an immigrant. It had a ludicrous beginning. My sister, as usual, prepared the morning meal, porridge and milk, and as we were in a hurry she set the porridge out to cool it off, and beside it was the can of milk left by the milkman. A dog came and ate up the porridge, and the dog's master took the can of milk. There we were without anything in the house, except the two or three spoonfuls of oatmeal left in the utensil in which the meal had been prepared. I went to my work, a walk of three miles, worked till noon, went away and sat by myself while the other workmen were eating their lunch, returned and worked till six o'clock, walked three miles, sold my watch, walked three miles more, and my sister and I had our first meal at nine o'clock in the evening. Why? Because villainous employers refused to pay wages when they were due. But that experience stiffened me and they paid me the next day. It should be added that these experiences are typical; that thousands of ignorant human beings pass through similar ill-treatment; that 'man's inhumanity to man' is nowhere more potent and cruel than in the first years of an immigrant's life.

What has been said is a source of light as to the psychological change through which the immigrant is likely to pass. There is at this period an exaggerated idealization of the old country. Everything was beautiful there, all early troubles are forgotten, life as it was shines in mild and lovely splendor. All this is, of course, pure exaggeration; still, it is inevitable. I remember a remark of my good sister, who died two years and eight months after we came here, 'If I could only see my native land again, I would kneel and reverently kiss the soil.'

There follows the revulsion against the new country. These accursed Yankees, what a bad lot they are! They are keen, they can outwit any Scot alive, and their keenness is unmodified and unsoftened by any religion. Again exaggeration is as plain here as it was in the idealization of the past.

Disillusionment is apt to appear at this stage of experience; vigorous persons come here to make money, honestly, by hard work, and great workmen have been sent from all European countries to these shores; they come to make money by hard work, and to save, and after a term of years to return home; almost all of them expect to return home. The immigrant finds that, although he gets more money, it costs him more to live, and he is hardly any better off than he was before. I recall the remark of a very close Scot newly arrived who went to buy overalls. He saw that they cost ninety-seven cents; that did not sound so bad. He handed out a dollar and got three cents change; then what had happened dawned upon him, and he exclaimed, 'That knocks a terrible hole in a dollar.'

The next thing is the discovery of the world mind, the greatest discovery that a man can make; the discovery of the resources in the human spirit, the wealth there, the independence, the character, and the open door into fellowship with great minds all over the world. Here was the Republic of America; in it there was a republic of letters, a republic of poets, of thinkers, who had taken the greatest ideas of mankind and put them into the most beautiful form. What an escape this was from the disappointment, the humiliation, and the sorrow of life, this vast and precious discovery of mind! The immigrant himself had a mind, and there was an intellectual world all about him waiting to bid him welcome to its fellowship, its communion, its treasure, its joy. And in the case of one immigrant, there was soon to be the discovery of a new vocation, and the vast romance of preparation for that vocation.

Here I must pay a tribute to a fine soul in a sordid environment, the kindest and most helpful soul to me in all Boston in the day of my distress and trouble. I was getting on very well with my work, and with my studies when, in June, 1872, I came down with typhoid fever. It took me four months to recover, and I got into debt again. When I was convalescent I owed my doctor fifty dollars. He was a wise and good man, moderate in his charges, and patient as to the time of payment. The woman who with her husband kept the boarding-house and bar in Pitts Street, where I had lived for six months, knew that I had been sick. She came to me and asked, 'Where are you boarding?' I replied, 'I don't know where I am going to live, my money is gone, and I cannot work for three months.' Her response was this: 'Come to my house and live there; pay me when you can, and if you want anything at the bar to strengthen you, it shall be yours free.' This last privilege, I am happy to say, I never improved. During the many weeks of my convalescence I had in this home the best of food, a good room, and I never met anything but a smile, a word of sympathy and hope from that most generous woman. I remember her with reverence and gratitude; she was like a pond lily, lifting above the stagnant and poisoned element in which her life was rooted, a soul of unsullied purity and loveliness. I still owed her five dollars when I took my leave, and I was not able to pay this till the middle of my first year in Bangor Seminary. When she saw me, dressed somewhat clerically, her greeting was, 'Lord bless you, what have you gone and become now?' 'A Protestant priest' was my reply, and her warm Celtic and Catholic nature burst into rich and delightful laughter. I may say that I had to fight to make her take that last payment of five dollars. Within the year she had lost by death her only child, a lovely daughter of twelve years of age. It was for the daughter an infinite boon, to be taken on the breath of death from that terrible environment, but for the poor mother and her nature, great in tender feeling, it was a crushing sorrow. We sat down and talked it all over while the great tears rolled down her kindly and sorrow-stricken face. The end of the dialogue was the only one that carries in it heart's ease. God's will is best, for us, for all whom we love, and for the whole troubled race of man.

I have often thought of that fine soul as a type of many others in this dark and ugly world. There are many of them, of all creeds and persuasions — souls with God's love in them, and human kindness, whose hands are stretched toward struggling fellow-mortals, and who are indeed Christ's ministers. That woman was the best friend that I, a youth of nineteen, had at that time; in the crowded city of Boston, where there are so many good men and women, she was the best.

In the end of September I went back to work, and this time I was engaged by the American Steam Safe Company of South Boston. During the winter preceding three hundred and fifty panes of glass had been broken in the factory, and during the autumn these windows were to be repaired. When I asked for a job, I was questioned as to whether I could set glass. I had seen a carpenter cut with his diamond one pane and set it. I was fearful lest I might lose this job which would keep me a month, in fine weather, out of doors, and thus confirm my recovery from typhoid fever, and I replied that I knew how to cut and set glass. I started in with fear and trembling; I got on famously, and no one ever knew that my previous experience had been so limited. I set every pane of glass in the factory and afterwards joined the force of painters indoors.

Toward the end of my painting experience I had a fine time of it, if I did not produce any great works of art. I was sent out to paint vaults, and the doors of vaults, in the Lowell Station, now part of the North Station, Boston & Maine Railway. I did the same sort of work for the Franklin Street Bank, the Suffolk Bank, and the then new Post Office on Devonshire Street. The company gave me fifty cents for my lunch or dinner; a cup of coffee and a piece of pie would cost ten cents, and the remaining forty cents went into my book-account. A new book a week came out of this achievement, and in the course of the winter a small library, of which I was inexpressibly proud, rewarded my self-denial in noonday meals. An unusually heavy breakfast and supper enabled me to endure this self-denial without any conscious injury to my health, and as the mistress of the boarding-house saved one meal each day by this arrangement she made no complaint.

In March, 1874, I again changed my occupation. I had been in succession safe-builder, stonemason, painter; now I became assistant editor to a monthly paper called 'The Cherub,' which I believe has long ago returned to heaven. I wrote one or two pieces for this paper and I did secretarial work of a miscellaneous character. The office correspondence was new to me; it was exceedingly interesting and I greatly enjoyed it. Events in my life were, however, shaping themselves into something higher; I was indeed on the dim frontier of a new career.

CHAPTER XI

A GREAT SURPRISE

I HAD been brought up to think very modestly of my abilities. At school I had met many boys who seemed to me to be much brighter scholars than I, and to possess much more mental power. It is true that, while I could not learn quickly, I could retain permanently what I had learnt and in this way the accumulation would tell in my favor over most of my associates; it is also true that I could think, but as this did not count with my teachers it was of little help in raising my self-estecm. My wise father, who regarded conceit as a form of lying, and an odious form of it, a feeling that I surely inherited, and which has become stronger with the years, told me with solemn earnestness that as my abilities were below the average I could only hope to succeed by unusual industry and good behavior. I have never been able to escape for any length of time from the wholesome shelter of that stern judgment. There has been perpetual peace under the shadow of my father's estimate of my powers, and another thing of the happiest character. Any success that has come to me as a student, preacher, thinker, and writer has always come as a surprise, as when one goes to bed expecting the next day to be one of tempest and wakes to find it a morning without clouds.

In December, 1871, I called upon my pastor the Reverend Luther H. Angier, minister of the Fourth Presbyterian Church, South Boston, with reference to joining the church.

I received from him a warm welcome and he unsealed the fountains of speech in me to such an extent that, the religious question being settled, I spoke of my interest in books, and in the great struggle of the Civil War whose close was only six years in the past. The interview was delightful to me, and the fine-looking, eloquent, and cordial old man of sixty-one made upon me a deep impression.

I seldom went to the weekly meeting, but my comrades were faithful in their attendance. On the week following my interview with the minister, at the usual mid-week meeting, Mr. Angier launched into a tribute to my abilities that startled my chums, who eagerly took in what was said, and amid much laughter repeated the eulogy to me, as a first-class joke. I was more than pleased, I was indeed inspired by this high opinion; at the same time I was afraid that the next interview with the minister might result in the cancellation of his first judgment. This did not happen and, after many interviews and ever-growing intimacy, the minister became more and more confident that there was in my mental endowment something worth while.

I now for the first time began to believe in myself, in a wholesome and just sense, and I am under everlasting obligations to the good and generous minister for the light he shed upon my life, and for the inspiration that for several years I continued to receive from him. I began to listen to his discourses on Sunday with the closest attention, and with sincere sympathy. He had one of the two best voices for public speaking to which I have ever listened. The other voice was that of President Charles W. Eliot in his prime. President Eliot's voice was superior to that of Mr. Angier for academic address; it had as great a range;

it was equally musical, and bell-like in tone, and it had far greater dignity due in part to the great mind and character behind it. Mr. Angier's voice, in its turn, excelled in awakening power, in fire, force, and sympathy; to listen to it was a delight. He was not a scholar, not in any sense a thoughtful preacher, nor did he have, in any department, other than a very limited range of information. But he was intensely practical, with good observational powers, and from his intimate association through life with many persons of distinction he had acquired a good measure of culture. He was not in any way a strong character, but he was generous, quick-witted, full of the juices and forces of genuine manhood, and he was, in addition to all this, a sincere Christian man.

His preaching took a tremendous hold upon me at the beginning; and even to the end, and after the meagerness of his thought had become evident to me, I heartily admired his extraordinary gift of natural eloquence. He could make a five minutes' speech in the General Assembly of the Presbyterian Church unsurpassable in wit, fervor, and telling power. He was fond of alliteration, and one of his famous passages lingers clear in my memory: 'Jesus taught more with lilies than with logic, with mustard seed than with metaphysics, with ravens than with rhetoric, with dough than with dogma, with parables than with nicely rounded periods.' In his bursts of eloquence he would speak of the Gospel as 'hanging out the lamps of immortality on the snow-peaks of Greenland'; he would contend that 'it had made the jungles of Africa and the palm groves of India vocal with the praise of Immanuel.' This sort of thing uttered with great oratorical force and complete sincerity, was captivating to an immature and sympathetic youth.

His praise of me was excessive and became more and more one of the humiliations of my days. The effect of his praise of me upon critical minds one may judge from a single example. Meeting for the first time Dr. George Ellis, of Boston, famous for his historical learning and pungent speech, and whom I came to regard as a friend of cruel truthfulness, he remarked to me, 'From what your friend Angier said to me about you I expected to find in you the quintessence of the twelve apostles.' About this cruelly truthful man I may tell another tale. When he was a minister in Charlestown, a lady of some social but of no other distinction, called upon Dr. Ellis, saying she would like to join his church, and begging him for a statement of his beliefs and that of his religious society. This the Doctor gave with great clearness and fullness of detail. He parted with this hopeful convert from Episcopacy and he never set eyes on her again till at an important social function she danced lightly up to the Doctor and said: 'On thinking the matter over I concluded to stay in my own church'; the reply to which was: 'That is right, Madam! There's no use changing the labels on empty bottles.'

There is another tale worthy of preservation of this same cruelly truthful man. A certain rather prominent Unitarian minister had been converted to Episcopacy. He was duly ordained, and he was to preach his first sermon as a priest of the Episcopal Church in Trinity Church, Boston. Phillips Brooks, from whose lips I received the story, presided over the august ceremony. Mrs. Robert C. Winthrop invited Dr. Ellis to come to Trinity, occupy a seat in her pew, and hear his former Unitarian friend preach under his new anointing. The invitation was accepted and Dr. Ellis was there with Mrs. Winthrop to listen and reflect. According to Phillips Brooks, the sermon was the worst he ever heard, rant, unreality, bombast, an endurance test from end to end. The service over, Dr. Ellis, who had sat bolt upright, looking steadfastly at the preacher through the whole ordeal, as if he were listening to an oracle of the Lord, rose and walked slowly down the aisle with his courteous hostess, saying to her when they parted, with a tone of voice that cannot be printed, 'Well, Mrs. Winthrop, you may have him.'

Annie Louise Lanman was the wife of my minister, the youngest in a family of twelve, five sons and seven daughters, born to James Lanman and his wife, of Norwich, Connecticut. Her father was a distinguished man; for one term he was United States Senator from Connecticut, and later he was Chief Justice of the Supreme Court of that State. His home was one in which the best books were read, where literature was a passion, where good breeding was a fixed habit, and high manners, and where rich culture abounded. Mrs. Angier's reverence for her father was unbounded, and, as her mother died a few months after this daughter was born, the tie between the father and this youngest child was of unusual strength and tenderness. A better minister's wife never lived than Mrs. Angier. She supported her husband in all things worthy, held him to his highest ideals, and lived as the soul of culture, and religious light and consolation, in the life of his parishes. Mr. Angier introduced me to his wife, and we became fast friends. My debt to her is simply inexpressible along many lines, but especially for encouraging me to prepare for the vocation of minister, and for opening the way. She it was who called upon Dr. Tarbox, then Secretary of the Education Society, after which an interview was arranged between this high-minded official and me. He was convinced that I had ability enough eventually to become a preacher. He wrote to Dr. Pond, then President of Bangor Theological Seminary, on my behalf. This letter from Dr. Tarbox to Dr. Pond brought from Dr. Pond to me a letter inviting me to enter the Seminary that autumn, September 16, 1874. This invitation I accepted; on September 16, 1874, I faced a new vocation with many misgivings and fears; in spite of them I have been able to fare forward.

The friendship of these two beloved old people made an epoch in my life. Without them I could have done nothing; with their sympathy I was able to make a beginning; with their parental regard and affection I was happy all through the strenuous years during which we lived together. I lived with them in Cambridge during the years of my course in Harvard College from 1878 to 1881. From that date till my marriage in 1890 they lived with me, three years in Greenwich, Connecticut, and six years in the Old South Parsonage, nine years in all. Mrs. Angier died at the age of seventy-seven in 1893, and Mr. Angier in 1898, in his eighty-ninth year. It was my privilege to conduct the last sacred service for both; they sleep side by side in Mount Auburn, and as I think of their heavenly love for me their remembrance is like music, and of them it can truly be said:

'Only the actions of the just
Smell sweet and blossom in the dust.'

I shall speak of Harvard College later, and shall here only remark that Mr. Angier went at my request to see

President Eliot about my entrance into Harvard as a special student, and to arrange for a brief interview with the President. Behind Mr. Angier was the compulsion of his wife, whose faith in education was hereditary and boundless, and my own ardent desire and determined purpose. I saw the august President the next day, June 15th, at nine o'clock in the morning, at 17 Quincy Street. He received me with the utmost kindness, spoke words of encouragement and hope, sent me away, with little waste of time to him or to me, with an exalted mind, and a purpose more determined than ever. The mood of the President toward me never changed, except from one degree of kindness to a greater, and it was the astonishment of my days then, and still is, that a man with so great a multitude of cares resting upon him could spare a moment even to think of a poor academic waif such as I surely was. Among all the glories of President Eliot's administration of Harvard College, none is brighter than his sympathy with aspiring and struggling youth; this vast merit of his spirit invaded the teaching staff under him, and made Harvard College then the most democratic society that I have ever known, and the most cordially human atmosphere that I have ever breathed.

CHAPTER XII

THE USE OF SPARE HOURS

NEXT to work and the hours of work the most important thing in a man's life is the use that he makes of his spare time. Work stands first; by that a man earns his living, by it he takes his place among effective and useful human beings, by it he expresses the serious and responsible purpose of his life, and by it the crude material of his nature is wrought over into character, genuine character, the character of a manly man. There are no more significant words in the New Testament than these: 'My Father worketh hitherto, and I work.' According to Jesus, the Deity was a working Deity, incessantly in the service of His universe, and Jesus himself, in his Father's name, was incessantly in the service of his Father's children; and his disciples are called upon in one form or another always to be serving. There is no finer basis of fellowship between God and Christ and man than honest work, contributive to the welfare and happiness of the community and the world.

Work comes first of all. Next to work, as I have said, is the use that a man makes of his spare hours, and especially is this true of young people. They may use their spare hours in a way to undermine health, soundness of mind, truth of character. That is what dissipation means; it means spending one's spare hours in such a way as to make certain the early collapse of the body, the mind, and the character. Spare hours should be so spent, or may be so spent, as to increase vitality, to develop the intellect, and when the intellect is pervaded with human sentiment it is always spiritual in its exercise, and necessarily brings into existence a noble character.

Spare time may be profitably spent in the enjoyment and study of Nature. Take, for example, a man like Lord Bryce; his early education was in this field. He knew every weed as well as every flower in the British Isles. Many love to study birds, their habits, their music. For many Nature is a perpetual æsthetic wonder, and surely here is a sphere in which time may be profitably spent. Thus in art: the monumental buildings of a great city, and the monuments themselves, how they touch imagination! They combine history and biography, with an appeal to imagination and feeling. Consider the enlargement of mind that one will get from going to a good museum and studying, for example, the remains of Egyptian art, those forms of beauty and of power coming down to us from five thousand years ago. One cannot get inside these works without an immense expansion of imagination and an infinitely greater expansion of human sentiment. I can never forget two figures that I saw in the museum at Cairo, the figure of a prince and of a princess newly wedded. There they sit side by side with the glow of love like a perpetual sunrise on their faces, with the most exquisite tenderness playing over their features, and truth, beauty, joy; and these two figures have come down to us from five thousand years ago. Here is a revelation of the essential identity of human beings in all the ages, and surely he was a master who opened the fountains of our humanity at their purest in that great work.

One may profitably spend one's time with exalted and

exalting friends. I do not here refer to love, because if a man is in love he has no spare time. Then there are books. This I have especially in view. Books differ as Nature in its various aspects differs. We have in Nature the mountain and the valley, the river and the swamp. You say the swamp and the river are both water. Yes; but one is perpetually running and pure, and the other is stagnant and unwholesome. We have the cultivated field and the waste places, the woods, glorious with foliage and filled with song birds, and we have the great desert and its solemn and mysterious appeal. Books differ as human beings differ. There is the stupid book, the boresome book, and it reminds one of the people one meets in actual life. There is the vicious book, brilliant, it may be, and fascinating, but reminding one of the unscrupulous and the immoral human beings by whom one is surrounded, a book that one may look at as he would at a rattlesnake, taking good care that it does not get its fang into his life. Then there is the loquacious and gushing book, reminding us of the loquacious and gushing human beings all about us; men may come and men may go, but they go on forever. Last of all there is the good book. Milton describes it as 'the precious life-blood of a master spirit.' That is the book to live with.

Perhaps it may be of interest here to say something about the books that a young man of eighteen read fifty-four years ago in South Boston — one who did not, as a boy, like books. It is a great thing for a young person to be isolated, to be thrown upon his own resources, to be dropped down into the heart of solitude where he must think and make connections with the thought of the world. Too much society is an invention for the prevention of thought. To be always babbling with one's friends stops the operation of the mind; the great forces of the human spirit get no adequate chance unless men are now and then thrown into a great, and it may be a terrible, isolation. What is a lad to do in a foreign country, one who had no time to enjoy Nature, or to study birds or flowers, and to whom museums were rather mausoleums, and who had no real friends or acquaintances in the new world, what is he to do? He is bound to read — or die. That discipline I have often thought would be beneficial part of the time to all the young persons in the community; it would force them, by the sorrow of life, the desolation of life, into one great path of intellectual salvation.

It may seem strange when I remark that the first book I read here was 'The Lady of the Lake'; and I remember well the impression that it produced — too much lake and too little lady — not that I cared particularly for the lady, but I said it to myself for politeness' sake. There was only one canto that really interested me, that of the combat between Roderick Dhu and James Fitz James.

Then followed 'Marmion,' an awfully long-winded poem, redeemed also by a battle, the battle of Flodden, the turning-point in Scottish and English history, and a really splendid piece of description. I will not stop to quote the parts of it that have remained in my memory ever since, from which it would seem they cannot fall away. I believe that to-day one of the books that our children are compelled to read at school is 'Marmion.'

About this time I read a book that made my blood boil with indignation at the treatment meted out to the Incas by the so-called Christian Spaniard. The disclosure of the

Spanish spirit in Prescott's 'History' made clear to me the cause of the decay of the Spanish people, and the end of their significance in the world.

How to get books was a serious problem with me. By severe self-denial I made some headway. A few of the books which I bought were Byron, Dryden, Pope, Cowper, Coleridge, and these were boon companions. A friend loaned me Shakespeare as the greatest of them all, Shakespeare, a name of wonder and mystery. There were a thousand things in this book which I could not begin to understand, but the really best things told their own story and fastened themselves forever in the mind.

I found that there was a Public Library in Boston, and from that I got Milton. I spent six months with Milton. I had heard his name mentioned by a schoolmaster with awe, as one would speak of Mount Everest after he had tried to climb it. The Bible helped me to understand Milton; the Westminster Shorter Catechism was also a help, the only good use to which I was ever able to put that document.

About this time I found a book of criticism, whose author I have forgotten, but he was a scholar, a man of ripe judgment and of acknowledged taste. The reading of this book did more to give me confidence in my own instincts, in the workings of my own nature, than any other book that I have ever read. The critic went over the authors that I have just named, selecting their most gorgeous passages, commenting upon them and commending them with critical skill, and I found that these I had already selected, and that they had gone into my memory. It was, indeed, a great discovery that one might trust one's nature working spontaneously as it went forth to seek what is best in the embodied truth and beauty of the world, and to find it able to discriminate and lay to heart the really great things. The young reader knows not why he loves this rather than that; his nature instinctively decides, and the critic comes and justifies while he clarifies and corrects the instinctive movement. I repeat that the reading of this book gave me the first intimation that after all I might be in possession of a mind which would enable me to know things really worth knowing. And here I made another discovery, one that has been with me throughout my life — that the stuff, the materials, of which the literary masterpieces are made are the thoughts and feelings of common men and women, their joys, sorrows, faith, despair, and the whole range of human experience; these the masterpieces take and express as the subjects of those experiences could not possibly hope to express. Genius gives the people back its own, its mind clarified and glorified, its heart exalted, inspired, and its life idealized, filled with beauty and power.

Really successful lives, so called, lives that are like cloudless days, that know nothing about disappointment, sorrow, defeat, despair, are really shut out from the best thing in life, the privilege of being a communicant in the great temple of human experience as that is built by the geniuses of the world. Why do men enjoy the Iliad? Because all life is a struggle, a battle. Why do the generations continue to read the Odyssey? Because all life is an adventure, an epic pilgrimage. Why do they enjoy reading about Antigone, a glorious woman who deserved the best and was sent to her doom? Because they know that in life. Again, why do they enjoy Œdipus at Colonus? Because, as a day of

storm sometimes issues in a golden evening, in that drama
a life that has traveled from birth to death in cloud, in
tempest, comes to an end of splendor and peace. And why
is the Bible, the greatest literature in the world, enjoyed?
Because it embodies the deepest, widest, loftiest experiences of the world, and they who enjoy it have shared in
those experiences; they come to its immortal words and
feel as if the Infinite, in music like thunder, were breaking
over them. If men have never had any sorrows, any disappointments, any failures, any reverses, they are to be
pitied. They have no seat in God's temple of universal
sorrow, triumph, hope, peace.

About this time I found in an American schoolbook the
imaginary speeches which Daniel Webster, in his eulogy on
Adams and Jefferson, puts into the mouth of a Continental Congressman opposed to the Declaration of Independence, and the reply of John Adams. These speeches
carried me away. Here was intellect, sentiment, eloquence,
all developed out of the fiery process of life. I purchased at
once 'Marsh's Reminiscences of Congress,' a book commended by Edward Everett and afterwards published as
'Daniel Webster and His Companions,' and containing altogether the finest report in existence of the great debate
between Senators Hayne and Webster. I went through
the further debates between Calhoun and Webster; and at
this time a friend made me the great gift of the six-volume
edition of Webster's works. These were for years a perpetual joy to me, and in this discipline I found myself being
prepared for intelligent American citizenship. I went backward and learnt what Hamilton and Jefferson had to say
to one another and to the world about the new nation. I

had a few wise friends, who knew well the history of their country, who guided my studies, and corrected my notions when they were wrong.   In this way I grew up into an appreciation of the constitutional structure of my adopted country, as any youth grows up into the same thing who has been bred in a family of intelligence and knowledge of American institutional history.   Later, a course in Greek, under Professor Goodwin, in the 'Politics' of Aristotle, the profoundest and wisest book in the world, upon political institutions and their basis in human thought and feeling, did much to expand and clarify my knowledge of American affairs.   The result was that when I came to read Lord Bryce's 'American Commonwealth' I found it to be little more than an orderly and well-written statement of what I already knew; and I believe that this is the universal experience of the American youths who have, as I have said, grown up into a clear apprehension of our political institutions and attachment to them.   This kind of training I consider the best.   The intelligent and patriotic home is the best possible school in which to learn about the Constitution and the constitutional history of the American Republic.   In this way one's knowledge becomes bone of his bone and flesh of his flesh; it is not so much knowledge held by him as knowledge that has taken possession of him, and that holds him fast.

I never was much of a theater-goer, but the few occasions on which I went were a genuine help in education. I heard and saw Edwin Booth in 'Hamlet' and in 'Macbeth.' In 'Hamlet' he was so superior to the supporting actors that he was, as it were, 'a star and dwelt apart.' I admired and enjoyed him, and I was impatient for his return to the stage, and on account of this concentration on Booth, I did not get the full benefit of the tragic evolution of the drama. I never enjoyed anything so much as Booth's Macbeth. He was well supported, the rapidity of the movement of the play was one of the elements of its power, and the more tragic scenes were acted with extraordinary sympathy and impressiveness. In the scene in which Macbeth sees Banquo's ghost, Booth was supremely powerful. His color went and came, changed from deadly pallor to red, with instantaneous suddenness, the frenzy of the actor was indeed that of the guilty king; it was not acting, it was living and terrible impersonation. Booth by his power in this scene raised the whole audience to its feet and held them spellbound. I have never known anything approaching this display of histrionic power.

Miss Neilson was impersonating Juliet, in another Shakespearean play. She was considered a very great artist on the stage. As I was only about twenty years old, and wholly without the experiences of rapture and despair depicted in that beautiful and wonderful tragedy, I must confess that I did not enjoy Miss Neilson. The 'balcony scene' seemed to me in bad taste; no young woman should talk as she did to her lover, before a crowded theater. Instead of a tragedy there was comedy in the whole performance, and I who came to pray went home to scoff. Such intensely passionate love affairs should be screened from the eyes of unbelievers, if indeed the whole thing was not humbug. So I thought in my immaturity, and so I behaved. Cast not your pearls before those who have no basis in experience for appreciating their beauty and worth. The delightful Warren I heard a number of times at the Museum, and Dion Boucicault in his charming Irish characters, and a few other minor things. I concluded that the art of the actor and the vocation of the preacher are totally different. The actor at his best impersonates his character; the preacher at his best is the character that he describes. Skill and sympathy are the foundation of an actor's success; reality and sincerity, the one objective and the other subjective, are the ground of all public address tolerable among intelligent and honest human beings.

Music was all but wholly left out of my early interests. The Jubilee of 1872, in Boston, I had sense enough to enjoy. The violin was common in my boyhood and many played it, and played it well, but the music that most appealed to me was that of the dance or the love song, the Burns love song. I never could appreciate the bagpipe; and I never heard even the best pipers without an irresistible impulse to laugh. This is, I well know, to a Scottish ear, more than profanity; it is blasphemy, but the truth must be told. Later experience and training have enabled me to enjoy thoroughly the works of the great German composers, and other classical artists in music, but I still love above everything else in music a Burns song truly rendered. Let a great artist sing, 'My love is like a red, red rose,' or 'O' a' the airts, the wind can blow,' or, 'O wert thou in the cauld blast,' or, 'John Anderson my jo,' or, 'Scots wha hae wi' Wallace bled,' which Carlyle truly says should be sung with the throat of the whirlwind, and the effect upon the universal human heart is simply transcendent. I regret that my musical education was so slight, that it played such a minor part in my earlier life, but I am thankful that the sacred temple of melody has some power over my being, and I have often wished that, like Luther, I could utter the otherwise unutterable as he did upon a really great violin.

When Niel Gow, the famous Scottish musician, was on his travels through the British Isles, that he might meet the best in his art, he came upon a wonder of musical genius in Ireland. Gow listened for a long time to the performer; at length he ventured to ask, 'Do you play by note?' 'No,' was the quick answer. 'By ear?' 'No.' 'Will you be so good as to tell me how you do play?' 'By main strength, be jabers!'

Returning to the use of books, John Morley in one of his essays makes a calculation of the amount of good literature that one will be able to read understandingly if he reads fifteen minutes a day continuously, we will say, for ten, fifteen, or twenty years. One would be astonished at the achievement that simply fifteen minutes a day, every day throughout the year, for fifteen or twenty years, would enable one to make. Change fifteen minutes into three hours a day, and keep that going for a quarter of a century, and how rich an introduction that will give one to the best minds of the world. For this is what reading does; it gives one a place in the best society of the world, really good society, not humbug society. This association with the greatest minds of the world, or with a selection of them, is on the intellectual side what we mean by the 'communion of saints,' what is meant by the great sentence in the Apostles' Creed, 'I believe in the communion of saints.'

> 'Let saints on earth in concert sing
> With those to glory gone;
> For all the servants of our King
> In earth and heaven are one.'

Wesley's fine hymn gives the spiritual side of this communion. There is, however, an analogue to that in the purely intellectual life, in the affiliation of mind with mind, the fellowship of the immature, appreciative, admiring, absorbing individual mind in the presence of a selected group of the great masters of the world. That surely is education; there is no education worthy of the name, in college or out, that does not have that as its heart and soul.

In 1846, Daniel Webster delivered his great speech in defense of the Treaty of Washington, in the United States Senate. The treaty had been ratified by the Senate four years earlier, but Mr. Dickinson, of New York, opened the vials of his wrath on Mr. Webster, heedless of what he was about to bring down on his own head, for Mr. Webster showed that every point made by Mr. Dickinson was without foundation in fact, and that the treaty stood as a solid achievement for the good of this Nation and for the peace of the world. When he got to the end of his debate with Mr. Dickinson, Mr. Webster said, 'And now I am done with the gentleman; I leave him, Mr. President, I leave him in the worst company in the world, I leave him with himself.'

There is another story. When Mr. Webster came home from the Senate, he was met by a delegation of his friends and constituents at the United States Hotel, an address of welcome was presented, and the chairman, the spokesman of the meeting, closed by saying, 'Now, Mr. Webster, we know you are weary with your work and your journey, and we will no longer detain you; we leave you, Sir, we leave you in the best company in the world, we leave you with yourself.'

When young men are left, with open mind, with reverent and receptive heart, in communion with a selection of the great intellects of the world, we may say to them truly, 'We leave you in the best company in the world, we leave you with yourself at your best, under the enlightenment and inspiration of the best.'

CHAPTER XIII

A TRAGIC STORY

THE story I am to tell in this chapter is no part of my life; the events which it describes do not fall within the circle of my experience; they appear in the field of intimate and sympathetic observation, and they concern me as part of the noble tragedy of the world, accentuated by ties of blood. The person about whom I am to write was a kinswoman, many years my senior, one of the loveliest of young women, and one of the best of human beings. As she lived, struggled, loved, suffered, went in the whiteness of her soul, more than fifty years ago, into the Unseen, why lift the veil of the past, why break oblivion's seal, why speak when a sacred silence has for half a century taken possession of its own? Because of the truth, the beauty, the exalting tenderness of the tale; because the universal tragedy of human life shines and gleams through this simple, typical instance.

Kate Fraser was the oldest child of her parents, so near in age to her mother as to seem more of a sister than a daughter. The love between them was like a religion for depth, sanctity, and permanence. While Kate was still a mere child, misfortune struck her family, and she was compelled to go into service in the homes of uncles, and of friends of her parents. In energy, endurance, vitality, and temper she resembled the Shetland ponies on which she often rode; of mixed Lowland and Highland blood, she yet seemed in her whole temperament a typical Celt. Her religion was her life; the daily reading of the Bible, the morning and evening prayer, the church on Sunday were never forgotten. The sense of time, and things earthly, was pervaded even in her girlhood by the sense of eternity; and human life seemed to her grand, and at the same time terrible, and God's salvation the sole refuge of strength and peace.

When Kate was six years old, she went with her father and mother and two younger brothers to Uist in the outer Hebrides. During the two years spent in this lonely island her nature responded quickly and deeply to the scene and the people. In the natives she found overflowing kindness, and she never ceased to love them and to speak with admiration of their life of courage, hazard, affection, sorrow, imagination, pathos, and faith. The wild birds were her delight, and she came to be almost one of them, her imagination carrying her where the wings of the wild birds could not take them. Beyond all was she affected by the Gaelic which she learnt to speak like a native. The soft accents of that tongue, its capacity for expressing sentiment, the feelings of the universal human heart, its capacity for carrying in it the whole tragedy of man's life on this earth, the force and fury that could breathe through it, and the sorrow and rapture of the soul face to face with God, all entered into Kate's soul in these early days of her existence. The scenery, too, was affecting, the loneliness, the desolation, the fact that it left man less with man than with God. It was a place made for dreams and for prayer. The wild storms from the Atlantic and the gales from the mainland of Scotland beat upon the little island, and made it the symbol of the tempestuous environment in which all human beings, but especially the poor, and the children of the poor, must pass their days. From 1853 to 1855, Kate lived with her father and mother and brothers in this desolate but enchanting place. She came back to the mainland more of a Celt than ever, and with the great qualities of that race living in her blood.

While still young, very young, Kate had two noticeable traits of character. There was her efficiency in service, something on account of which she was always highly regarded, and her capacity for love. Her father she admired and tenderly regarded, her mother, as has been intimated, she loved with a glorious and endless devotion; her brothers and sisters, one and all, she carried in her heart. She had distinction of figure and feature and something more; she had clearness and strength of understanding and something more; she had rare capacity for exalted friendship and something higher; she had a genius for heavenly love.

At the age of ten she went into service, doing while a girl the work of a mature woman. Her force and fire were taken advantage of by mean masters of her own kith and kin, and she was allowed to do things so hard that only men could do them without risk to health. Without intention on the part of her uncles, but through brutal indifference bred in them by the severities of their own existence and lot, this spirit of energy and light was overtaxed and the seeds of disease sown in one of the best constitutions ever given to a mortal. Through it all she led a studious life, read the best books, put herself to school when she should have been asleep, grew swiftly in richness of nature, in depth of sympathy, never complaining of her lot, writing home the regular letter full of cheer, ambition, and hope,

setting before her brothers, especially, glowing images of
the careers to which they should aspire. Her occasional
visits to her early home were simply inexpressible in their
happiness; there were the gifts that she brought, and there
was the radiance and triumph of her spirit. She returned
always with new ideas, and with the programme and passion of a reformer. She was allowed to have her way because of the wisdom of her plans and the pure unselfishness
of her heart. She was goodness embodied, and goodness
filled with bright intelligence, and therefore she was invincible.

It is strange that uncles and aunts, wholly respectable
and even high-minded, should have taken undue advantage
of the working capacity of this bright and gifted girl of ten.
The only explanation I have ever been able to arrive at is
that already intimated. They themselves led lives of hardship and suffering. They were obliged to rise early, retire
late, and every day, Sunday excepted, from dawn to dark,
wring the means of existence from one of the sternest of environments. The conditions of life were pitiless; they themselves looked for pity neither from God nor Nature nor
man. Life ordained of the Most High who could do no wrong
was a hand-to-hand battle with adversity from the cradle to
the grave. In this way came into being the pitiless heart,
without intentional unkindness, the lack of sympathy for
women, for mothers and for their children; in this way originated the one classification for all human beings. They
must all of them work, and they must do this in conditions
as they found them, and to the utmost of their strength
and even beyond it.

One would hardly believe credible the story of the pitiless

tasks that a girl of ten or twelve was set to do, and the insensibility to her mute sufferings, the want of appreciation, too, of her dash and unconquerable spirit. Uncles were a synonym in my boyhood for taskmasters and slave-drivers; like Shylock they were after the pound of flesh to the last ounce. They were not ignoble; they were not cruel; they were bred by gales and hurricanes, and they knew nothing but the gospel of endurance and conquest by heroism. A good gospel in part, as winter in Northern latitudes is a good climate part of the year; but as winter needs to be balanced by summer, so the gospel of heroism needs to be softened by that of sympathy. Blessed is he that considereth the poor, and blessed is he that considereth the children whose only fault is that they are too willing to work. These beatitudes did not originate with the gospel of unmitigated heroism, nor with that idiom of hell, the survival of the fittest.

At the age of fifteen Kate went to Aberdeen, Scotland, and entered service for two old people, distant relatives of her mother. With these dear old people she lived more like a daughter than a servant, for nine happy years. Here she had more opportunities for reading and schooling, and these were diligently and eagerly improved. Her letters home became more and more reflective, and, while still bright with news and imagination, clearly showed the growth of her naturally strong understanding. In Aberdeen she made many good friends, and among them a young man named Robert, several years older than she. He was, like herself, deeply religious, and again, like herself, eager to rise in the world, by cultivated abilities and faithful service. At the age of seventeen she became engaged to this aspiring and most lovable youth of twenty, and for the next seven years they walked together as if in Paradise. Frequently they went together to Kate's home; the welcome they received was one of pure gladness; and when they went away to their several places of service, they left the hearts and home of Kate's parents as in an everlasting evening glow. This relation of truth, beauty, fidelity, and hope continued without a cloud for seven supremely happy years. These two young people were in the strength and honor of a tide of love from the Author of their being.

It must here be noted that this wonderful young woman had two infirmities, if such they could be called, and infirmities they were only in their fierce strength. Kate Fraser had always given evidence of a quick temper, easily appeased, and, when found to have been mistakenly excited, followed at once by a flood of penitence. When convinced that she had been insulted, her temper was wild and terrible. The other infirmity was her pride; that under stress of appeal rose higher than the heavens. Here was the slack in Kate's armor, the chance for the tragic force in life to enter and destroy a whole world of beauty and promise. One evening Kate met two sisters of her gallant lover, who in the presence of a numerous company taunted her with her inferiority in station to their brother whom she was to marry, and repeatedly told her how extremely fortunate she was to have won the love of a person so much superior to herself. After this meeting the fire was kept burning by correspondence, the devoted, high-minded lover himself being in total ignorance of what was going on. Kate's nature rose in a flame of indignation over the insult that she had publicly received, for which there could be neither excuse nor pardon. Her pride came to the help of her indignation, and together the fierce force demolished in a few weeks the fair fabric that had been built from two devoted hearts, securely as they had thought, through seven years of tested and perfect friendship. Kate felt that she was rightly indignant, and no doubt she was, but she was not right in sending forth the hot flames of an insulted nature against her innocent and chivalrous lover. It was no use for him to reason, to protest, to extract from the offending sisters an apology; Kate felt she could not live a happy life even with him in an environment of taunt and disparagement. The engagement was broken; all the beautiful things he had given her, all the precious tokens of love were returned, all save one thing, most precious of all, to be named later.

Probably the break, though terrible, might have been mended had not another who had long been a candidate for her hand appeared. He was fifteen years older than Kate, a widower, with a scheming mind, desperately in love, but not honorable enough to consider the affliction that had come upon his rival whose claims he had no right to dispute. This man further fanned the flame of indignation and pride, said prudently everything that could be said against the defeated and dishonored lover, and, although he did not dare to question the integrity of that lover's life, or the ideal beauty of his devotion, he succeeded by schemes and wiles in winning the affection of Kate. They were hurriedly married, and together sailed for America, to try the world and meet their fate there.

Kate's husband was good-looking, generous, industrious,

but common in mind and character. He loved his wife truly and with fidelity, but her soul he could not satisfy. Kate threw the whole energy of her life into helping her husband, and a measure of prosperity came to them; still the vision of the past haunted her. She had done wrong to the best human being she had ever known, filled his life with incurable sorrow, and brought it to the verge of disaster. When she was alone or unoccupied, his face would appear before her, full of unearthly love as of old, but pale, sorrow-stricken, and with the question written on it, in lines of agony, What had I done to deserve this? How could you, perfect in honor and in every form of truth, do what you did? Kate's face became a mask behind which on the stage of her mind the tragedy of her life was enacted. Often would she rehearse the sad story to the kinsman whom she trusted, and he listened in reverence and sympathy, and because of the respite which the recital brought to her. From a Paradise she felt that she was self-driven; that world of beauty, peace, and joy, was irrecoverably gone; regret and grief could not bring back what had been disdainfully cast away. Thus the months went by filled with a woman's work, with friendship, with a noble wife's perfect fidelity, and with profound penitential religious experience. Still that face continued to haunt her; it was the last pale image before her eyes as they closed in sleep, and the first to greet her on awaking.

'Whither shall I go from Thy Spirit?
Or whither shall I flee from Thy presence?'

One day a message of vast relief came to Kate; he was married, and therefore he could no longer be unhappy.

This message became the litany of her new joy. He is married; he sorrows no more; he must be happy; those seven years have at last passed into quiet oblivion. Then came the birth of her first child, a son. Her marriage had now the sanction of the Lord and Giver of life, and she would sorrow no longer; she would think that all that had happened was according to the mysterious purpose of God; it must be added that Kate was a Presbyterian, and a supralapsarian Calvinist. Her child grew in strength and loveliness; he became the joy of all who knew him, and the heart's ease of his mother, her strength and joy. A new world seemed to be about to dawn; old things seemed passing away, all things seemed about to become new. It was not to be. The lovely boy, who had never known a moment's pain since his birth, was taken with scarlet fever, and in less than two days lay dead. A lioness robbed of her young was Kate, with a majesty of pain, but with all the fierceness gone from her being. Inconsolable she was and yet subject to the guidance of sympathy and to the calm brought her by religious faith. This was her punishment, and she must bear it. She had been to her early devoted and blameless lover as the apple of his eye, and she had torn from him his chief joy in this world. Her child was to her the object of fondest attachment, the source of sweet self-oblivion, the fountain of healing grace, and endless consolation. Her Maker had dealt with her in the death of her darling boy, as she had dealt with her first, best, and only supreme lover. Her Maker had shown her, in this bereavement of her life, the enormity of her sin against him. The revelation and the retribution were from God, and they must be accepted in perfect faith and com-

plete resignation. 'Though He slay me yet will I trust in
Him,' became the secret chant of her heart. For the rest of
her life in this world Kate lived a purgatorial existence.
She went about her duties; she laid large plans for bringing
to America her younger sisters; she set her heart upon
bringing to her side her wise and beautiful mother; stronger
than ever, greater than ever, lovelier than ever she seemed
to all who knew her. The old world still remained in her
memory, and to the trusted kinsman she would still speak
of it as something 'that having been must ever be.' She
confided to this kinsman the fact that the one precious gift
she had not returned when she broke her engagement was a
gold ring; that she had sewed this ring into the waist of her
rich black silk dress. There she could feel it near her heart,
and there it would remain unknown, and where it could
give no pain. It would be an endless link with that hallowed past, and it would continue to be a fountain of love,
regret, truth, and hope. This dress she was to be buried in,
if the end should come suddenly.

The end did come suddenly. Her second son was born
on May the thirteenth. She was exhausted by grief and
motherhood, and did not have the strength to come through
her trial. She lingered eight days, named her son with sac-
ramental beauty and solemnity, saw and conversed with
her minister, became conscious of the happiest reconciliation to the will of the Highest, retained clearness of mind
to the last, and wonderful elevation, frequently breaking
into song, in the old evangelical hymns in which she had
been trained:

> 'O happy day that fixed my choice
> On Thee, my Savior and my God';

especially these lines, which seemed to sum up the whole sad and yet beautiful story of her life,

'He taught me how to watch and pray
And live rejoicing every day.'

Thus believing and singing, she went her way into the great Unseen at twenty-seven years and five months. After simple and devout services her body, dressed, according to her request, in her black silk dress, was laid in the grave of her infant son, in Mount Hope Cemetery. No stone marks the grave. Her husband soon married again, and for the third time, and that soul of light and beauty passed forever from his memory. She had been to him a charming convenience; time had convinced her that, struggle against the thought as she might, he was but an incident, a troubled and painful incident, in her existence. The truth of her life came to light by one of those accidents that seem revelations from the heart of the Infinite. Many years after her burial in her lonely grave, with her sacred secret in the waist of her black silk dress, in digging the grave next to hers, invasion of her grave was accidentally made, the lid of her casket was broken, and there, in the poor handful of dust that remained, was the gold ring, keeper in its shining circle of the troth that could not be broken, imperishable symbol of the love that never faileth, and of the faith of all suffering and pious souls that the Lord is their Keeper, in life and in death, and of the whole treasure of their being.

The kinsman by whom this moving tale has been preserved is still living. A thousand times, in the last fifty years, she had appeared to him in his dreams, always with triumphant grace, and always 'crowned with attributes of

woe,' still expiating the error of her life, but serenely, in-
effably happy so to do. Those meetings in dreamland have
been, if not in heaven, yet on the topmost round of purga-
tory, where the purified soul prepares for higher things.
The kinsman would confess that these dreams have been
among the most sacred and exalting experiences of his existence; they have kept him mindful of his past and made it
unforgettable; they have told him with the solemnity of
the Invisible of the woe that haste, hot indignation, and
uncontrolled pride may create; above all, they have made
part of his life the union of time and eternity, the visible and
the invisible. This kinsman, wandering in the city where
she lived for two years and eleven months, and wondering
if any outward token still remained that would speak to
him audibly, truly, in melody, of Kate Fraser, went to the
old house on Cambridge Street where she had a room.
The old house had been rebuilt, but exactly on the same
lines, and of the same size. The new window of the new
room was the old window of the old room; and this kinsman could see that fine head with its hair of raven black,
and that radiant face and those eyes aflame with goodness
and affection, thrust out to greet him as of a Sunday afternoon he went to see her. He found the stone pavement
from the street to the side door the same old pavement,
worn by the feet of numberless other men and women with
their soul histories. Over these worn stones her blessed feet
had passed so many times, and over them on a Sunday
afternoon fifty-two years later, the feet of this kinsman
passed, hoping in this way to renew and intensify the exalting consciousness of her presence. In this new and hospitable land to which she fled, and which, before her death,

she learnt to love, nothing now remains to mark or indicate that she had ever been but the flagstones in the old pavement and the gold ring in the handful of sacred dust.

'We pass; the path that each man trod
Is dim, or will be dim, with weeds;
What fame is left for human deeds
In endless age? It rests with God.'

CHAPTER XIV

MY FIRST PARISH

THE old-fashioned people used to talk emphatically about a 'call' to preach. The first question put to a man headed that way was, 'Are you sure of your call from the Invisible?' I was far from sure. The fact is I was induced to try by very dear friends who thought they knew me better than I knew myself. I accepted their judgment tentatively, and I am free to confess that the call was so feeble that if I had met with any serious reverse, with anything other than the unqualified kindness and unbounded encouragement which I did meet, I should have turned back. If I had met with any such experience as one of the greatest preachers I ever knew had when he was a young man, it would have finished me. Dr. George W. Field, of Bangor, was a man of penetrating intellectual power, rich imagination and genuine eloquence, but of very unimpressive appearance, and he was exceedingly shy. He told us students of his first attempt to preach. His text was, 'Woe is unto me if I preach not the gospel,' and he was so manifestly confused — although the literary quality of his sermon could not have been missed — and so utterly afraid to look human beings in the face that the most important member of the congregation, and the most pompous, went to him, after the service was over, and said, 'Well, Brother Field, there will be no woe upon you if you don't preach the gospel.' If I had met with that, or anything like it, it would have been the end of me.

I was admitted to Bangor Seminary on the 16th day of September, 1874, as a member of the first, or junior, class. There I spent three as happy years as any mortal ever spent in this world. One might not imagine it, but a theological school can be a very jolly place, when from forty-five to fifty young men meet in noble fellowship, and with no sense of responsibility — that being laid on the shoulders of the faculty.

As to the course of study: we had the New Testament in Greek and the Old Testament in Hebrew. We were taught Hebrew from the foundation by a master. It was an ideal language to learn and we greatly enjoyed it and proposed to keep up the study of it till our last breath — which none of us did. We had the history of the Christian Church, from its foundation in apostolic times till well into the nineteenth century. There was an important course in Systematic Theology, a good version clearly and sincerely delivered, of the old New England Calvinism. We had all sorts of advice and criticism in the making of sermons; and outside of that, for those of us who wished, endless reading of English literature and all good things. The power of a healthy young man to study twelve to fourteen hours a day is something amazing as one looks back upon it from the years of lessening vitality.

We had in the Seminary a class prayer meeting, ever memorable to every one of us. No word of criticism was ever passed by one member upon another, however poorly he addressed his classmates, however poorly he spoke to God. I believe that that class prayer meeting was the beginning for us of really effective speech and of power to express our sincerest thoughts and feelings to our Maker.

The President of the Seminary was a patriarchal man — Dr. Pond, who lived to be ninety-two, impressive in appearance, in character, in piety. Another extraordinary teacher of a type entirely different was Professor Talcott, a Greek and Hebrew scholar of highest rank, a man of deep insight, a master in the range of his learning, in the method of his investigation, in his spirit as a Christian and a gentleman. A few words must be added about this remarkable man. He was a vast storehouse of learning and judgment, but he could never be induced to publish anything. He was an astonishing linguist, the master of some nineteen different languages and literature; his whole strength went into acquisition with the intention of eventual publication, but when the date at which publication was fixed arrived, he again and again postponed it, till delay destroyed desire. I have spoken of this scholar to many learned men who knew him, and all of them put him in the front rank. In range of learning, in exactness of method, in maturity of judgment, in conscientious care in reaching his conclusions, in imaginative sweep and glow, and in reality and beauty of his religious life, this teacher has been in my mind through all these years an image of what the scholar and thinker should be. His nearest parallel was Ezra Abbott for whom he had the highest admiration and esteem.

Professor Talcott called upon me in my room in the Seminary one day and my questions received answers which I have not forgotten. I was reading a speech of Daniel Webster, and in rapt admiration asked, 'Was not Webster's mind the greatest in all history?' He looked at me and said gently, 'Bacon had a more far-reaching mind, Burke had a more affluent mind, Aristotle had a mind immeasurably greater.' The fine old teacher saw that he had spoiled my joy utterly, and he added, 'Webster's mind was one of vast strength, he had an immediate command over his intellectual resources never surpassed, and in the statement of his arguments and conclusions he often showed colossal power.' Under this concession my soul revived, and I went on my way rejoicing. The judgments of Professor Talcott were of this final sort over the whole breadth of his learning.

He was at home in the new learning on the Old Testament, but he never uttered one word on the subject to his students. He doubtless thought we were not mature enough for such discussion, and here I think he was wrong. He looked upon us as morally earnest young men, with very limited intellectual capabilities, likely enough to do good honest service in humble churches, where there would be no serious call for learning. In all this lay the one great mistake of his honorable and wonderful life.

Professor Levi L. Paine was our teacher in Ecclesiastical History. He was a competent scholar judged by the highest standard, an acute but almost wholly negative intellect, a really great teacher, but over-fond of controversy, somewhat eccentric and inclined to confuse in his perspective the essential and the formal in religious belief. He was a good man, and yet religion in his treatment did not appear as the joy and consecration of existence, its perfecting grace, but rather as something to debate, to talk and write about. Christianity in his hands lost its magnificence and glory.

Passing from the faculty, there was our janitor, Wing; I never knew his first name; I must recall him. We had in

Maine some snow when I was there, and I believe this custom still holds during the winter months. Forty-five to fifty young men, whose usual behavior is proper, let loose in a Maine snowstorm are likely to have a little fun. In a contest at snow-balling we forgot that the Seminary windows were in the way and we broke them by the dozen. Wing came round and said, 'I swear, boys, I will go to the faculty and report every one of you.' We knew that he would rather die than do any such thing. We paid for the broken windows and then we hugged him till he cried out, 'Boys, I love you!' and that ended the matter. The last time I saw Wing was in January, 1877, as our class was leaving the Seminary forever; he was leaning against one of the buildings and crying as if his heart would break. Honest, upright, truthful, full of kindness and full of devotion, he was one of the best human beings that I ever met; always saying that he would do such horrible things to us, and we knew perfectly that he would not do one of them.

In those days, at the end of the junior year, the students were assigned to Home Missionary parishes to preach during the vacation, at the salary of seven dollars a week and our board. That sounds small, but it was better than nothing — probably it was all that the preaching was worth. I was assigned to Temple, in Franklin County, Maine, at the foot of Mount Blue. A half-dozen of us started on the train, to go our several ways; one would drop off at this junction, another at that, till finally I was left alone, and it seemed as if I was bound for the end of the earth. I got off at Farmington; that looked a nice place; Sandy River flowed through the village. I hoped this

THE CONGREGATIONAL MEETING-HOUSE IN TEMPLE, MAINE

might prove the end of the journey; but, no; a team was there waiting to take me seven and a half miles farther, and every mile took me farther away from things human. The valley itself is one of the most beautiful in New England. Mount Blue is indeed blue in the morning light, at noon, and in the evening; and the pathway to the intervale is lined on either side of the road with elm trees that make an avenue of delight; and the human beings who lived there in my time were of the best New England blood. Some of them had never been on a train and could not have been hired to get on to one any more than many men to-day could be induced to ride through the air in an airplane. They were intelligent, industrious, absolutely temperate, and with an amazing faculty for affection and loyalty. I served this parish two vacations of three months each; in this place I was ordained a Christian minister, June 20, 1877, and I remained the minister of this dear people for one year, or till I went to Harvard College.

About the Sundays. Think of it, two sermons in one day, for a theologue! All that we had on hand was only about a half-dozen, and those almost too poor to preach. The first Sunday came, with the first sermon at eleven o'clock; then Sunday-School from twelve to one, followed by the second sermon from one to two. In those early times things were crowded together into the middle of the day; it was not worth while to go to church for one sermon only. Those who did not go to the Sunday-School would hang round the outside till the hour for the next sermon arrived; they wanted to take it all in, such as it was. I shall never forget the feeling that I had after I got through the first sermon. Exhaustion! I do not know how the audience felt, but for me there was utter exhaustion. After an hour's rest I was at it again and trembling in every fiber.

I met at my first service one of the best critics that I have ever met, Lemuel Jenkins, veteran of the War of 1812, eighty-one years of age, a man who served in Lake Champlain under Commodore Perry. He had in his possession a certificate of honor given him by the United States Government, a shining letter of credit from the Commodore himself, medals and trophies galore. That same man volunteered, when the Civil War broke out; he was too old to go into the ranks, but he served as a body servant to a superior officer. He was one of the most extraordinary parishioners that I have ever had — and I have had a lot of extraordinary ones in my ministry. He was extraordinary for his combination of fearless honesty and absolute kindness, genuine religion and genuine profanity, utmost cleanness in his life and the most passionate patriotism. He was a man with an intellect, and he was a good speaker. He came to church that first Sunday, and after the two sermons he addressed me in this way: 'Elder,' — I was then twenty-two years of age — 'I liked your preaching immensely.' That seemed to me propitious. Then he added, 'Yes, while you were preaching I had the best sleep that I have had in three months; your voice reminded me of my mother's lullaby.' What did I do? I saluted the old veteran, and from that moment he and I were fast friends.

A little later he sent word to me that I had lied. I saddled the horse and rode down to see him, and I put on an expression of deep grief and said, 'Mr. Jenkins, I did not think that you would ever accuse me of such horrible wickedness, that you would ever say that I had lied.'

'Well, you did lie; you know you did; you promised to come
and see me in three weeks, and here it is five weeks; you
know you lied. It 'most broke my heart to find that you
lied. I love you better than I do my own wife, I do.' That
is not so great a compliment as it might seem; Jenkins's
married life was not particularly happy.

One of the most impressive addresses I ever heard, piercing in its pathos, overwhelming in force, was delivered by
this man at a meeting for the children. There were about
forty to fifty nicely dressed little boys and sweet little girls
gathered there; they were such as would charm the heart
of any normal human being. The deacons were present
discussing the question — which might have been discussed here in Boston two hundred years ago — whether
there was really any hope that children would go to heaven
if they died before they were baptized. Old Jenkins was
there in his overalls, his usual dress. He was bald-headed,
there was a rim of white hair round his ears and the back
of his neck. He looked like an immense orang-outang;
powerful, fearless, and yet universally beloved by the children; they would follow him and keep company with him
for hours, so tender was he to them, so full of interest, so
wonderful in the way he would enter into their life. He
listened to the speeches, and then he said: 'I would like to
say a few words, if I may.' He was a good contributor and
a good citizen, and of course, he was permitted to speak. I
will try to reproduce his speech briefly — he was no gram-
marian — 'Them's the sentiments that kept me out of the
Christian Church. I don't want to belong to an institution
that holds them views about children'; and he went on in
the fiercest kind of address, full of native eloquence, pene-

trating power; and with tears running down his cheeks he turned and spoke to the children: 'You're the ones that go to heaven. The Master said so. "Suffer the little children to come unto me, and forbid them not, for of such is the Kingdom of God." You're the ones that go to heaven. It's old devils like me that go to hell.' There was no laughter; he meant just what he said. The purity and innocence, the capacity for service and everything noble that he saw in the children, entitled them to heaven, while those who had lived wild lives were fit for some other place.

One day he came up to the deacon with whom I lived and said, 'Hitch up your horse and drive me to Farmington; I have a bill there that I want to pay.' Everybody obeyed Jenkins. We went in the evening; it was a fine summer evening, and there were twenty or thirty young men round the store, lounging. He said to the grocer, 'I owe you a bill for seventeen dollars.' The grocer told him that he did not think that was so. Jenkins told him to look it up. The grocer did so, and found that it was charged to another man. Jenkins said, 'Them goods were received by me. That bill is mine; I must pay it.' The grocer said that he didn't know the goods were delivered to him. The man against whom the seventeen dollars was charged was worthless, and the grocer never expected to get anything; he was extremely happy to get the seventeen dollars. It must be added that this grocer was a thoroughly unpopular man, and deservedly so. After he got the money, he came outside and spoke to the men there and said, 'Young men, I want to show you the finest character in Franklin County,' and he went on in praise of Jenkins. Jenkins at first started to go, but paused, looking down all the time; he remained silent till the grocer got through, and then he spoke: 'Young men, he has told you what kind of a man I be. I am going to tell you what kind of a man he is. He is a damned copperhead; that's what he is. When I went into the army, he sent a man all the way to Augusta after me because I owed him a bill for two dollars. He is nothing but a damned copperhead.' That grocer was absolutely used up in that community, and deservedly so. There he was in the presence of an honorable, a great character, and he brought this retribution upon himself.

The effect was something tremendous. A mean character stood exposed and condemned in the presence of a great citizen, a great patriot, a sound human being, to whose depth of feeling clean profanity was a necessity owing to an otherwise limited command of words.

The free-thinker in the country town fifty years ago was a phenomenon. Temple had one. He believed in God, but rejected the Old Testament; he believed in Jesus Christ, but he had no use for the New Testament; he believed in religion and in the life of prayer, but the Christian Church and its people seemed to him hardly worthy of notice. Jenkins had been rather wild for two or three days; nobody could calm his wrath or arrest the flow of his profanity. His wife had misbehaved and he had turned her out of doors. The tempest must rage till its force was spent. So said we all, except the free-thinker. He could and would tame Jenkins. He went to the old man's house, talked with him about God, and the real Christ and true religion, and then he said, 'Jenkins, you and I are religious men, men of prayer, and I want you to lead in prayer.' Down went Jenkins on his knees and poured forth a speech to God wonderful for penitential feeling and thanksgiving, and the hope of forgiveness for all his sins, but finishing and finding his free-thinking friend half asleep, he called him by name, and in a fierce voice said, 'Now, damn it, Jones, you pray.' Jones had never been known to offer a prayer in his life and naturally felt ill at ease. Pray he had to, and of course he made a bad job of it. Jenkins could not stand this. 'Jones, a rat in a trap could pray better than you. Go home and get your wife to larn you how to pray, and don't come back and talk to me about prayer till you kin pray, damn you.'

The last scene of all was a particularly touching one. On one of my visits to Temple, while I was in college, I went to see my old friend. He was ill with gangrene of the foot and leg. Everybody knows what the issue of that is in the case of a man eighty-five years old. Our talk was serious and affectionate; at length he said, 'When you come back again, I shall not be here.' There was no use whimpering and sniffling over Jenkins. I said, 'Where do you expect to be?' He answered, 'Part of me will be up there in the graveyard, I suppose.' 'And where will the other part be?' 'Oh, in hell, I suppose.' I replied, 'I hope not. Remember who says He came to seek and to save the lost.' He answered, 'I know the good Lord has saved bigger sinners than I be. I never drank no rum, never chewed or smoked no tobacker, always paid my debts, always loved and served my country, and always voted the Republican ticket.' To get the full significance of this last claim to Divine Compassion, it should be said that it was spoken during the Greenback heresy in the politics of Maine, when the Democratic Party and the Greenbackers went wild and nearly ruined the financial standing of the State. I assured old Jenkins that many a man had died in hope without having nearly so good a ground of hope as he had.

One more incident. After my arrival in that beautiful lonely town we had the County Conference; all the churches sent delegates, and people from all over the county came to the religious exercises in the forenoon and afternoon. At lunch-time I was deputed to take a dozen people to the home of Jenkins to lunch. Of course, I did not know him then as I knew him afterwards. The food was excellent and abundant and beautifully served. He showed us his trophies of the War of 1812, was entertaining and charming, and everything went swimmingly till an indiscreet man took his pipe out of his pocket and began to light it. Then came a glare from the eyes of the host, and the protest, 'You shan't smoke in my house, you shan't.' The gentleman took it very pleasantly and said, 'All right, I will go outside and smoke.' 'You have no business to soil God Almighty's pure air with your tobacker smoke,' was the rejoinder. 'Well, where shall I go to smoke?' asked the poor man. 'Go to hell and smoke there!' I gathered my friends together as quietly as I could and took them back to church.

This is only the fringe of the life that I have presented of this remarkable man, remarkable for his deeds, his benevolence, his sterling character, remarkable for his religion — and for his profanity, which was, with him, a sort of High Church ritual. I have hoped that I might have time, before I leave the world, to write a fitting memorial of this Yankee patriot, this extraordinary human being; his wit, his humor, all so memorable. I have given here only glimpses into his character and circumstances, that one might thereby get a sense of the character of the town and a vision of what a green theologue had to face in the management of that kind of a community. If one should ever have a six-horse team to hitch up and to drive, full of life, ready to shy, one would know something of what the theologue in question had to do in that Maine town.

The first funeral at which a theologue officiates, the first wedding, the first baptism, how these open up his sympathies, how they conduct him into the sorrows, the sanctities, the joys of human life; he is taken into a new world! The education that he receives is unspeakably tender and lasting in its influence.

We had in the town the beloved physician, one of the least sophisticated, one of the most charming of men. He had gone into politics and been successful; he had the habit of talking to himself, and one of his sons, who loved his father and at the same time had a sense of humor, overheard the Doctor in soliloquy: '"Samuel Small, Representative," that sounds well; "Samuel Small, Senator," that sounds better; "Governor of the State of Maine," still better; "Representative in Congress," better yet; "United States Senator from Maine," somewhat unlikely, but that may come; "Secretary of State in the Cabinet in a Republican Administration," rather unlikely, but not impossible; "Vice-President of the United States," doubtful, but not absolutely hopeless; "President of the United States," damned doubtful.' The Doctor and his wife were the most cultivated, the most important persons in the town. They had three lovely children, two daughters married, and a son younger. The eldest daughter, well educated, a woman of fine personal appearance and of charming manner, after three years of wedded life came home to die of old-fashioned consumption. It was a tremendous blow, not only to the father and mother, but also to herself to go out of life when life had so much for her here. She asked the young minister if he would call to see her in her decline, which he did, three times a week, conversed with her on life, death, judgment, eternity. She wasted away, and at the last she had a sense of fear as to what the end might be. She asked the minister if he would be present with her when she died. He promised that when the call came, day or night, at any hour, he would come and be with her at the end. One morning at one o'clock, one hour past midnight, the thermometer twenty degrees below zero, an open sleigh called at my house to take me to the Doctor's residence three miles away. When we reached there, I sat down beside her; her father, mother, sister, brother, and her husband were all present. She suffered greatly for two hours, from two o'clock till four, but spoke constantly on the deepest things and of her desire to be in perfect accord with the will of the Highest, and in appreciation of the light and beauty of the way that had been opened up for such as she to the heart of God by our Lord Jesus. From four o'clock till six she was in a deep smooth sleep, but before she went to sleep she placed in certain positions round her bed her husband, father and mother, her brother and sister, and her minister. When the end came, it was just as sudden as I had expected it to be; she could not have seen us, but she knew where each one was, opened her eyes and gave each one a bow of recognition, and then passed sweetly into the Eternal World.

One cannot easily imagine what an educational power that event was in a young minister's life, what it meant to the whole town; how out of it came a sense of God and of the reality of worship and preaching that crowded the little meeting-house, that made one feel that the prophetic office was part of the power of all genuine Christianity.

I must not leave the impression that this incident was sad. It was not so; it was rich to overflowing with everything beautiful, tender, and sacred. It did emphasize one thing; that there is no use preaching unless one shall deal with reality. That is in my judgment the first great discovery that must be made when one is studying and preparing for the ministry. Eloquence is nothing, dramatic power nothing, fire and passion are nothing, unless they represent reality. It is reality that sways the mind, that moves the heart, that controls the will, in genuine human speech. There is no respectable, no tolerable speech except the speech that represents things that are believed to be real, ultimate, part of the constitution of the Universe.

I met an illustration of this the other day, a humorous one, an instance of utter humbug where reality is absent. A young man who had spent the evening with his fiancée, on returning home thought that he would write her a letter before he retired. The letter ran like this: 'My dearest, I would climb the most precipitous and barbarous mountain to see the light of your eyes, I would swim any body of water far wilder and wider than the Hellespont to sit at your side, I would go through tempests and torrential rains to sit at your feet. Yours forever. P.S. I hope to make a call upon you to-morrow, if it doesn't rain.'

CHAPTER XV

COLLEGE AND GREAT EXPERIENCES

IN his great address to the students, as Lord Rector of Edinburgh University, in 1865, in some ways the climax of his career, Carlyle speaks with unconcealed pathos, as he looks back upon it, of the eyes of wonder and of awe-struck expectation with which, as a boy under fourteen, he entered Edinburgh and looked upon what was to be his university. Most reasonable was the feeling of the boy, and surely a tender, moving, and beautiful recollection on the part of the old man, for he was then seventy. Edinburgh was the capital of his country, and the university stood to him as the record of science, philosophy, literature, shining with a thousand glorious names. Most fitting it was that a boy under fourteen should look with eyes of wonder and with awe-struck expectation at this symbol of his race at its greatest and best.

I can never forget the wonder and delight with which I looked at the old irregular buildings in the Harvard Yard, or my happiness when I found that I was to be a student in this fellowship. I went to Harvard, not to play football or row on the University Crew — although I was invited to do so — but to work, with an open mind and heart, and to avail myself of every help that might come in my way toward intellectual development; and I am happy to say that the kindness which I experienced was unsurpassable and universal, all the way from the great President,

President Eliot, down to the humblest tutor — if there ever was a humble tutor.

The feeling for the university, of which I speak, may not be so common to people who take admission to college as matter of course; but in my native country it is hard work financially to get to college, and a larger number of the students in the Scottish universities are from poor homes than perhaps in any other country in Europe. Such students are naturally full of the sense of the privilege before them, of the sacrifices that are being made for them to go there, and imagination and conscience together are stirred, as they are not so often stirred among universities in richer communities. It is pleasant to recall what Daniel Webster reports of himself when his father, driving along the road in his buggy, his son with him, stopped and said to him, 'Daniel, I am going to send you to college.' The spot in the road was held in sacred remembrance, and Mr. Webster often related in after years that for perfect joy he burst into a flood of tears. There is the kind of a boy for whom college was made, and the kind of a boy that college will make into something more and better.

I can best indicate what college meant to me by describing briefly certain experiences that at the time seemed to me to be great, and which have proved to be, with the passage of the years, of fundamental and permanent moment.

First, as to what the university meant — to feeling, and later to understanding. The university meant to me in feeling, and later, on reflection, two things: it meant a symbol of the total intellectual achievement of mankind; and, second, it meant a center of creative activity and power whereby new additions were made, all round, to the knowledge of the world. In the university all that was best in the intellectual life of the race could be studied and known better than anywhere else; here scientific scholars, philosophers of many shapes and hues were pushing back the surrounding ignorance and making new gains to the fields of knowledge and of light. The university was the great mediator of what had been done and what had been thought by the race at its best in all the past, and, besides this, it was the pioneer into new fields of learning, science, thought. This was the conception of the university that lay in my feeling, that ultimately rose up into clear vision, that gave me veneration for university life, a conception that has had an increasing influence over mind and character, that has been a source of unalloyed and unspent happiness. Where a university exists and where it is true to its high calling, nothing that man has discovered as knowledge, or that he has proved to be essential to life, or that he has wrought into forms of beauty and power, no view of existence or of the universe of distinction and influence, no great personality in science, literature, art, or philosophy, can ever be lost to the memory of the world. The university is the mighty memory of the race, and its active, achieving, progressive intellect.

My second experience of moment was in meeting great teachers. All the teachers that I had at Harvard were men of distinction; they were unusual men. I shall here name only three. There was Professor George H. Palmer, who is still living and well at eighty-three. He was then thirty-six years of age, a young man, working upon the highest thought of the world that he might master it, that he might be an expounder of it, that he might be an intelligent critic of it, working that he, too, might find the supreme meaning of human life. It was education in the highest sense, and delight, to listen to his expositions of the thought of thinkers of the first magnitude in other days, to listen also to his critical appreciation of their thought, to watch the process of his mind in passing from premise to conclusion, to watch the still more ultimate process of moving toward his own final intellectual home.

Professor Palmer did two things for his receptive students. He gave a faithful and luminous exposition of English Empiricism and German Idealism side by side, and he brought to bear upon both movements of thought an acute and sound criticism. He showed that these systems of thought are not so much antagonistic as complementary, that English Individualism needs German Universalism, and German Universalism needs English Individualism, to complete their thought, to save each from fatal self-contradiction.

Professor Palmer did another thing of highest moment; he connected great philosophic movements with the great philosophic personalities that initiated them. A lecture from Palmer on Socrates, Plato, Berkeley, Kant, or Hegel added so many heroes of the mind to the student's hall of fame, his ample imagination. The love of literature blended with Palmer's abstract studies; his mastery, for example, of Homer's Greek, made his appeal wide, rich, human. Palmer was one of the best teachers that I ever knew; he was luminous, simple, learned, rich, subtle in intellect, a great teacher, a great character, a great friend. I have lived in the field that he made visible and fruitful for me a great part of my days. The following letter will, as many others in my possession might, show that he has admitted me to the sacred degree of friendship, *cum laude*.

HARVARD UNIVERSITY
Feb. 23, 1897

DEAR MR. GORDON:

Thank you for your little book on immortality, which I have read with interest from cover to cover. I half fear I never acknowledged your previous volume, the Christ of Today, which was sent me before I returned from Europe.

I wonder if you know the extreme satisfaction a teacher feels in seeing those who were once his boys become leaders, instructors even of himself. I watch your large success with great pleasure and know how important for the community is the grave work you are doing. Our denomination has always stood as the champion of human interest in divine problems. But never more than today has it needed to be kept true to this its characteristic work by ministers willing to neglect ecclesiasticism, church activities, and sensational appeals. Such men as you do much to maintain the sound Orthodox tradition.

Sincerely yours

G. H. PALMER

Palmer as the master of Ethical Studies was after my time; he was in my day historian of philosophy, expert and subtle metaphysician.

There was William James, no longer among the living; he, too, was thirty-six when I was his pupil, a young man, working slowly upon his great book 'Principles of Psychology,' a book which upon its publication placed him at once among the famous men in his subject all over the world. He was brilliant, erratic, for weeks at a time languid and nearly useless, and then all at once for two or three weeks following he would be incomparably original and suggestive. He was not great as a metaphysician, but he was in psychology a man of genius, and his gift of expression has made his books literature.

When he retired from active teaching and became Professor Emeritus, I, as one of his oldest pupils, ventured to write him a letter in which, among other things, I said that I was happy that I knew him before he became famous; that I never knew a fairer mind, one more sensitive to evidence for or against himself, one more candid or more willing to give even the Devil his due. He was a noble and most lovable man, and at the same time occasionally provoking owing to his eccentricity. Professor Palmer was a wise but frank religionist; Professor James was equally religious, but he was fond of hiding it; the truth, however, could not be concealed. He was too high in tone, too fine in fiber, too deep in his sympathy with the best in the life of his kind, to be other than a profoundly religious man.

Professor James's father was a remarkable character, a kind of glorified Greek Fury. When I came to know him he was old, white-haired, lame, and wore a skull-cap. On one occasion his son sent me for a book to his father's house on Quincy Street, where William James lived before he was married. I thought it was strange to send me, an unknown student, to an unknown home, to unknown inhabitants, to find a book, but I went. The old man met me at the door with the question, 'What do you want?' 'I want a book,' I replied. 'What's your name, and who are you?' I told him my name and who I was. 'Are you one of William's students?' 'I am.' He looked me all over with a good deal of suspicion, still glaring at me with eyes like flames of fire. 'Come in,' he finally said. I went in and I looked him over, and I was perfectly sure that I could take care of him physically, if it should come to that. I sat down. 'Are you a believer?' he asked. I said that I counted myself on that side. Then every sentence was kinder than the one that went before, and mellower, and before the conversation ended he had taken me into his heart, a great heart it was, and he told me some things about his two sons, of whom he was very proud, William and Henry. They were always debating when they were boys, he said, and I learnt afterward from another friend that this was true. The old man further reported that Henry was quicker both in speech and in argument than William; William was deeper, and usually, before the debate ended, got the better of his brother. Henry announced one day, 'I believe in God; but I have no use for the church.' William said, 'If you believe in God, you have got to believe in the church because God is the church.' This remarkable statement staggered the younger brother, being a sort of solar plexus blow, and it ended the debate for that day.

William James was the simplest and most confiding person with his students. His eyes were weak, and he invited some of the more mature of us to come and read our examination-books to him. Then he would ask us what we thought we ought to get on the book. There was, however, in reserve a judgment, absolutely upright, that could not be twisted by kindness or by comradeship; in that true mind there was a standard that was fixed as fate. We debated with him, but without avail. This sort of thing will show the comradeship that existed between James and his students, and his absolute integrity as a teacher. He loved and trusted us, but we could not fool him, if indeed we had ever wanted to do so.

I recall an incident in his section that contributed to my admiration for him, an incident which in most cases would have destroyed the influence of another type of man. He was explaining some subtle point in psychology, and he wished to use a mathematical illustration. He went to the blackboard and was in the midst of his process when one of the men in the section who was an expert mathematician inquired respectfully, 'Professor James, are you sure that you are right there?' He continued with his figuring, and the further he proceeded in the illustration the profounder became the confusion into which he went. At last he turned and said, 'Well, I knew that once, but I must have forgotten all about it; let it go.' This confession of absolute candor in his confusion called forth a round of applause, and greatly increased our admiration for our teacher and our loyalty to him.

When Professor James died, his wife wrote me a note asking me to officiate at his funeral, in which she said, 'I want you to officiate at the funeral as one of William's friends and also as a man of faith. That is what he was; I want no hesitation or diluted utterance at William's funeral.'

The letters that follow have long been precious to me, yet am I glad to share them with his friends and mine.

95 Irving Street
Cambridge, *Jan. 24*, 1907

Dear Gordon:

I am deeply touched by your letter — on the whole the finest compliment I ever received. To be held in such remembrance by men like you spells indeed success for a teacher. Within a year or two I seem to be getting 'recognized' as I never was before, and feel in consequence as if my place in the world was warmer. No one can tell how he really appears to 'outsiders,' least of all, perhaps, after they have tried to tell him; so I am well content to take the conclusion without chopping logic over the premises. You and I seem to be working (along with most other decent people) towards the same end (the Kingdom of Heaven, namely), you more openly and immediately, I more subterraneanly and remotely, but I believe we are converging upon the same thing ultimately, and the best thing I can hope for is that our successes may not be too uneven.

With thanks — and thanks — believe me ever

Affectionately yours

WM. JAMES

95 IRVING STREET, CAMBRIDGE
30. IV. '09

DEAR GORDON:

Your letter has given me acute pleasure, both substantively that *you* should show such sympathy with what I am trying to do, and representatively as the first swallow of what I hope may be a summer flock. You seem to be the first person to have read the book through, and from its effect on you I am encouraged to hope for a similar effect on others. My intent is indeed deeply conciliatory, as you may see by the advertisement which I wrote and which I enclose.

Have you read Elwood Worcester's Fechnerian book of devotion, which seems to me a very living word indeed?

What a reader you must be! It is very good of you to write to me at such length, and so warmly. I much regretted not being able to get to your anniversary dinner. I have perforce to cut all such things out of my life nowadays — you had enough without me!

Believe me, again, dear Gordon, with heartfelt thanks, in which the good wife joins

Yours always truly

WM. JAMES

95 IRVING STREET
CAMBRIDGE, *Oct.* 31, 1909

DEAR GORDON:

I have just finished reading your 'Religion and Miracle,' and have found it even more full of the 'Spirit' than your previous books — extraordinarily rich and superabounding in moral and rhetorical momentum as well, of course, as true in the thesis it urges with such convincing power. I should think it would have a strong effect in the Church, I mean on the Clergy, for I found myself wondering often, as I read, how much your very respectable Old South Congregation really relished the wild-horse freedom of some of your rushes of feeling and thought — they must feel a little breathless, like poor Mazeppa.

How times have changed in theology! How could people ever have taken these paltry miracles as the cornerstone of the whole system? God's 'credentials,' forsooth! Bah!

Always truly yours

WM. JAMES

95 IRVING STREET
CAMBRIDGE, *March 24*, '09

DEAR GORDON:

I have just had to refuse a gracious invitation to the dinner to be given to you. I regret exceedingly to have done this, for I should like above all things to swell any crowd assembled to do you honour, but dinners and crowds do me nothing but harm nowadays and my 'doctor's orders' are to abstain peremptorily. You are having so splendid a career that I grow prouder than ever of having had anything to do with you in your infancy, and I hope that fifteen years hence I may still be alive to witness your 85th jubilee.

With warmest regards from both of us, to Mrs. Gordon as well as to yourself, believe me

Ever truly yours

WM. JAMES

The third teacher whom I will mention was William Watson Goodwin, one of America's greatest scholars, and, in his own department of classical Greek, almost, if not altogether, without a rival. He could not force the unwilling, he could not drive the obstinate, but for those who were eager to learn he was, in my time, without a peer. His kindness to me, whose opportunities to learn Greek in earlier years had been so miserably poor, is simply beyond description. He advised, directed, encouraged me with unfailing patience, and when I discovered an identity of phrase in the 'Politics' of Aristotle and in Paul's 'Letter to the Galatians' he looked as pleased as if I had found in Tarsus the copy of Aristotle's 'Politics' that Paul might have owned and read.[1]

The influence of these three men upon me was deep and abiding. What was of greatest value to me was, perhaps, the chance as a student to watch the use they made of their intellectual wealth, to get now and then a survey of their learning, to brood upon their ideas as scholars and thinkers, to observe their methods of study, and the ways which led them to mastery. When these teachers became permanent personal friends, mind was lifted to its happiest exercise, and its highest hope.

I have two letters of introduction, given me by Professor Goodwin on June 18, 1884, one to Mr. Lowell, then Minister to England, and the other to Mr. Bryce, afterward Lord Bryce, so good that I did not dare to present them. I have kept them as consolation and inspiration, and no one outside my family has ever seen them. As the two letters were almost word for word the same, I will give here only one, that to Mr. Lowell.

June 18, 1884

DEAR MR. LOWELL:
   The bearer of this is the Rev. George A. Gordon, the new minister of the Old South Church in Boston. He is one of our graduates, and was the best student in Plato and Aristotle that I ever had. He is a Scotchman by birth, but hopes to appear in regular standing as an American citizen in London.
                Yours very truly
                          W. W. GOODWIN

[1] *Politics*, III, 13, 14, and Gal. v, 23.

I had one course in Fine Arts under Professor Charles Eliot Norton which has been a distinct and permanent influence in my education. His course on Egyptian and Greek Art, while sufficiently erudite, was of peculiar significance because it derived the monumental works of Art from the thoughts and feelings of the people of the various nations; the instrumental force was the individual artistic genius; the source of it was in the soul of the particular race of human beings. This thought took complete possession of my mind, and it has been an abiding and happy conviction. Professor Norton, it is well known, rejected all metaphysical views, including the great metaphysic of Christianity that God is love. I met Mr. Norton more and more in his last years, and I found him reasonable and delightful as a comrade in service. He could with ease transcend personal considerations, and look at the most delicate questions without bias, and with a clear and disinterested mind. While conducting prayers at Appleton Chapel, in October, 1908, I learned one morning from President Eliot that Mr. Norton was very near his end. I ventured to write him from the fullness of my heart, and here is his response, dictated eleven days before his death.

SHADY HILL, *Oct.* 10, 1908

DEAR DR. GORDON:

If my thanks to you for your very kind letter were expressed in any degree of proportion to the pleasure it has given me, they would be too much for my little remaining strength, but I can at least tell you that your words touch my heart, and find there most cordial reciprocation. With true regard and respect

Sincerely yours

C. E. NORTON

by S. NORTON

As I look back upon college days, and the influence exerted upon me for good, the office of the teacher rises into a greatness surpassed only by noble parenthood. The teacher may be forgotten; the effect of the teacher upon mind and life is as enduring as the race to which he belongs. His character through the character of his pupils passes into the biological stream; it remains there forever to cleanse and exalt. The character of the American people, so far as it is worthy, carries in it the saving grace of all the great teachers we have ever had, the noblest example, perhaps, of the doctrine of the conservation of energy. It was a true instinct, it was genuine piety that led the German people to inscribe the monument to Fichte, a very great teacher, with these words: 'The teacher shall shine as the brightness of the firmament and they that turn many to righteousness as the stars for ever and ever'; and this although only the eyes of the Eternal may behold them.

Another experience of moment in college was the fact that the student was led by such teachers as I have described into open communion with a company of the greatest minds in human history. I was led by these and other teachers mainly along one line. There were Locke, Berkeley, and Hume in English thought, there were Descartes, Malebranche, and Spinoza in French thought, there were Leibnitz, Kant, Fichte, and Hegel in German thought, and there was that interesting old reprobate Schopenhauer; and behind them all, there was the supreme mountain range of the intellectual life of the world, Plato and Aristotle.

This is only one line. But to be thus advanced, to be enabled by one's teachers to understand these men, their achievement and its limitation, to gain faith and courage under one's guides, to push on toward the attainment of one's own personal view of the meaning of life and the universe, marks another superlative college experience. I should say that intellectually the best thing that college did for me was to procure for me open communion with a single line of the world's greatest minds. I am unable to express the happiness that this privilege has brought me. Veneration for the minds that have controlled the thought of the world has become habitual with me; to know some of them, and to have had them as life companions, guides, and friends, has been a source of help and happiness too great for utterance. For this chief service I can never be thankful enough to my Alma Mater.

I have so deep a respect for Emerson, and so high an estimate of his good influence, that I regret to seem to think less generously of him than I do think. When he is compared with Plato, as he has often been by writers of distinction, it has always appeared to me as if these writers understood neither Plato nor Emerson. Emerson is not Greek; he is New England in his flesh and bone, one of the purest, one of the most radiant souls, with gifts of expression full of charm and power, and with an undefined and mystic relation to man's world and man's universe, the guide, as Arnold truly said, to those who would live in the spirit. Plato is one of the most magnificent of human intellects, one of the strongest and most original of metaphysicians, a technical thinker and a man of letters at the same time of the first order, whose insights into human society, the soul of man, and the universe as construed through reason and moral feeling have enriched the world; one with surpassing wealth, who must be regarded as the greatest writer of prose of whom we have any record, and a dramatic genius in the history of philosophy, the most difficult of all spheres for the display of successful dramatic power, the equal of any man who ever lived. Let him who would lightly dispute this last judgment read again the 'Phædo,' the 'Symposium,' the 'Protagoras,' the 'Theatetus,' and the 'Republic.' We love Emerson, and we are prouder of him as the years roll by, but he is no more like Plato than 'I to Hercules.'

The comparison of Aristotle to the English Empiricists, which was in vogue in the nineteenth century and earlier, while somewhat different, was equally wanting in insight with that between Emerson and Plato. Until enlightened by German scholars and thinkers, particularly by Hegel in his 'History of Philosophy,' and by Zeller in his monumental work on 'Greek Philosophy,' English writers were singularly meager in their conception and treatment of Aristotle. Good men the English have had in more recent times, Ross and his great edition of the 'Metaphysics'; Burnet, the Oxford Aristotelians, Smith, T. Case, Joachim, and above all Bywater; still it remains true that the most adequate works on this great Greek master are in German, and these set him where he belongs, greatest among the great, a world teacher for all time. His 'Physics' are indeed worthless, or nearly so, and there are many things even in his marvelous biological works that are clear mistakes; yet, when we think that he lived more than twenty-two centuries ago, the substantial value of his works in the human sphere, and their surpassing merit, are indeed amazing. The discoverer of the process of syllogistic reasoning is still the deepest and the most exact expounder of it; the best treatise on 'Rhetoric' ever written, one that contains all of good ever said on that difficult subject since his time and infinitely more, is from Aristotle's hand; his essay on 'Poetry,' only half of which has survived the wreck of time, has been and still remains an unequaled fountain of light, and carries in its fifty pages more comprehension of the soul of tragedy and more insight into poetry than does any other book in existence; his 'Ethics,' excelled in single aspects by Butler, Kant, Green, and others, for mastery in its vision of the supreme end of human conduct, in its analytic insight, in its serious, luminous, and unbiased treatment of ethical phenomena, in its rational strength, elevation, and charm, is without a parallel. Witness its treatment of friendship, and its contention that the sex relations of husband and wife are capable of rising into a true part of virtuous character. This every good man knows, yet one will look far and wide to find a recognition of it in ethical writings; and it would do them good to ponder Aristotle's words who think it blasphemy to claim that Jesus came into the world by the path of natural human parenthood. It is interesting to find Jonathan Edwards and Aristotle in fellowship here. Edwards's last message to his wife, one to be forever cherished by those who find in the human home the heart of the world, runs thus: 'Give my kindest love to my dear wife, and tell her that the uncommon union which has so long subsisted between us, has been of such a nature, as I trust is spiritual, and, therefore, will continue forever.' To the works of Aristotle already mentioned must be added his treatise on 'Politics,' which experts tell us is without a rival in wisdom and political insight, and his great book on 'Metaphysics,' the first, and still the richest treatise on the subject. Here we find the Greek master, throwing the whole world of rich and wonderful detail into the simple classifications of substance and accident, matter and form, the world and God; surveying the universe, in its amazing development from formless and therefore meaningless matter, through the ever-ascending presence and sovereignty of form in matter, till we reach the perfect Spirit, the Divine Being, matterless, the Absolute Life, by the love of whom organic, instinctive, and rational, the universe is sustained and moved. I once wrote that Aristotle had no religion; this I now believe is a mistake. I ground my new conclusion on two things; Aristotle's 'Hymn to God,' in the seventh chapter of the eleventh book of his 'Metaphysics,' and upon the turn, a perfectly natural turn, given to Aristotle's ethical teaching by Eudemus: the end of life is 'to behold God and to serve him,' which might have served as a model for the Westminster Divines when they framed their famous answer to the question, What is man's chief end? 'Man's chief end is to glorify God and to enjoy him forever.' Respect for experience combined with a lofty idealism sustained by the profoundest insight is characteristic of Aristotle. His great qualities are knowledge, acuteness, analytic and synthetic vision, sagacity, comprehensiveness, strength, critical and constructive genius, and a mind as purely devoted to the search for truth as ever lived among men. When Jerome, one of the greatest scholars of the early Church, spoke of Aristotle as 'Miraculum Mundi,' he came as near as may be to saying the best word about this thinker.

Passing from Plato to Aristotle, many complain of finding the latter cold and formal. I have not found him so; I have found him one of the greatest of teachers, one of the best of friends, an eternal protestant against the overdone statement, the wild rhetoric, and the weak sentimentalism to which every preacher is exposed, and I commend to my brethren, and to others similarly exposed, as a delightful companion for life, as a teacher of truth, and a correcter of errors, this champion intellectual athlete of the world.

Among men of supreme genius of the Greek race there is no one whose works come closer to the modern mind than those of Sophocles. Sir Richard C. Jebb has made the seven dramas of Sophocles a part of English literature by his translation. Tragedy as calamity, pure calamity, has never had a greater presentation than in 'Œdipus the King,' and I know of nothing more tender and beautiful than 'Œdipus at Colonus,' Œdipus coming to Athens to die, and guided in his old age and blindness by his two faithful daughters. Here the tempestuous life clears in the evening into transcendent beauty, and Œdipus goes hence leaving the world in the glow of a benedictive death.

Nor is there anywhere depicted a loftier or grander woman than Antigone. It is only saying what all Greek scholars know that the Greek of Sophocles is beautiful as the living world in early summer. This poet 'saw life steadily and saw it whole,' as Arnold says; so deep and pure was his vision that his works are contemporary with all generations of human beings.

Professor Goodwin would urge his students to read another great Greek writer, Thucydides. His Greek is admittedly the hardest of all the classic authors, and it has always been a matter of regret to me that I have had time to read only a little of him. He recorded the greatest historical tragedy of ancient times, and in doing so he filled his pages with political wisdom that modern times should be slow to overlook. The seventh book of the 'History' of Thucydides rises into a grandeur of form and of movement unsurpassed by any tragedy known to me, and the last words of Nicias, the Athenian commander, to his doomed army, Andrew Lang might well class among the greatest and most piercing utterances of despair: 'We must do what men may, and bear what men must.'

Another experience I gained from college of great importance to me was this, that the past is the background of the present, that we inherit a world of interests still imperfectly comprehended, and that it is the duty of every educated mind to do something somewhere to move these human interests one step more at least out of their imperfection. Professor Palmer has a striking essay on 'The Glory of the Imperfect.' This is the condition not only of American interests, but also of the total of those interests that constitute our world. We have inherited this world; we are under obligations to it in science, in history, in philosophy, in religion, and the philosophy of religion. From the wealth of the past, and with the intuitions and inspirations of the present, we must help the Eternal Spirit in the creation of the new heaven and the new earth wherein dwelleth righteousness. The call of the college, in the name of the goodness and incompleteness of the past, to serve the present by the power of the past, and by the light of the Perfect under which both past and present stand revealed, in their achievement and failure, is one of the great awakening calls of the world; it rang then in my soul, it rings to-day in ten thousand souls, prophetic of the consciousness of power and ampler and better service.

There was at length a great religious experience. Because I took serious subjects, I met only the serious men in college; they all were devout, even those of them who believed nothing. I recall an experience in Appleton Chapel that has been central in my life; it came like a flash, it came to stay, it has been a permanent light. One day in Appleton Chapel, weary with work, tired in every nerve, waiting for the service to begin, I asked myself this question: What is it all for, this toil and struggle, living in the heart of intellectual conflict, nothing sure, everything called into question, what is the good of it? Then came this thought: Life stands at the center of the world, human life; whatever cleanses that, whatever redeems it from the power of evil, whatever gives it freedom, whatever greatens it and glorifies it, must be true. Religion then appeared to me to mean sovereign insight into life's meaning, insight that generates power to overcome the world, the flesh, and the Devil, insight that brings one into humble but happy service in the Kingdom of God, that leads a man to consecrate his being to the improvement of the life of his kind, and that gives him a song in the night and in the light. Life is central and supreme; life is the judge from whom there is no appeal as to what is true, beautiful, and good; the verdict of life overrides all other verdicts; what life approves, through its growth, power, joy, becomes our Divine Gospel; what life condemns, through its waste, weakness, and woe, has no right to be except in the synagogue of Satan.

This fundamental and generative idea came to me in college, and out of it have flowed the faith and service of my subsequent life.

CHAPTER XVI
MY SECOND PARISH

ONE of the happiest days in my life was that on which I knew that I was to be an alumnus of Harvard College. I had not expected any such honor; I had been content to pursue knowledge and to seek intellectual power for their own sakes; now by the unanimous vote of the Faculty, after two years as a special student, I had joined the Class of 1881 in its senior year, passed all required examinations, with the result that I took the degree of A.B. *magna cum laude*, with honors in Philosophy. While this issue had never been in doubt, yet when it became a fact I was indeed lifted to the summit of happiness. I was to be proclaimed, by the highest academic authority, as an educated man, and qualified as a member in the fellowship of educated men. Money was decidedly scarce in those days, yet I had enough to hire a horse and buggy, and with a similarly happy classmate as companion to drive for four hours, in the merry month of June, through the whole region adjacent to Cambridge. The fine air and the beauty of the fields, flowers, and trees induced a measure of self-oblivion, and I returned after this excess of joy to a sane and sober view of myself and my small but still happy place in the great world of men and things.

It is strange how one's career is kept from deflection by the circumstances of one's life. President Eliot wanted me to go abroad on a fellowship for two years to be devoted to study in the English and German universities, and to return to Harvard and teach Ecclesiastical History. This opportunity I should have embraced at once but for the death of my father in 1881. His death left my good mother and two minor children without support, and I was the only son to whom the bereaved household could at that time look for aid. I must earn money, and I must do it at once.

Another crisis arose when I came to the Old South Church. I had an informal invitation to go to Johns Hopkins University to teach Ethics; I preferred to remain in the ministry, but if the council that examined me when I sought installation as minister of the Old South had rejected me, I should have accepted the new academic opening. The council voted forty-eight to eighteen to settle me and again my way was determined for me by the turn of events. It was many years before I was at all sure that I was in the right place in the Christian ministry; this doubt was raised and intensified by the incredibly conservative atmosphere of my denomination in Boston. Completely and honorably sincere as the orthodox body was in Massachusetts, a more provincial or unenlightened mind, upon the nature of religion in general, and of Christianity in particular, probably never existed than in my denominational environment in those painful early years of my ministry in Boston. Among the conservatives there was no learning nor any desire for it, no high intellect nor any regard for it. The New England scheme of theology was fighting its last battle; its generals were without skill, its army ineffectual, but generals and army alike were bound to fight to the bitter end. A few liberal and fine spirits there were, but they were objects of distrust and disparagement on the part of the organization. So much for the circumstances that in one sense meant deflection from the ministry, and that in another sense prevented it. Whether for better or for worse God only knows; what actually happened has on the whole seemed to me the better and the happier.

My second parish was in Greenwich, Connecticut. I began my service with the Second Congregational Church of that lovely town August 1, 1881. Shorn of the traditional Introduction to the Old and New Testaments as the verbally inspired utterance of God, and shorn of all faith in the New England theology as an adequate philosophy of Christianity, I was now to undergo a further form of education. I was to discover that the Bible, in all its greater parts, speaks for itself; that it needs no theories to commend it to morally earnest men and women; that as a record of the highest human experience it makes an irresistible appeal; that its intrinsic worth and beauty is the ground of its permanent power over the mind and heart of man. I was further to discover that the Christianity of Jesus is an order of ideas filled with His purpose and life, and that these ideas are independent of all ecclesiastical theology, old and new. Thus denuded of the traditional view of the Bible and of traditional theology, I was to prove by actual service whether I had or had not a gospel for my fellowmen.

Connecticut was then, on the whole, a liberal State. Bushnell's great life and ministry had told everywhere within its borders. There was little doubt that I would be settled by the Ecclesiastical Council called for that purpose. Eternal punishment was still a necessary article of

SECOND CHURCH, GREENWICH, CONNECTICUT

belief in the creed of a Congregational minister, and I was obliged to frame my answers upon this point with some care. This I did, affirming that I believed in the everlasting punishment of the finally impenitent. When questioned if I believed in the final impenitence of any individual person, I replied that on that question I was wholly without knowledge; that the only adequate authority on such a matter was the omniscient God, and that so far as I was aware, He had not made known His judgment. I was installed, with only two votes against me, and with the church and congregation wholly with me.

I heard recently of a revival of the doctrine of everlasting punishment in a strange connection. A man of very bad repute had died, and the Episcopalian, Presbyterian, Methodist, Baptist, and Congregationalist ministers declined to officiate at the funeral of this wicked person on account of previous engagements. The only minister available was the Unitarian. The widow of the deceased refused to allow him to conduct the service, declaring with much warmth of feeling: 'No minister is fit to conduct that service who does not believe in hell.'

I began my ministry in Greenwich, Connecticut, with a message small in mass, but charged with the vitality of a personal experience from which it mainly came. Every man has power for good over the character of his life and God helps the man who helps himself in the things of the Spirit. Jesus Christ had greater power over the character of His life than any other recorded human being, and therefore God was with Him without measure. These were my fundamental convictions; the first was a direct issue of personal experience; the second was a judgment from history.

A small body of belief this surely was set against the ecumenical creeds of the Christian Church; I found it enough to begin with, and I found in it the genius of inevitable evolution into a philosophy of the Christian religion that has proved fairly adequate. I am obliged to confess that I look back with genuine respect to my ministry of nearly three years in Greenwich. It was wild, one-sided, in many ways immature; but it was a ministry of utter sincerity, and it went onward as by a hurricane of moral passion. It has been a perpetual comfort to me to reflect upon the power of a few vital ideas, sincerely held and uttered, to awaken, organize, and lead forward in a life of worship and service a whole community. Those three years convinced me that life and truth belong together, that true ideas by their own might call into their fellowship the souls of men and women, and that the might of true ideas becomes manifest through the sympathies, purposes, and personality of the preacher. The cry that the pulpit has lost its power is old and idle. Faith as a grain of mustard seed, moral idealism in meager form, moral passion, and the breath of humanity in the preacher will raise from the dead any pulpit in the land. Learning is not needed at first, great learning, nor maturity of judgment, nor an elaborate and thorough philosophy of religion, nor genius in any sense; sound ideas charged with the life-blood of the preacher to whom the moral tragedy of the world is of all sad things the saddest, to whom the possible moral triumph is of all joys the greatest, are sufficient equipment for the beginning. My outfit from my theological seminary had become obsolete; its Introduction to the Old and New Testaments had to be thrown away as untrue; its systematic theology had become incredible. The seminary was not much to blame; the rush of ideas in the new era made the theological outfit a Saul's armor that could not be worn; and the smooth stones from the ever-flowing stream of Christian life, the sling of the moral will, and the passion to serve were an availing equipment for the militant soul. Thus it comes that the Christian religion is born anew out of the experience of every fresh generation of the disciples of Jesus. What refuses to be melted back into this furnace of the soul cannot be essential Christianity; all that comes forth from the courses of great and free religious experience attests itself, as at least part of the essential message of Christianity to mankind.

The Second Congregational Church of Greenwich has always seemed to me one of the healthiest in its attitude toward its ministers. It had but one test. Does our preacher enlighten and help us in the great struggle of life? If he does this, he is orthodox and we will stand by him against the world. Calling one day upon a venerable woman who lived with her son, this crumb of comfort was handed me. 'Eliphalet, how do you like the young minister?' 'Well; but, by George, Mother, he does whet a fellow up unaccountable.'

The first year I made four hundred calls in a parish that formed a square ten miles on each of the four sides. I had a horse with a record of two-forty, which was good then, and as horses go, if they go at all, is not bad now. My horse was fond of racing, and I did not object. The excuse made for the young minister was that he had no other known bad habit, and that probably he was on his way to see some person dangerously ill, which was now and then the truth. Once my horse tore off a front shoe, and two spokes in one of the wheels of my buggy got broken. I went to the blacksmith and to the carriage carpenter and asked, in a tone of mystery, how he could account for these mishaps. Looking gravely at me, suppressing the sense of humor for which he was well known, he replied, 'Too slow driving'!

It is strange how physical strength and courage will add to a man's influence even in a calling so spiritual as that of the Christian minister. John, the saloon-keeper, was not the worst man in town; in fact he had many rather good qualities, but he was a bully. He ruled the street, and within hearing of the persons described would say unpleasant things about them. John and I passed the time of day on several occasions with the result that John said: 'I respect that young minister at the stone church because I know he could thrash me.' John spoke the truth, and his word became a classic among a certain section of his fellow-citizens. Going into the smithy one day the young minister took the forge on the floor with one hand and set it on the block. Only one man in the shop could do this feat with both hands. Here was another distinct recommendation. At that time the young minister could put the shot a fair distance. His reputation again so grew that the distances which, it was said, he could heave the sixteen-pound shot, had they been true, would have remained records to this day. Youth has many disadvantages in a calling of high seriousness, but in a community of strong and healthy human beings, strength and skill and courage wield an enormous appeal.

A vastly nobler appeal comes from searching out the poor who are fighting to keep their heads above water. The pride of the poor who will not acknowledge to themselves or to any one else that they are poor is simply magnificent. They are among the finest of the unconquerable; I know them, for I have marched with them. Much can be done at Thanksgiving, Christmas, and other seasons of generous feeling, to signify admiration for this heroic class of human beings, and it was the young minister's delight to move among them, walking often as upon eggs, but easing the terrible economic pressure without saying so, like Lincoln's total abstainer who said to a friend of the opposite persuasion: 'Can you give me a drink unbeknown to me?' Nothing in life is sweeter or more rewarding in the way of influence than help given by stealth in this section of society. A young minister, with a good salary, without family, and a lover of the simple life, may gain in this fellowship such credits as no ecclesiastical council or college can bestow. 'Blessed is the man who considereth the poor,' without letting them know it.

In Greenwich I came in contact, for the first time in my life, with great wealth. Jeremiah Milbank, of New York, and his family, William Rockefeller and his family, Mr. Benedict and his family, and a group of others, less prominent, but all very rich, came to the church of which I was minister, during the four summer months. They were all of them men and women of the utmost kindness to me, and my intercourse with them was altogether pleasant. They were always present at the morning service, and invariably liberal in their contributions to the good causes in which the church was interested. Mrs. William Rockefeller I recall as one of the best of mothers. If the sermon was austere in its moral appeal, if it happened to be unusually faithful in dealing with the sins of the rich, Mrs. Rockefeller with her children was sure to come forward with generous thanks to the preacher. I learned then that love fears nothing so much as the waste of the beloved life that comes from wrong-doing, and that in all the world love has no friend or helper to be compared with truth. Moral cowardice in the preacher has two sources, failure to perceive that loving hearts desire nothing so much as the security of the human lives that are dear to them, and indifference to the tragedy of the world, in particular to the immolation of youth in each new generation. Insight and love in the preacher are the ever-flowing fountains of moral courage; insight and love will move the hostile community, so far as it has insight and love, so far as it is capable of insight and love, wholly to the side of the faithful preacher and in utter friendliness to him. Mothers know that without righteousness there can be no abiding beauty or worth in human homes.

Another bit of enlightenment came to me in Greenwich; that what we call calamity may become one of the chief blessings of life. There was born to a father and mother in Greenwich, a quarter of a century before I knew them, a child horribly deformed. To a stranger the sight of this boy or young man was painful in the extreme; it was, indeed, at first revolting. The young man was not an idiot; he was in no way deficient in intelligence, although in every member of his body utterly without human shape; he was unable to speak except in a series of cries which his parents and friends had learnt to read. Only two redeem-

ing things there were in this poor creature, his amazingly
bright intelligence, struggling to be free, and his capacity,
a truly divine capacity, for love. His father had been a
drunkard till this child was born to him, and a spendthrift.
The sight of this child, as he grew, his craving for love, his
infinitely tender response to love, his intelligence and
character and helplessness so wrought upon the father as
completely to revolutionize his life. He broke up his drinking habits at once, he began to save for the future of this
son, he became a new man in the whole habit of his behavior, and in the character of his thoughts and purposes
because of the helpless mass of intelligence and love whose
parent he was. When I knew him he was able to put in
trust a large sum for the proper and tender care of this unfortunate being, after the death of his father and mother.
We became friends to an unwonted depth of loyal attachment because I often called to see this son, and because,
after the first revulsion of feeling, I was able in all sincerity
to regard this prisoner in unsightly form with affectionate
respect and true sympathy. His delight in life was profoundly moving, and recognition from a friend was like
sunrise to him. The light in his eyes, light of the intellect
and of the soul, was indeed something strangely beautiful
and affecting, especially in a form otherwise so hard to
look upon. The father said to me, while caressing this son:
'Here is God's best gift to me. Through this child God has
changed my whole life from selfishness to love. In him, so
unsightly to others, I see nothing but the beauty of the
Lord our God.' The young minister must be made of poor
stuff whose education was not permanently advanced by
an experience like that. The father and mother and son,

long ago, were dissolved in God, and after the sore discipline of time range free in mind, in spirit, and in service, all the more heroically happy because of what they endured here.

I learnt another thing, that a rich man with attention to the subject could get an $8000 horse taxed for a value of $100, while a thoughtless young minister, whose horse cost him $175, was taxed at that value. This young minister became a political protestant at once, had the tax reduced, and henceforth was not regarded as so much of a fool as he had formerly been.

Greenwich is beautiful for situation, particularly so from the Second Congregational Church and from the parsonage near it. The church is one of the finest between New York and Boston, standing on the highest elevation on the shore at any point between these two cities; it is beautiful in its proportions, lifting its spire, in my time, two hundred and twelve feet in the air, and now, since it has been rebuilt, two hundred and seventeen feet. It is to me an affecting witness of the character of the men and women by whose love and self-sacrifice it was erected, a witness of the pride and devotion of those who guard its life to-day. The tides of toil and fashion ebb and flow at its base; the generations come and go, but there it stands, the symbol of man's origin and home in God.

From the windows of the parsonage, 'looking eastward to the sea,' there was Long Island Sound, where of a summer evening as many as six steamers might be seen going or coming from their ports of clearance to their ports of entry; a symphony on the placid waters, a movement in the peace and beauty of nature, whose burden was hu-

manity and the service of humanity. From my study window, looking westward, the impressive sight was the principal village graveyard, transfigured in the sunset, the radiant heavenly visitation of the hallowed dust of God's
servants who had finished the work given them to do.
Those sunset hours are an ineffaceable memory, and the
splendid pageant of planets and stars that followed. Those
windows of the little parsonage had outlooks over the face
of the earth and up into the infinite spaces, and they
taught this young minister that the Gospel that he was set
to preach was for all mankind and that it came out of the
mind and heart of the Absolute Soul.

I have never known a church better organized than this
Greenwich Church. It ran of its own accord; the consequence was that I was left free to study, to prepare for my
pulpit, and to cultivate the friendship of my people. There
were humorous incidents. Hamilton Wright Mabie, so
long associate editor of the 'Christian Union' and the 'Outlook,' and I went to one of the bathing beaches, in company with Mrs. Mabie and other young women of high
character, and there, plentifully dressed surely, was a fat
old lady, plunging in the tide, who looked, for all the world
like Judy, Punch's wife. I still recall the enormous difficulty with which Mabie and I controlled our laughter, and
how when I said, 'Is that Judy, Punch's wife or widow?'
all further restraint was impossible, and I never understood
before the Homeric impulse expressed in the lines, so se-
verely criticized by Plato,

'Unquenchable laughter broke out among the blessed Gods
As they beheld Hephæstus hurrying breathless from room to room.'

Mabie and I were as austerely criticized by our friends as

Homer was by Plato, but with no result except more laughter at Widow Judy's expense.

There were many marked characters in this church, typical of earlier generations of New England people. One, a Mr. Sherwood, told me that when I was called to this parish he voted against me, not because he did not like me, not because he did not want me for his minister, but because he thought unanimous calls were unhealthy, showed little individuality in any group of men, and because it would do a young minister good to know that there were some who had their suspicions about him. He and I became fast friends, and his thanksgiving in the weekly prayer meeting, after his marriage to his third wife, was true to the fact, and indeed memorable: 'O Lord, we thank Thee for the mercies of these latter days'!

Greenwich was an ideal parish for a 'young minister. The old, sturdy, high-bred New England stock predominated, and the community was composed of men and women of unusual intelligence and character, free in their thinking and with a passion for reality in faith and practice. There were many families of merit, a few of extraordinary character, and all the people had the capacity for high and enduring friendship. I was their minister for only two years and eight months, yet, because I had lived in their life intensely and with great happiness, the whole community rewarded me with the noblest sort of friendship. Here in the changing loveliness of nature, in the character of the people, in the kind of service required of me was a position as near to the ideal as one could wish in this world. I felt easily on the level of my work; it gave me no sense of strain; the responsibilities were such as to give joy

without anxiety. Why change or think of change while
life shall last?

Such was my mood when the incredible happened. In
January, 1883, the Old South Church of Boston called me
to become its minister in succession to Jacob Merrill Manning recently deceased. All Greenwich rose up in protest,
and this protest made it impossible for me to leave.
Another year, with further correspondence with the leaders
of the Old South, convinced me that should the call be renewed I must go. The call was renewed in January, 1884,
and on the last day of March that year I had said farewell
to Greenwich. It was with a sense of vast bereavement
that I turned my face toward Boston. Had I known what
was coming, my regret would doubtless have been deeper.
But the decision had been made, and by Providence I was
driven out of Paradise. A wonderful group of friends
awaited my arrival in Boston, but, on the whole, a stormy
reception was prepared for me, and a hostile environment
was my lot for the first decade of my ministry in the Old
South Church.

It was altogether good for me that it should have been
so. The intellectual life of the young minister needed the
spur of adversity to drive it into the strenuous process that
leads at length to clearness and maturity; character had
to be remade and built upon deeper foundations, and opposition and withheld confidence aided in this work; a task
larger than his powers was likewise a necessity, one to
which he must look up, against which he must measure
his abilities, to discover how inadequate they then were, a
sense of the future and the glorious privilege of growth,
silence under misunderstandings, under misrepresenta-

tion, under sure prophecies of his coming failure; above all, a foe strong enough and noble enough to compel him to retreat upon God and there reorganize and reëquip his life for the grand campaign that was opening before him. The courage of youth kept him calm, the sense of truth gave him assurance. The perception, now dim, now clear, that God was on the field, that the tides of the Eternal Spirit were running with the Kingdom of which he was a humble minister, made it easy for him to surrender comfort, appreciation, praise, made the acceptance of laborious years and high combat an heroic delight. Another chapter in my education had begun.

CHAPTER XVII

INSTALLATION MEMORIES

WHAT possible interest can there be to-day in an installation of a minister, in the Old South Church in Boston, that took place April 2, 1884? There may be some amusement in this event, and the event itself may suggest other bits of amusement. For it must never be forgotten that religion and humor are close friends, and theology, the most serious and grand of studies, has ever been accompanied with comic incidents. When Massachusetts was greatly agitated over the question whether man has or has not the natural ability to obey God, whether sinful men have any part in their conversion to righteousness, an ecclesiastical council for the examination of a young minister was as exciting and absorbing as the theater at its best. Both sides, believers in man's natural ability to fulfill the law's demands, and deniers of this supposedly dangerous doctrine, fell upon the young minister with holy fury, each determined by logic to win a new witness for the faith about which the saints were sadly divided. On one occasion the pastor-elect, as he was called, allowed himself to be led to the affirmation that the sinner has a part in his conversion, whereupon the question was flung at him from the other side: 'What part? Did the man with the withered hand, whom Jesus healed, have any part in the healing?' After a pause, during which the excitement became intense, the young minister answered: 'Yes, he had a hand in it.' Then logic dissolved in laughter.

Another case may be cited in which the fierce examination ended in a still more obvious relief to feeling. After an extended and severe test ranging all the way from the eternal purposes of God to the bliss of the righteous and the woe of the wicked in the world to come, the exhausted candidate was asked if he were willing to be damned for the glory of God. This was more than he could bear. His answer was that he was not willing to be damned for the glory of God, but if it were for the glory of God that this ecclesiastical council be damned, he would in no way raise any objection. Further questions about the moment of an installation over forty years old may be answered by a poem of Browning:

> 'Ah! did you once see Shelley plain,
>   And did he stop and speak to you,
> And did you speak to him again?
>   How strange it seems, and new!
>
> 'But you were living before that,
>   And also you are living after;
> And the memory I started at —
>   My starting moves your laughter!
>
> 'I crossed a moor, with a name of its own
>   And a certain use in the world, no doubt,
> Yet a hand's-breadth of it shines alone
>   'Mid the blank miles round about:
>
> 'For there I picked up on the heather,
>   And there I put inside my breast
> A moulted feather, an eagle feather!
>   Well, I forget the rest.'

This reporter of having seen Shelley, and having heard him speak, and being spoken to by him, was a plain man, probably a very stupid person, otherwise absolutely uninteresting, with no significance for any one anywhere. But

OLD SOUTH CHURCH, BOSTON

the fact that he had seen Shelley, that Shelley had spoken to him, gave him distinction to the end of his days and made him of moment to every one with whom he came in contact.

And there is that heath, the moor, bleak, barren, desolate, ugly, forlorn enough. What relation can that have to the joyful life? What significance is there there for any wide-awake, normal human being? There is just one star on that moor that shines, and the lonely traveler over it found that an eagle had flown over it and shed a feather and the feather of the royal bird gave significance to the moor which otherwise would have had none. There is my parable.

What on earth is there in an installation that occurred nearly forty-two years ago to interest any living being to-day? It may be that there is an eagle's feather, and all the rest of it, waste and forlorn enough, is made worth while by the Shelley idea and the eagle's feather. What is the Shelley idea? What is the eagle's feather?

The men who composed that council, ministers and laymen alike, to the number of sixty-six or so, believed that there was something sacred in human life. The worst type of man is the person who sees nothing to revere, nothing to care for or in any way to regard in human life. It is easy to be liberal when one cares for nothing. Old Gallio, the Roman judge, looked upon the quarrels that were brought to him as simply what Carlyle would have called Semitic anti-Semitic street riots, and so Gallio cared for none of these things.

We have to-day a mood of this kind, very prevalent. You can believe anything you like about life, say anything

you like about it. Who cares? That mood is infinitely below the mood of conviction even when confused, even when
intolerant. There were two sides represented at that council and both were at one in this respect, that life has infinite sanctity in it, that it holds a treasure of immeasurable moment. There is the Shelley idea.

And what is the eagle's feather? Up to the time of my
settlement here, especially in New England, the New England Calvinism had ruled every pulpit in the Commonwealth. Only one type of minister should be acknowledged.
This was the issue before that council. The members of
the council could have compromised, as I learned from the
outside afterward; they could have decided that, all things
considered, this man is satisfactory, and we will pass him.
But, no; the liberal men would have none of that. The result might have been unanimous if the council had gone
upon a compromise. The liberals said: 'This man believes
in God, the Father of Jesus Christ, and he believes in the
programme of Jesus for the help and salvation of man, and
he is going in on his record, New England theology to the
contrary notwithstanding.' They fought that battle; it
took them three long hours to do it, and they settled that
question for all time. There has not been a word upon this
subject since in any council. It seems a small thing, but
look at our Presbyterian brethren, going through what we
Congregationalists went through and finished forty years
ago. Look at the distemper of the Presbyterian body.
Dr. Fosdick must not be allowed to preach in a Presbyterian Church unless he subscribes to the Westminster
Confession, a faith which no intelligent man who knows
anything about the world he is living in to-day could pos-

sibly accept. It contains 'the doctrine of reprobation, that God made some men to be saved and some to be damned.' That is the Westminster Confession. Now I say the Presbyterians are having it a great deal worse than we had it and they are forty years behind. But even so, I have a great deal of respect for the conservatives and their fundamentalist followers, because they recognize that there is something in the faith and the life of man of infinite moment. They deserve respect and respectful regard, because life is not empty to them. They would go to the stake, these men, for what they believe, and we believe as they do, that life has infinite worth from God in it, that it has a treasure in it which all honest men ought to do their utmost to conserve. They have not yet come to the other point, the Presbyterians have not, of saying: 'You fundamentalists have a perfect right to preach in a Presbyterian Church if anybody wants you to preach there, but you have absolutely no right to prescribe one type of theist, one type of Christian, one type of Prophet of the Gospel of Jesus Christ.' They have not arrived. They are forty years behind, and that old council looms to-day with its great meaning, that for Congregationalism over the whole country there is room for the conservative and there is room for the liberal, there is room for every man who recognizes in Jesus Christ Our Lord the revelation of God and His programme of help for man.

Nothing done in our history was more complete in its effect than the work of that council. There followed several other installations within a year or two, and I attended to see what might be done. Nothing was done. The pastors-elect were far more careless in expression than I was, and yet they sailed through the straits, not a shot was fired from any fort, and not a rock was struck in the channel. There is the eagle's feather.

Extreme opinions were wont to meet in the ancient councils of our body and the clash of logic was inevitable and of general interest. Thinkers would aver that man, shorn of all ability, both natural and moral, was yet in duty bound to fulfill the Divine will, as a soldier would still be under bonds to serve his country who had voluntarily cut off his hand, to which Lyman Beecher is reported to have replied: 'Suppose that soldier had cut off his head?' There was a famous professor of mathematics in Bowdoin College two generations ago, whose pet phrase in demonstrations was this: 'Paradoxical as this may seem to you, it is nevertheless true, as I shall now proceed to show.' Occasionally this famous man, who was a Calvinist of the austerest type, would be called upon to lead morning prayers in the chapel. It was reported to me, by one of his students, who was famous in his generation, that on one occasion the Professor prayed thus: 'O Lord, Thou art infinite in majesty, goodness, and power. In Thy presence man is as nothing. He is destitute of all power to obey Thee and to do Thy will, yet is he under strict and eternal obligation to obey Thee and to do Thy will, and paradoxical as this may seem to Thee, it is nevertheless true, as I shall now proceed to show.'

The humorous side of the council that examined me was so obvious that it was with difficulty that the pastor-elect could be entirely serious. There was great excitement in the council, evident alarm at what the Old South Church had done, resentment, too, as if the advice of wise men had been disregarded by the church, and an attitude toward the young minister of cold courtesy, covering a suspicion that he was an unworthy adventurer, without true faith, with spiritual credentials altogether inadequate. The candidate felt that he was in the presence of men panic-stricken, half-wild; and therefore as facing the inevitable he was completely calm; he made no effort to persuade, but did all he could to be sincere and clear. On the question of the Being of God, the Person of Jesus Christ, the Holy Spirit, the value of the Bible, the eternal distinctness of the righteous and the unrighteous life, and the purpose of the minister to endeavor by the grace of God to save souls, and to lead them in the hope of a new heaven and a new earth wherein dwelleth righteousness, there was no trouble. One would imagine that this should have been enough, but it was not; it was a mere unimportant incident when what was left out was considered. The New England theory of the Atonement was set aside, and the everlasting punishment of the wicked was not affirmed. What these good men were concerned about, what stirred their souls with a great and holy fear, was the New England scheme of Divinity. The Gospel of Jesus Christ might be affirmed, but that did not count, because it could not take care of itself; it was impotent without the guardianship of New England Calvinism.

Here was the humor of the situation and close by it the fountain of tears. Few things have I seen more amusing, few things sadder, than this utter failure on the part of able and good men who had given their lives in Christian service, in the just perspective of the values of the faith which they held and preached. I speak of the conservative leaders, noble men they were, heroic in a way, but without insight into the most precious possession of their race, without vision in the Kingdom of God. One delegate asked me if I believed in a personal Devil, evidently thinking that a more serious thing than the question of belief in a personal God. On the failure to affirm the everlasting condemnation of those who died in their wickedness, and the New England theory of the reconciliation of God to man and man to God, the moderator of the council who had consented to offer the installing prayer withdrew his consent, and eighteen members of the council voted against my installation. The humor and the pathos of the whole affair lie in the perverse perspective of spiritual reality characteristic of these good men.

Dr. E. B. Webb, the moderator of the council, came to be friendly and kindly to the young heretic. His words to a friend eleven years later, on reading 'The Christ of To-day,' were: 'Of all the men whom I have expected to turn out badly, Gordon has disappointed me the most'; not an honor degree, indeed, but a sincere word and meant to be friendly. When Dr. Webb was ill with the trouble of which he soon after died, he sent for me to come to see him. I went, and we had a most friendly conversation. He alluded to the council and his part in it, but I protested, saying: 'Dr. Webb, you were true to your convictions of duty; you thought I was all wrong, and you said so. I have always respected you for your moral courage in doing the thing you believed to be right, and which you knew would be extremely unpopular.' He then asked me to pray with him, which I did from a full heart. We parted forever in this world, and when I returned home the thought, which till then had not occurred to me, came into my mind with a strange feeling of the dramatic contrasts in this life of ours: when we first met, Dr. Webb refused to pray for me; when we met for the last time, he asked me to pray for him, and I gladly did.

Another amusing incident related to the superb supper prepared by the Old South Church for the council and invited guests. The council went into secret session about five-thirty in the afternoon. The supper was set for six-thirty. At that hour the council was still in debate. The committee in charge delayed till they could delay no longer. The invited guests, representing all religious denominations, were escorted to the dining-room and partook of the supper. Speeches of welcome to the new minister were made, and greetings extended by Phillips Brooks, and others. Still no council appeared. At a few minutes before nine o'clock the result was given out, forty-eight in favor, eighteen against installation. All were tired after three hours of debate, and all were somewhat out of temper to find the supper had been eaten for them, that only cold fragments remained. I fancied when the council assembled for the installation service that the light in the eyes of those who fought for me signified that they wondered whether I was really worth it all, while those who lost had two disappointments; they had been beaten, and they had lost their supper! Under the circumstances, the service did not impress me as inspiring. A small blizzard was raging without, an equal moral chill reigned within. Dr. Tucker's fine sermon I recall, delivered as a tired eagle might fly against the wind; Dr. Herrick's admirable address to the people of the Old South Church, containing generous but audacious words of prophecy concerning the young minister, Dr. Merriman's prayer as substitute for Dr. Webb, which gave one the feeling that there was still one man left who could honestly pray for me, and Dr. Barbour's charge to the minister. He had been my teacher in Bangor, and with great caution made this statement: 'All signs will fail if you do not make a good minister of Jesus Christ to this people.' To be sure, this did not carry far, but it was good as far as it went. It was close to twelve o'clock when I pronounced the benediction as minister, duly installed, of the Old South Church in Boston. When I retired for the night in the parsonage, I felt as if the council had done its best to place the tower of the church upon my chest. It was another instance of the ridiculous panic and cruelty of which good men are, in times of excitement, all too capable.

The council did not kill me, because I was able, after a night's rest, to laugh at its wild absurdities and strident nonsense. There were, of course, many splendid men on the council, who knew the significance for the denomination of the occasion, and who fought this battle with conspicuous skill, and by their victory obtained a lasting peace for New England Congregationalism.

Good fighters never know when they are beaten. It was thus with the defeated minority in this council. They carried on the warfare in the prominent pulpits of Greater Boston, in the 'Congregationalist,' and in other papers, particularly the 'Boston Traveler' of that day. Their attitude has often reminded me of one of Professor Park's experiences told me by himself. Dr. Lyman Beecher, then an old man, was Park's guest at Andover. After dinner a dispute arose between Beecher and Park upon a series of subtle points in theology concerning which Park was a consummate master, and Beecher simply a thoughtful and eloquent preacher. The dispute ran on to one o'clock in the morning. After they parted, Park's social conscience greatly troubled him. It said: 'Here is your guest, an old and honored man whom you were in duty bound to treat with affectionate reverence. Instead, you have beaten him by your logic into insensibility, and sent him to bed in utter humiliation. Your conduct is unworthy of a gentleman.' Park slept little that night, crept down in miserably low spirits to breakfast, sat in silence with Dr. Edward Beecher, oldest son of Dr. Lyman Beecher, when the old hero appeared and greeted his host: 'Well, Park, how do you feel after the tremendous mauling I gave you last night?'

Congregationalists have always been rationalists. However much they may have made of religious experience, they have always held a reasoned philosophy of man's life and man's universe. They have always been rationalists, and at times extremely disputatious. Many of them like Edwards, Emmons, Taylor, and Park have been expert logicians and consummate dialecticians. Dialectical encounters were their sport; they began this joyous and serious play of the mind in boyhood, in homes where theology was the chief interest, and they continued this behavior, in a way, to their last breath. Professor Park used to relate of his senior colleague Moses Stuart an amusing instance of this habit. For two years before his death Professor Stuart was ill. His colleagues took turns in passing the long weary evenings with him. Fond of Park, a much younger man, Stuart was concerned about the looseness of some of his views. One evening the debate was intense and loud when there was a knock on the door of the Professor's room. An old pupil was shown in to see him. Stuart's annoyance at this interruption in the debate with Park was acute. He made as if he were fainting. The visitor inquired how his venerated teacher was and got for reply this: 'More dead than alive.' The visitor added, 'It is lovely to think that your faith does not fail'; and again was answered that this was his chief trouble. 'I have no faith, no opinions, no convictions, one proposition is to me as meaningless as another. I am in a mean and miserable collapse.' 'Well, good-bye, and God bless you, my great friend and guide of my youth,' said the retreating visitor. In a voice reduced to a hollow whisper, Stuart said, 'Good-bye.' Then, listening till the retreating steps were far enough away, he resumed the debate, raising his voice till it resembled the roar of a lion: 'Park, as I was saying, and as I maintain against you —' the ruling sport and passion strong in death. Some one, some day, will awaken and recover for all our churches this slumbering tradition of the intellectual play and strength of these generations of extraordinary men. For wit and humor, no less than for subtlety and strength of intellect, men like Emmons and Park should not be allowed to fade from the memory of educated persons. That they had failings, not of the flesh, but of the spirit, is altogether true. They were pious men with a flavor of the Devil in them at times, and their utter reality in all things and at all seasons is more than compensation for their lack of sainthood. Most saints are too well aware of their sainthood, and sometimes are driven to the manufacture of evidence for it. The Christianity that streams through all life as the sunshine streams through the clouds that would obscure it, that transfigures them, fighting human infirmity while disclosing it, and on the whole prevailing over it, is perhaps the healthiest Christianity, as it is the most dramatic and real, in a world of sadly imperfect men and women.

I have long wanted to write a book upon this subject: From Authority through Anarchy to Insight. I have not read Dr. Jack's book 'From Authority to Freedom,' but I am sure it must be admirable. My thought is that when authority is lifted anarchy is the first result, and that the terrible discipline of anarchy brings insight which is the condition essential to all freedom and peace. Those under authority in the world of thought must ever be without insight; when the authority is broken, be it of the Church or of the Bible, the first issue of incompetent minds, in trying to reduce to order the intellectual puzzle of the world, is Babel on a large scale. The ideal end, toward which this Babel works, is insight, and the unity and peace that can come only from insight.

Authority both of Church and of the Bible has been lifted from a large part of the Christian world. The result is an indefinite number of conflicting opinions upon every subject in the whole range of Christian faith. Many sigh over this shattered unity of the Christian mind and compare it to a bursting bomb, which not only breaks itself into a thousand pieces, but also works disaster upon its environment. There is much truth in this description and sound reasons for regret that it should be so. Yet it must be added that heroic men do not weep over the inevitable.

Men under authority are men without training in the powers of the mind, and in character as it bears upon the things of the mind. When the authority that has kept them ignorant has gone, men seek for truth as those try to find their way home from afar in midnight darkness. Intellectual anarchy is the inevitable issue of cancelled authority; it is a beginning in independent intellectual life, it is a start toward the far-away goal of competent judgment.

Bernard Bosanquet's last book, 'Contemporary Philosophy,' in which that admirable thinker seeks to find the centers of identity in the opposing opinions of present-day philosophers, made upon one reader one overwhelming impression, the sense of anarchy reigning in the entire philosophic field. For those for whom philosophy is novelty and sport, this is delightful; for those for whom philosophy is a struggle and conflict in the dark toward the light, this is interesting; for those for whom philosophy is the sure grasp of the meaning of man's life and universe, this is simply the revelation of primitive incompetence, barbarian ignorance. When philosophy has become an assemblage of contradictions, that grand science is not discredited nor are those who cultivate it to be treated with disrespect. Doubtless they are doing their level best. They are children working at a task too big for them; they are learning to think, but have not yet attained mastery; they are free from authority, but they are still far away from the freedom and unity of adequate insight.

There is a similar anarchy among Biblical scholars. No two books agree over any great extent of investigation. Tradition has been set aside, and the multitude of questions thus set free no scholar and no college of scholars can answer. These books upon the New Testament are remarkable above all things in the reasoned contradiction of the opinions of other scholars; they are sincerest where they confess complete ignorance about things which tradition has taught the Christian world to believe as historic truth. Break the authority of tradition, and you lift the lid of Pandora's box. Out fly a swarm of unanswerable questions to plague the seeker for truth. Tradition must be broken, of course, but the first result, and a long result it is, brings anarchy in the world of scholarly opinion.

The chief end of the ecclesiastical council that finally, and after difficulty, installed me as minister of the Old South Church, was the disclosure of the variety and conflict of ideas that came with the loss of authority in the New England theology. The old views and the new views, in endless mixture and modification, came into the light of day. The intellect of our churches, split into a thousand forms, was facing the task of finding a new and more adequate philosophy of the Christian religion, the experience of Christian men, and the meaning of God's great world in time. Honesty and ignorance, high purpose and sheer incompetence, heroic struggle and heroic failure were everywhere manifest. We were free from a great but tyrannous tradition, but we confronted a task requiring a thousand generations for its adequate performance. The bees were out of the old hive forever; who can collect the ever-increasing swarm and provide an adequate home for it? A thousand answers, often in conflict one with another, all of them imperfect in wisdom, came, making many precious things clear and sure, but rendering clearest and surest of all that the mind of the Christian Church had entered the vast, painful, and prophetic discipline of anarchy. This I take to be the chief merit and lesson of the council that met in the Old South Church April 2, 1884.

Heresy, tolerated heresy, had always lived within the Congregational fold, to speak only of this branch of the Christian Church important for the American people, especially for New England. There is Edwards's famous dictum in the discussion of the Freedom of the Will, that 'the will is as the greatest apparent good.' This heresy lived on through much of the history of New England theology. The maxim was never brought to the test of experience; it is not only not true, it is demonstrably false. The will never is as the greatest apparent good; it is as the real good from the point of view of the person making the choice. The moment the good is known to be apparent and not real, the will is in opposition to it; then it is seen to be a cheat and a sham. Edwards was profoundly right in connecting the will with good; indeed, they cannot be separated. He was profoundly wrong in not taking account of the illuminating power of experience by which the will, set to the good when that good turns out to be apparent and not real, is reset. Let us suppose that coffee is the greatest morning good at breakfast; it turns out to be a disturber of digestion, a poison to the nervous system, a cause of sleeplessness, and the will that before this experience was as the greatest good — that is, coffee — now regards it as an evil. In thousands of instances this process is repeated, with the same issue, in respect to certain foods, drinks, habits of behavior, customs of the mind, ways of thinking and feeling, which were at one time believed to

be good, but which turn out to be evil under the great recti-
fying principle of human life, the illuminating power of
experience.   This heresy, error, falsehood, that 'the will is
as the greatest apparent good,' ducked its ugly head under
the bedclothes of New England theology, was never
dragged from its hiding-place and exposed as it should be
as a pure misrepresentation of the fact. No honest man
wants appearance, he wants reality; show him that this
greatest good is appearance only and he surrenders it at
once; show him that what he has hitherto regarded as evil,
the greatest evil, is good, the greatest good, and his will
instinctively turns toward that.   Edwards's name is
rightly connected with the denial of freedom to man. His
substitution of apparent for real good left the will like the
log in the whirlpool. There was no way out. The question
of freedom is inseparable from the question of good. Experience teaches man what appears to be good and is not,
and what is real, essential, changeless good. The will of
man guided by the eternal good comes under its sovereignty; and here it must be said that apart from good freedom has no meaning. To be forever under the sway of the
greatest good is to be perfect in freedom. The will, good,
real and unreal, and freedom belong together; they constitute the field in which our moral life moves. Edwards failed
in moral insight, failed to see that essential good at its best
is the inevitable goal of will; he failed to see in human experience the Divine Teacher of real good and evil; he failed
to provide a way of emergence from mistaken good such as
every honest man finds in the courses of time; he failed to
ground the ultimate dominion of God over men in the ultimate inseparableness of the human will and the greatest

real good. Edwards's treatise on 'The Will' has been immensely stimulating to American thought, but it is far from valid in insight or in reasoning. Edwards remains a great speculative intellect, a chief distinction of American thought, one of whom it may be said as it was of Israel, 'Thy God is thy glory'; still it must be added that he is as often manifestly wrong as he is right, and that he sent into American theology a whole swarm of heresies.

One more heretic who dwelt within the Orthodox fold in comparative peace must be mentioned here. Nathanael Emmons, who trained more men for the ministry than any other single thinker in our history, whose sermons were read all over New England, held the astounding opinion that God was a growing being. Here is a strange coincidence with the thought of the English philosopher of to-day, Alexander, who, if he is understood, is said to begin without a God, and from space and time and their contents, in the course of the ages, to evolve God under the form of perfection. Emmons held that the universe of matter and mind is the operation of God, that man's soul consists in exercises, that these exercises are the determinations of the Divine Will. Here is pantheism working through human forms. Again we are reminded of the thoughts of certain contemporary English idealists, whose position would seem to be that the universe does our thinking for us, that there is no other meaning to the soul of man than that it is a temporal form through which the universe does its thinking; poor universe if this is all it can do. High Calvinism, whether in philosophy or in theology, is forever the same. The One Being is alone real; all the rest is field and plaything for that One Being, whether men call it The

All, The Absolute, or God. New England theology is of permanent interest to thinkers, because, like Jacob and Esau before their birth, true ideas and false, realities and semblances, contend within it. The election of time will save what is truly worthy in it and reprobate the rest.

Councils such as that which examined me were the meeting-places of conflicting opinions. The endeavor was to force the candidate into the acceptance of certain beliefs or fight him the rest of his days. There were always two sides, often in numbers unequally matched; and again the two main parties held within them a whole lot of jarring minds. A representative ecclesiastical council carried with it an emotional value somewhat similar to a gladiatorial exhibition in ancient Rome. The whole community was stirred to the depths, and controversy took from these occasions a new birth. The council whose memories I am recalling is an instance of the conflict of mind with mind on the most serious subjects out of which much that is greatest in our New England life has come. They afford amusement as we survey them, and they bring before us one of the best things in any age, the conflict of intellect with intellect upon the interpretation of the sovereign interests of human beings.

In Professor Park's 'Memoir of Dr. Emmons' we read:

'A divine of no small eminence, having read Dr. Emmons's sermon on the Atonement, a sermon which was encountering at that time some opposition, sent to the Franklin minister the following epistle, which was considered too laconic, magisterial, and patronizing to comport with the Apostle's rule for the treatment of elders: "May 1st, My dear brother, I have read your sermon on the Atonement, and have wept over it. Yours affectionately, A. B. A." These admonitory words were no sooner read than the following reply was written and sent to the post-office: "May 3rd, Dear Sir, I have read your letter and laughed at it. Yours, Nathanael Emmons." '

This is perhaps the best way to end this chapter. One may survey the whole, note its high character and serious purpose, recall with honor all the combatants in the struggle, lay to heart many important lessons of that far-away council, rest the entire turbulent mood of the day in respectful and tender recollection and close the interview through memory, not with tears, but with laughter. Three friends went to the Adirondacks for their vacation. One of the three was elected cook for the party. He consented to serve till criticized, and further stipulated that whoever found fault with his cooking should be made to take his place. One day the cook in making apple pie used salt instead of sugar as sweetener. The first member of the party to partake of the pie shouted, 'That is the awfulest pie that I ever tasted,' and then, recollecting himself, he added swiftly, 'but I like it!' I should like my memories of my installing council to be taken in this way. 'It was the fiercest council I ever knew, but I have always been fond of it.'

CHAPTER XVIII

THE SENSE OF A MISSION

A LARGE part of a man's education comes through his vocation. In the case of his character this is evident; in the case of his intellect it becomes equally evident when wide and enlightened views are entertained about the things which one has undertaken to do. William II of Germany said on one occasion that he was emperor of the German people, not by their will, but by the will of God, and, when met by the indignant protest of the nation, he replied that he was claiming for himself only what every Christian man might claim, and indeed should claim, that he was sent forth into this world to do the will of the Highest. Whether this answer was made by William II or made for him, whether it was meant in solemn sincerity or was framed to get the impulsive ruler out of a hole, it was in strict truth an answer wholly justifiable. It meant what Bushnell meant when he wrote his famous sermon, 'Every Man's Life a Plan of God.' It is, indeed, an extremely offensive thing to think too highly of what one has been set to do in comparison with what other men have been set to do; overestimate of one's self and underestimate of others is one of the meanest of all mean traits, and exposes one of the most contemptible moods of the human spirit. When one's view of his calling is no more than a particular instance of the universal calling of men, his exalted ideas of what he has been set to do stands free from egotism, and becomes a prophetic announcement of the high vocation of his kind. In this universal vocation there are diversities of gifts, diversities of operation, but the same spirit. The Eternal Will is seeking expression through the entire circle of His human apostles.

To perceive a purpose in one's life growing clearer with the years, to find one's keenest intellectual exercise and one's chief joy in fulfilling that purpose, is, I suppose, what we mean by the sense of a mission. In the light of a great example we may see the meaning of the little errands we are called upon to run. There is General Grant, one of the most modest and magnanimous of all great Americans. He went into the war for the preservation of the Union as the colonel of a regiment, and rose by clean and clear steps of merit to be supreme commander of all the armies in the field fighting for the life of the United States. The sense of a mission must have grown within him, the sense of a purpose working through him mightier than he, for the good of his nation. His deepest and most careful thinking was done in the service of that purpose; here, too, lay his highest happiness. Such was the Hebrew prophet and the Christian apostle. The Hebrew prophet was a man of towering dignity because he felt that his God had sent him to proclaim the truth to his nation. The splendor of his intellect was brought forth by his fidelity to the high purpose working through him, and, while denunciation formed a large part of his message, I cannot doubt that this sacred profanity brought with it an exhilarating emotional accompaniment. Even Jeremiah seems to have enjoyed his tears, as so many with a similar genius have done. I am here reminded of the Scottish woman who had a regular order of weeping for every day except the Sabbath. She

had a short period of weeping before breakfast, a longer
period before dinner, and after, stopping for afternoon tea,
and not resuming the business till supper was well over,
closing the day with a moderate outpouring, and all this
for the poor mother who had been dead for more than
twenty years. Having wept in an orderly and rational
manner all through the six days of the week, she rested on
the seventh day, as the Lord did from all his works. This
good woman had a mission; she fulfilled it, and had much
happiness in so doing.

The primary mission of the preacher of the Christian
Gospel is to make Christian character by the grace and
power of Christian ideas. Nothing is more disheartening
than the insensibility that the preacher meets, in many
instances, to the attractive power of goodness; and on the
other hand nothing could be more exhilarating than the
responsiveness of the human heart, in the majority of men
and women, to the appeal of Christian ideals. Human
nature was made to be swayed, satisfied, and saved by the
vision of the supreme good; when truly presented and truly
beheld, the supreme good is irresistible in its power over
the human soul. Augustine speaks for the deep, eternal
nature of man when he says, 'Thou hast made us for Thy-
self, and we are restless till we repose in Thee.' The minister's calling, to one who is fond of it, is an endless romance.
The Gospel of Jesus is the sovereign version of the *summum bonum* for man; when it gets a fair chance, it has the
wonder-working power of the greatest music; it calls to
what is universal in man and he answers, and cannot but
answer. Call this determinism, if you will, necessity, or any
other name to which unpleasant associations are attached,

but be it remembered that the appeal and sovereignty of the highest good carry in them the life and freedom for which man was made, and outside of which life is slavery and misery. To show human beings that the Gospel of Jesus is the highest good is the chief purpose of the Christian preacher, since out of the vision of the highest good must come a new man, a new humanity. The care of a parish carries with it this great primary privilege; it is an incessant call upon the minister to be the prophet of the highest good. As under the ministry of sunshine and showers, in the springtime, the earth covers itself with the beauty of new life and new promise, so under the Christian Gospel presented as good, as the chief good, human nature comes again to the bloom of love and the service of love and the prophecy of a new social world filled with righteousness and peace.

The question of good is blended with the question of truth. Under the Calvinistic scheme, which is the Augustinian and medieval scheme of belief passed through the logical life and power of the Protestant Reformation, the good was not true and the truth was not good. At the heart of the whole business this was the fatal contradiction in our inherited faith. The love of God for man is the highest good, creating in man love among men for one another. This is essential Christianity as it lives in our great Master. What now is the truth? God looks out upon a world of fallen and depraved men and women. He elects some to life eternal, reprobates others to eternal death, or simply leaves them to perish everlastingly in their sins; whom He elects, for them He provides an atonement, them He regenerates, sanctifies, saves and glorifies. The vision of earth is a divided one; it consists of saints and sinners, saved and lost, God's children and the Devil's. This vision of a divided humanity is carried back into the will of the Deity. The division on earth is caused by the division in heaven. God's will is the will for the highest good of some of His creatures, and for others it is the will for their eternal misery. This is the logic of Augustinianism, Calvinism, Edwardeanism, of the whole tradition of systematic and speculative theology since the period of the great Greek theologians. If this is the truth, it cannot be good; if the good be the vision of God as the lover of every soul that He has made, its home and infinite peace, the good is not true.

It was here that the sense of a mission to my generation came to possess me. The critical problems of the Old and New Testaments did not concern me other than as a learner from those who were masters in this field; the historical questions about these ancient Scriptures concerned experts in historical learning and again they concerned me only as a student; the religions of the world as taught by great scholars were, indeed, an object of the deepest interest to me, but I had no call to do anything here but to gain light and width of sympathy from those who had qualified themselves by long and laborious investigations to enlighten their age upon this vast and alluring subject. My life had been devoted to two great spheres of human interest, to European philosophy from its beginning down to our own day, and to literature, especially Hebrew, Greek, and English. I was qualified to look critically into the philosophy of man's life and world offered to us in the theology of the Christian Church.

I well remember the day when the insight came to me, that what New England theology, historic theology, needed to save its life, and all the precious things bound up with its life, was to universalize it, from the Being of God to the first and last human being in time, and through the whole process of its thought. This insight came to one who knew the scheme, in all its varieties and modifications, as well as he knew the Greek or the English alphabet, and who had gone over the whole expanse of it, times without number, in the hope of finding the key to its reasonableness; this insight came like a flash, it stood the test of examination; the longer it was reflected upon, the profounder and the more evident its truth seemed to me to become. God's will must be a will of creative love; it must be a will that no accident of sin or lapse in man can change; it must be a will forever on the side of our whole humanity; and the forms of its expression in the processes and powers of the Spirit must have one goal and one goal only, the redemption of mankind into the liberty, the glorious liberty of the sons of God. If this is not accomplished in time, as it plainly is not, the scene of the redemptive drama must be indefinitely extended. God is under the bonds of His own nature as the creator and lover of man, to show man what his supreme good is, to persuade him, both by the experience of righteousness and the folly of unrighteousness, to lift up his heart to what is always and eternally good. Death is an incident in the discipline of the soul; judgment is the incessant examination implied in the Divine education of the world; the final examination is final only as regards what had been done in time. The Judgment Seat of Christ is forever; the rational being, man or angel, is before it forever; it measures and records; it is the revelation of progress or failure, and always as the illumination of love, always as the light and impulse to the grander existence. The character of God is the life of the Christian religion; the character of God must be saved, whatever in the thoughts of men may be lost or changed. Let the character of God as revealed in Jesus the Lord have free course, and the issue will be that the truth will be seen to be the highest good, and the highest good the absolute truth for man's life. Metaphysics and ethics thus meet in mutual eternal support; the highest metaphysics, the loving Being of God, becomes the highest ethics, love as the sovereign good, and the highest ethics, love as man's need and good becomes the ultimate truth of the universe, the eternal good will of God to all souls in all worlds.

My books have been, all of them, expositions of this fundamental change in theological thought. 'The Christ of To-day' asserted the ideal Sonship of Jesus to His Father; it contended for a special incarnation of God in our Lord in the light of which the universal sonship of man to God became a reality to Christian faith. Finding the meaning of the call of Jesus to be a mission of deliverance from darkness to light for all mankind, a mission from the Infinite Father, all texts in the Old Testament and in the New Testament, that asserted a limited love on God's part for His human creatures, were brushed aside as inconsistent with the mission of Jesus. Jesus embodied an idea, and that idea must rule and overrule all isolated texts. Historical criticism has introduced another answer. Jesus' mind could not be, evidently was not, consistently reflected in the minds of His greatest disciples. Their inheritance and their limitations made this impossible. In Paul, the greatest of them, this is plainly seen. It may be difficult to say how much of Judaism Paul left behind him when he became a Christian, how much he brought with him and embedded in his Christianity, how much he learnt from classical and Hellenistic Greece, how much from the mystery cults in the Roman Empire that was the wide field of his service, but it is perfectly clear that he did not reproduce, in all its purity and completeness, the mind of Jesus, its inwardness, its depth, its easy comprehensiveness, its unimpeded insight, its unity of thought and purpose, its majestic simplicity. When 'The Christ of To-day' was written, the voice of historical analysis was not heard in the land above a whisper, and a philosophical idea such as I still hold had to do duty in place of the critical method. Nothing in the New Testament can be admitted as true which contradicts or sets at naught the reality of Jesus' mission of love from God to the whole world.

'Ultimate Conceptions of Faith' was an attempt to replace the wreck of the New England theology, by a modern building, a house of faith for the intellect framed of irreducible realities, a shelter for my own generation till a grander edifice should appear. Personality, for the individual; humanity, for society; optimism, for history; Jesus Christ, for religion; the moral order, for the universe; and God, as the absolute ultimate: these were the irreducible realities which I thought I had found, and which rose spontaneously into a temple for the mind, like that of old, without the sound of hammer.

'Immortality and the New Theodicy,' the first Harvard lecture on the Ingersoll Foundation, gave me an opportunity to discuss in a new way the question of the destiny of man, upon which I had read and brooded for more than fifteen serious years. To limit to this life opportunity for man's spirit to recover itself to goodness seemed wholly arbitrary; to limit the redemptive purpose of God in Christ to this world seemed to me simply incredible. In that case God must be seen to be defeated in His purpose, which surely must not be a conclusion lightly held. The universe must be regarded as a redemptive universe, and God's purpose to lift to their best estate all the souls that He has made, however blinded by sense and passion they may have been, must be forever.

The harmony of this scheme with the reality of retribution for all wrong-doing is not difficult to perceive. If retribution is an act or process of retaliation, of course there can be no harmony between it and the religion of hope. If retribution be in its essence illumination filled with the purpose of reform of him to whom it comes, filled with hope for him upon whom it falls, then retribution is one of the two mighty wings — the other being approval — that carry the soul from the life of slavery to sense to that of freedom in God. There never was a more foolish fear than that an endless chance for the spirit of man under the eternal redemptive purpose of God might destroy the whole fabric of ethical Christianity. If Christianity is love, and if the sinful life is selfishness, an endless chance to change from selfishness to love could endanger nothing except the confederation of the loveless; and the woe of the loveless life is the endless ally of the timeless purpose of the Most High. The worst, perhaps, that might be said of the traditional theology was that it was without profound ethical discernment, and that what was best in the ethical life of the Christian ages had no home or shelter in the accepted theology. Many a thinker has been open to the criticism that Father Taylor, the sailor preacher, passed upon a contemporary divine of high Calvinistic bent: 'Your God stands for my Devil.'

My book on 'Religion and Miracle' brought me more abuse and persecution than anything I have ever done. It was written to vindicate the right of my younger ministerial brethren who could not believe in miracles, to preach the Gospel of Jesus Christ. The book was an extremely conservative one. It did not deny the reality of miracles; it simply undertook to show that on the supposition of the unreality of miracles Christianity still lived in its intrinsic integrity. I still regard the chapter in this book on 'An Eternal Gospel,' and the last chapter in 'Ultimate Conceptions of Faith,' as the best in thought and in expression that I have ever done.

When I began my ministry in Boston, my denomination, in its influential persons and organs, was strongly against me. Naturally the Old South Church, on account of its minister, was in practical excommunication except for financial appeals when the denominational order was hard up. My constituency was limited. Only heretical persons came to us from the outside, and, as there was a goodly number of such persons, the church rapidly filled, and with galleries added was no more than adequate for the congregation when the weather was favorable. When my books began to be published, strangers would come to us in greater numbers, and the church came to breathe an atmosphere brightened by the visits of many shining friends.

My books augmented the size, confirmed the dignity, and brightened the loyalty of my congregations. So it has continued to this day.

It may not be without interest here to refer briefly to the sustaining studies of a long life of continuous production. These sustaining studies have been chiefly in literature and in philosophy. In literature I have found the really great artists dealing with the experiences of men in their richest and darkest aspects, giving forms of everlasting beauty to the same ideas that engage the reflective intellect of the philosopher. The great instrument of the poet and the man of letters is imagination, a faculty as strikingly exhibited by Carlyle as by Wordsworth or Tennyson. The Bible I have found, in all its greater books, the richest and the most rewarding literature in the world. Next to this in substantial merit, and often superior in form, I place Greek literature; and next in order of worth our English literature. Dante is among the greatest, but he is solitary in Italian literature. Goethe is great, but again nearly solitary, and to me he has ever been a repulsive human being. Of French literature I am almost entirely ignorant, unless her philosophers are counted among the elect, as some of them must be, Pascal, for example.

In human experience there are things of sublime moment and of abysmal depths. The most precious possessions of the human spirit mount to heaven and sink to hell. The task of the great poet, whether in epic, dramatic, or lyric form, is to deal with these sacred things of the soul in a great way. To present the substance of man's heart, as that heart has suffered or rejoiced, in light and fire, is the vocation of the great poet, and of the great imagination in prose. In this field I have found the tree of life, bearing all manner of fruits, whose leaves are for the healing of the nations.

Philosophers are of two classes, acquaintances and friends. Among modern philosophers I have found Berkeley a permanent friend. For a theist, like myself, I can think of no modern name so bright as his, nor any philosophy more coherent than his Spiritual Realism. Locke must be read, but he is a milestone on wisdom's way, not an inn; truth-loving, honest, but everywhere and always commonplace. Hume I have always regarded as the greatest negative thinker in the history of speculation, a man of the keenest detective intellect, whose vocation it was to show that English empiricism began with nothing and led to nothing. The nineteenth century of British empiricism, a sad century, was done on the Humian basis, without any sort of perception that the disciples of Hume were building upon foundations that had been completely discredited by the master. Hume's homage to convention, his regular attendance upon Divine worship, his friendships among ministers and all sorts of intelligent people, and his sense of humor add to the interest of his strange character. When the street on which David Hume lived in Edinburgh was sarcastically named 'Saint David's Street,' his laconic reply was, 'Many worse men than I have been called saints.' Hume is keen and rewarding as an acquaintance, not by any possibility as a friend.

Of Descartes and Spinoza it must be said that, while they are interesting, even absorbing studies, they leave the life of a modern man nearly untouched. The maxim of Descartes, 'I think, that is to say, I am,' does indeed detain one, but the fabric that he weaves from this primary and wonderful thread does not look well, and does not wear well. Spinoza's life is one of the sacred things in the history of philosophy, and his philosophy as the sincere and ardent expression of his intellect and heart has called forth homage from many besides Schleiermacher. We put him down as an occasional friend.

German philosophy is the greatest treatment, by reflective mind, of the supreme interests of man, in modern times. Kant was serious where Hume was sportive; he was an austere moralist where Hume was a man of pleasure and ease; Kant was a constructive thinker through his critical adventure where Hume was wholly negative, with no great interests to conserve, because to him there were none. In all these respects Kant is great. He is great, too, in the magnitude of his plan as seen in his three 'Critiques,' in the thoroughness of his elaboration, and in the extent of his influence. It must be added that he did not greatly succeed in his philosophic task. He confined human knowledge to the sphere of phenomena, and, while asserting the existence of reality, banished it forever beyond the bounds of human knowledge. Kant is the father of modern agnosticism, and something more; he is the patron saint of bad writers. To get himself understood, he has wasted more of this world's precious time than perhaps any other recorded thinker in European history. We put him down as an essential friend, but one whose manners provoke impatience, indignation, sometimes even profanity. Hegel is the greatest of all modern philosophical scholars; by his insight, if not by the extent of his learning, one who has done more to enable students to penetrate to the heart of Greek

philosophy than any other modern; and besides, his
wealth of ideas is the greatest since the Greek era. He has
given rise to a strange variety of disciples and successors,
but the great master should not be held accountable for
the dragon's teeth that others have sown, or for the intellectual anarchy and woe of the harvest.

Plato and Aristotle, great master and equally great disciple, work upon a civilization, a concrete human possession, as rich and deep as ever existed in this world; and
when dealing not with physical science, in which they are
forever transcended, but with the possession which lay
before them in Greek experience, they are still our greatest
philosophic contemporaries. The life of the world has examined both these thinkers; what is true in them and what
is not true or not adequately true, the judgment of the
ages has made plain. They are often wrong, and infallible
nowhere; yet in originality, in the sense of reality, in the
pure disinterested mind, in the love of truth and the confidence of reason, and in the magnitude of their achievement, they remain incomparable, the best of all friends of
the reflective intellect, the best of all guides and teachers
in the long history of man's unfolding thought of his world.

In the Old Testament story when the Syrians encom-
passed a certain city during the night with horses and
chariots of fire, the servant of the prophet was terrified,
crying out: 'Alas, my master, how shall we do?' The calm
answer of the prophet was: 'Fear not; for they that are
with us are more than they that are with them.' Then the
eyes of the servant were opened, and he saw that the mountain was full of horses and of chariots of fire round about
the prophet. Thus is the world of high insight and true

wisdom round about every brave and faithful thinker; the solitary elevations on which he lives are crowded with august presences from all the great races and ages; they are his divinely commissioned allies; they strengthen the might of his fighting arm, and through their influence upon him become the living and invincible defenders of the supremely precious possessions of mankind.

CHAPTER XIX

MARRIAGE AND HOME

THE proverb has it that it takes several women to mould into acceptability the average man, at the very least four, his mother, his sister, his wife, and his daughter. No one has ever accused me of presuming upon the attention of women, of supposing that they had for me other than a kindly regard, that I was the object of anything beyond their good will, or of over-fondness for their company. And yet I am bold to claim the distinction of having as much admiration for refined and high-minded women as any man I have ever met, as profound a respect for the sacred purpose of their existence, as ready a recognition of their intellectual and emotional power, as much reverence for their capacity for service and self-sacrifice, as much delight in their exalted and wonderful sympathy. I have never been far away from the influence of such women. One of the best of good mothers, seven sisters, six of whom were my companions, over seventy first cousins more than half of them girls, six sisters-in-law, and, again, one of the best of all good wives, and one daughter, have assisted with much devotion in my education. They have not had an easy task, and in a representative way they all are to appear in the courage and hope of the supreme member of their group, the lady who on June 3, 1890, became my wife.

The following letter from Phillips Brooks has a place here.

MRS. GEORGE A. GORDON

MY DEAR GORDON:

I rejoice in your great happiness with all my heart. The morning mail has just brought me your letter, and I want at once to tell you how very glad I am. Little did I dream last night, when we sat and talked of Dr. Alden and other trifles, that all this was in your heart, and that we were so far away from you all the while. How blind we are. And yet I fancy that I did feel that there was something different from what had been, and can feel now that the new world which was with you was also unconsciously with us as we sat in your presence. I dare not try to tell you how sacred your happiness seems to me. Only you will believe that I rejoice in it profoundly and let my thoughts wander through the life which is opening before you, with thankfulness to Our Father that he has been so good to my friend.

It makes me very glad that you should wish me to have part in your joy and should have told me of it in such warm and friendly words. There will be many who will be very thankful for you, but no one of them will value his privilege of saying so to you more than I do. And the promise which you give me that I may have part in the fulfilment of your happiness by marrying you in June gives me the greatest pleasure. If I am here, as it now seems likely that I shall be, I shall count it a great privilege to do that service for you and Miss Manning.

Will you give her the assurance of my most earnest congratulations and regard? I hope that she will allow me to come and see her that I may ask her to count me as her friend also.

May God be ever good to you, my dear friend, as He has been.

Affectionately yours   PHILLIPS BROOKS

Miss Susan Huntington Manning, oldest daughter of my predecessor in the ministry of the Old South Church, Dr. Jacob Merrill Manning, and I were married in her mother's home, 29 Gloucester Street, Boston, on June 3, 1890, by Phillips Brooks, Dr. W. H. Fenn, of Portland, an uncle of the bride, and my old friend, the Reverend L. H. Angier, assisting.

Here is a note of noble sympathy and warning from my friend William James:

95 IRVING ST., CAMBRIDGE
June 13, 1890

MY DEAR GORDON:

So confused have my relations to my environment been of late that I only just awake to the knowledge that you are married.

Well! better late than never! So I send you my apostolic benediction and wishes for the happiness of you both. You ought to be happy because you deserve it. Only don't let the comfort of married life blunt the 'ragged edge' of the Ideal! Therein lies the danger!

With blessing also on the bride, I am yours always

WM. JAMES

Phillips Brooks called upon us, as was his wont, in the early autumn, and the next day this supremely graceful word came from him:

233 CLARENDON ST., BOSTON
Sept. 10, 1890

DEAR GORDON:

Perhaps you may care for this photograph of Maurice. Pray keep it.

It was good to see you in your own home with your own wife, and to feel that at least one bit of the world was all right.

Faithfully yours
PHILLIPS BROOKS

I shall speak of Phillips Brooks at length in another connection, but I must here remark that from the time of my settlement as minister of the Old South Church in April, 1884, till his death in 1893, our relations were to my joy increasingly intimate, and that the friendship between us was one of the loftiest experiences of my life. He was always crowned with success, and overflowing with heavenly sympathy and joy. One day I quoted to him, as expressive of my own feelings about life, Campbell's lines:

> 'The weary bird, blown o'er the deep,
> Would sooner quit the shore
> Than I would cross the gulf again
> That time has brought me o'er.'

To this Brooks called out, 'Gordon, I never felt that way five minutes in my life.' I protested that I had heard notes from the divine depths of sorrow in his sermons that told another story, which when uttered had given relief to a thousand overburdened souls. I continued that I thought, standing triumphant upon the heights, he had forgotten the severity of the ascent. He paused, reflected for a moment, and then replied, 'Yes, Gordon, we do forget, and it is a good thing that we do.' He was at all points, on all occasions, a sublimely incurable optimist. I often secretly thought in those years of my distress, although I never said so to him, being always careful of the utmost respect in behavior toward my great and good friend, 'Brooks, your life has been one long celestial joy-ride while mine has been through thick woods, and over rough hills with not even a footpath for a guide. The struggle onward and upward has been exhilarating, and now and then the outlooks rewarding and occasionally grand. Yet once over such a path is enough.' All this was changed by my marriage. Thirty-five years of unbroken, ever-increasing happiness has followed in this relation, and I should like to tell Phillips Brooks now that, since our wedding day, and what he did for us then, I should like to live it all over again.

There are two songs of Burns that seem to me the highest expression and consecration of true love. The first

song is the utterance of love at its beginning, the cry of
passionate joy and loyalty:

> 'O my luve's like a red, red rose,
>   That's newly sprung in June;
> My luve's like the melodie,
>   That's sweetly played in tune.
>
> 'As fair art thou, my bonnie lass,
>   So deep in luve am I;
> And I will luve thee still, my dear,
>   Till a' the seas gang dry.
>
> 'Till a' the seas gang dry, my dear,
>   And the rocks melt wi' the sun,
> I will luve thee still, my dear,
>   While the sands o' life shall run.'

This is the gorgeous sunrise of love in a true heart, it is
great and beautiful; but greater far, with its blending of
humor and infinite tenderness, is the glory of love at the
close of the day, as in this incomparable vesper hymn of
wedded lovers:

> 'John Anderson my jo, John,
>   We clamb the hill thegither,
> And monie a canty day, John,
>   We've had wi' ane anither:
> Now we maun totter down, John,
>   But hand in hand we'll go,
> And sleep thegither at the foot,
>   John Anderson my jo.'

There is no form of service nobler, none more self-
effacing than that of the minister's wife. None but the
minister knows of the constancy of her unrecorded and unrewarded kindnesses. Her allowance of money cannot be
large in any case, unless she is the exception, one with a
private fortune. This limited allowance goes not for fash-

ionable and gorgeous apparel, but for flowers to honored friends, to the sick at home or in hospitals; for tokens of remembrance when children are born in the parish, on festive and memorial occasions in the domestic circles inside the church, and sometimes outside. Then there is the incessant calling, the ministry of the affectionate note or letter, the quiet, dignified, sincere, and loving personal influence on Sunday. The ministries of such a life are like that of the snowflakes as they blend and disappear in the tide of the rushing stream. They bring to it a new purity and they add by their incessancy to its bounding life.

Then there is the defense of the minister's hours for study, the side-tracking of the axe-grinder and the bore, and the genius to know who should and who should not have access to the man often almost overwhelmed with approaches, reproaches, and appeals. The minister's wife is both cherubim and the flaming sword guarding the entrance to the Tree of Life, and even when her appearance is celestial beyond all peradventure, she must often sustain the blame and anger of the guilty ones whom she has turned away. This same person knows what foods produce health, what hours are necessary for sleep, and the whole character of the domestic economy that must lie behind the life of a student and preacher who is expected always to be ready for service, always to be clear in mind, vigorous in body, and abundant in nervous force. Such a wife is like the sunshine in the atmosphere, the source of vitality, motive, and joy. The people who praise her husband for the light, sympathy, comfort he brings them little know how vast is their debt to her. She lives like the Holy Spirit in the life of her home, in the life of her friends, in the life of her parish, an unseen but a divine influence. Unrecorded, unrewarded is her service, in one sense, in another and higher sense it is recorded and rewarded. It is visible in the dignity, peace, and sweetness of her face; it is known in a consciousness that has been filled with unearthly sympathies and loves, in an experience of faith and grace that is its own exceeding great reward. About the best thing on earth is a life so rich and good in itself that it can support itself in every kind of Christian service without human praise. Human praise comes at length, homage to beauty of soul, and such love as only the benedictive spirit may command.

Among our many guests I select for mention here a representative group. The Reverend Dr. Robert Horton, whose ministry of forty-five years and more in London has had in it every quality of a great ministry, was one of the earliest and one of the knightliest of our guests. He preached in the Old South Church with distinction in the morning, and with very unusual power in the evening. He was the sternest kind of a teetotaler, and innocently enough Mrs. Gordon had grapefruit for breakfast, properly qualified by sugar and sherry. Dr. Horton made no inquiries, offered no protest, but, as he was finishing the delicious fruit, then new to him, he turned to his hostess and asked: 'Mrs. Gordon, is this the natural flavor of the fruit?' We have often wished that we might again entertain this pure and exalted spirit, whose burning idealism and simplicity were so full of charm.

Dr. Watson (Ian Maclaren) and his wife were our guests on two occasions, in 1895, and again in 1907. Dr. Watson was an excellent and an abundant talker, and we were able to give him of the best to talk with; on his first visit President and Mrs. Eliot dined with us, and on his second Professor and Mrs. William James. These hours were rich in good things; it was pleasant to see as it is now pleasant to recall such eminent conversationalists in action. President Eliot matched Dr. Watson's popular tales with academic tales equally amusing and carrying in them more for the understanding, and Professor James was no whit behind Watson in the popular variety while contributing from his own brilliant mind both wit and humor. One of Watson's tales, known to every Scot, gave James infinite entertainment, I imagine because it made him sympathize anew with the self-defensive effort of a confused mind, and perhaps of his own Pragmatic Deity. A Scottish minister being questioned by a member of his Bible class, and called upon to show the justice of God, first, in foreordaining the course of the world, and all human actions, good and bad alike, and second, in making a distinction among the mere creatures of His will, and sending, as Burns says, 'Ane to heaven and ten to hell,' replied: 'You must understand that the Almighty in His public and judicial capacity is obliged to do many things that in a private and personal capacity He would be ashamed to do.'

Watson's first sermon in the Old South Church attracted a multitude so great that it would have filled the edifice at least five times. That sermon was sane and beautiful and gave universal satisfaction. Its subject was 'The Optimism of Jesus.' Zaccheus the publican was the New Testament example, and there were two of him — the Zaccheus that the world saw and the Zaccheus that

Jesus saw and brought forth into light and sovereignty. On the second visit Watson had lost somewhat in the level of his preaching. He had come to represent a British craze for novel character sermons. He had, so he informed me, a great sermon on the elder brother, in Jesus' parable, which contained a thoroughgoing exposure of the worthlessness of the lost or prodigal son. Amusing I am sure it would have been, entertaining in the highest degree, but utterly misleading, and a travesty upon perhaps the deepest and most sacred teaching of Jesus. I said to him: 'Dr. Watson, if you go into my pulpit and deliver a eulogy on the Pharisees of whom we have altogether too many in Boston now, and ignore the purpose of Jesus in uttering the parables of the lost sheep, the lost coin, and the lost son, which constituted his defense of his interest in poor sinful human beings, against the pride and inhumanity of the original Pharisees, I shall follow you next Sunday and skin you alive before the whole congregation.' Watson went to his room and returned in an hour saying his 'elder brother' sermon was really too good to preach to my people; they would be so carried away by it that they would not wish ever to hear me again, and in order that I might not lose my parish he had concluded to preach his sermon on Nicodemus. I replied that I approved his conclusion even if he had been led to it by bad reasoning. A vast audience heard Dr. Watson again, but the sermon itself was far below the Watson that I first knew. Witty, humorous, immensely entertaining, it was bad interpretation, vicious imagination, unacceptable in doctrine, being a stinging arraignment of the people and destitute of serious purpose. The popular lecturer had driven out the earnest minister of the Christian Gospel.

Watson's best books, 'The Bonnie Brier Bush' and 'Auld Lang Syne,' had little substance in them, and could not live any length of time, yet 'A Doctor of the Old School,' in the first volume, and 'Jamie Suter,' in the second, should not be allowed to perish. They were true to the heart of Scotland and instinct with beauty and moving power.

Dr. A. M. Fairbairn, famous as a scholar, theologian, and as principal for twenty-three years of Mansfield College, Oxford, spent eight days with us in the autumn of 1899. We were delighted with him, and especially delighted with him was our daughter of four years of age. She waited patiently outside his bedroom door every morning till he appeared, that she might be carried shoulder high to the dining-room. That autumn we had within one week something altogether unusual with us, a succession of maids, and this child introduced, on each occasion, this grave and learned Doctor to the new maid. His humor and humanity made the experience a delight to him. So happy had been the relations between this distinguished man and our little girl that when about to part he took her in his arms and asked her what she would like him to send to her from Oxford. Her answer was tremendous. 'Papa has sent us more gold pins than we want. Please send me a gold chain, with a gold locket set with diamonds and rubies.' The Doctor protested that it would take him years to earn enough money to pay for such a present. To this protest came the honest reply: 'That is the only present I want, and I will wait till you get enough money to pay for it.'

Dr. Fairbairn was much interested in a bit of child

sophistry which I reported to him. A father, being slightly annoyed by the too frequent use of the word 'love' by his daughter, a child under five years of age, told her that word must be reserved for great uses, for her mother and father especially. Somewhat angered by this rebuke the little girl asked: 'Do you love yourself?' The father answered that he did, and that it was proper to love one's self in a proper way. The child, flushed in face, flashed back these words: 'I do not love myself.' The father then inquired why it was, when he asked her to give him a piece of her cake, that she always gave him the smaller piece and kept the larger for herself. The reply was this: 'Papa, that is not because I love myself, it is because I love the cake.'

The following letter will be read with interest as giving a glimpse into the heart of a widely influential man.

R.M.S. MAJESTIC
Sept. 27, 1899

DEAR MRS. GORDON:

Here I am with my face homeward, but my thoughts turned backward to all the happy days spent in your home and the gracious hospitality which made them so delightful.

The visit to Wellesley was most interesting and enjoyable, and the journey to New York as pleasant as and no more restful than a night journey usually is. But I know nothing of fatigue to-day.

Tell Ruth I do not forget her. Her last kiss still lingers on my lips. The very memory of it is fragrant.

My love to my dear Brother Gordon; and when next he comes to Oxford he must come to us, and not come alone.

With best regards and thanks that cannot be written

Ever yours

A. M. FAIRBAIRN

Dr. George P. Fisher, of Yale, was our guest while Fairbairn was with us. He came to us in bad physical condition, having had little or no sleep on the boat from Bangor to Boston owing to the fog and the foghorn. He was to speak after luncheon before the International Council of Congregational Churches then in session in Boston, and seeing Dr. Fisher's condition I took him aside and said: 'We use no wine or spirits in this family, but we keep a little whiskey as medicine. Will you take a little now or with your luncheon?' He replied that he would take it now, and he did, a good solid dose. I got a carriage and took the Doctor to make his speech, and after it, I took him to his train for New Haven. On the way I said: 'Professor Fisher, I never heard you speak so well as you did to-day.' His answer was: 'I spoke by the power of the spirit.'

Professor Park, of Andover Theological Seminary, had looked upon me with disdain in my early years at the Old South, and thoroughly enjoyed the Reverend Joseph Cook's reference to me as 'that callow youth on the Back Bay.' After my marriage to the daughter of one of his favorite pupils, Dr. Jacob M. Manning, Professor Park adopted me with complete sincerity and unusual warmth into the fellowship of his friends. A memorable man he was, of great keenness of intellect, an accomplished mind in every sense, a mind in which the syllogistic movement had become, through discipline, second nature. Here is an instance. A lady of dignity and reserve whom Park greatly admired told him, in my presence, that she had just heard a marvelous address: after the speaker finished his discourse there was not a dry eye in the house. Park looked at her and said: 'You wept.' 'No,' protested this reserved woman, 'I did not.' 'You wept,' Park repeated, with assumed severity: 'there was not a dry eye in the

house, and you were in the house.' This remarkable
man had more knowledge of New England ministers and
churches than any other scholar I have ever met. Aside
from his prejudices, which were strong, and sometimes deplorable, he had the widest intellectual sympathies, the
keenest interest in the things of the mind, and the richest
store of anecdote that I have known. It is, indeed, a pity
that because of revolt from the theology he taught, this
brilliant intellect, with all its stores of anecdote, its wit and
humor, and its transcendent moral strength when dethrone-
ment came, when the king of influence saw that his day
of power was done, should be widely and utterly forgotten.
Nothing finer, nothing grander than this has passed under
my observation. I put my infant daughter in his lap one
day and remarked to the infant: 'You are in the lap of the
last New England theologian.' He met this with a victorious smile, turning to the infant of four months, and asking: 'Are you willing to subscribe to our Seminary Creed?
Would you use the phrase "for substance of doctrine?" Or
how would you take it?' The infant made no reply, which
being prophetically, or at least parentally, interpreted,
meant that she would not take the creed in any sense; a
mute witness of the new day that has spoken for itself in
words that may not be resisted.

Dr. T. T. Munger and his wife were frequent guests in
our home; they always brought with them a spirit and influence greatly valued by us, but as I intend in another
connection to speak of Dr. Munger, I shall let the sanctity
of his name and the radiance of his memory close this chapter on my domestic life.

CHAPTER XX
PRAISE AND BLAME

PRAISE and blame are the sources of two potent forms of pleasure and pain, and as they concern the minister's life as intimately and acutely as that of the members of any other profession, not excepting even the physician and the politician, it may not be without interest to consider them here as illustrated by some experiences of my own.

Praise and blame of the minister, as of other men, fall into three categories, the foolish, the unjust, the reasonable and intrinsically worthy. The foolish kind of praise comes first. Every minister, especially in his youth, has been told by some parishioner, usually a woman, that he was the greatest living preacher. Let that sort of praise be repeated often enough and, in the absence of the proper antitoxin, the poison would infect and damage the healthiest mind. The consequence is that young ministers are tempted to think of themselves more highly than they ought to think; they are apt to come to regard themselves, in the absence of chastisement, as the most important men in town. Excessive self-esteem gets into their way of walking, their manner of greeting other persons, their style of public address; this excessive self-esteem tends to harden into conceit, one of the deepest forms of self-delusion, and one of the most offensive. A conceited minister is indeed ridiculously funny, but he is more; he is a cruel contrast to the spirit of the Gospel, an afflictive instance of selfishness, a heinous example of littleness in one whose vocation is to measure all men and all things earthly by the greatness of eternity. Plato was right when he called flattery a dreadful beast, and foolish praise, when accepted as wise, surely works in the character of the minister as one of the deadliest of toxins. It is true that undue self-esteem, vanity it may be called, often exists side by side with many good qualities. The vain man will work hard, will achieve much good, will suffer that others may gain benefit, but always with his eyes on his wages, new and excessive supplies of praise for his vanity to feed upon. Take away the sure hope of praise, and he will fall as flat as a boy's kite when the wind goes down. The ageless cry of the man poisoned with foolish praise is the familiar one, 'Behold this great Babylon that I have built.'

There is, to be sure, an availing antitoxin for this disease, in the form of foolish blame. This comes usually, although not always, in the way of anonymous letters. 'What a liar you are, and what a lie you told in your sermon last evening; be a man next Sunday and tell the truth. From one who wishes you well.' Such was the communication which I received on a postcard, one Monday morning, many years ago. Relating this experience to my friend Dr. E. Winchester Donald, of Trinity Church, Boston, he read to me an anonymous note which he had received that same morning. 'Rev. E. Winchester Donald, D.D., rector of Trinity Church, and Preacher to Harvard University: You are a damned fool. A Friend.' These two notes will serve as examples of the continuous injection into the preacher's mind of the antitoxin of foolish blame to fight the poison of foolish praise. These persons are perhaps the cowardliest in character, the most venomous in motive, and the stupidest in intelligence of any class in the community, yet in result they often are real benefactors. They remind me of the visitor who came to see one who was a stranger to him, riding a donkey. This visitor dismounted at the gate of the garden, in which there was a wonderful grapevine, in the full blossom of early summer, and leaving the donkey outside, and the gate to the garden open, he went to make his call. He was kindly received by the stranger upon whom he called, stayed longer than was wise, and when visitor and visited came forth from the interview they found to their dismay that the donkey had eaten the grapevine clean of its blossoms. The owner bore the disaster as a gentleman should, parted courteously with his extraordinary guest, and returned to lament the complete loss, as he thought, of the fruit of the vine for that season. He was mistaken. Sunshine and rain brought forth new leafage and more abundant blossoms. The greatest harvest of grapes the owner gathered that year in the history of the vine. While bent upon the senseless satisfaction of its appetite, the donkey had proved the best vinedresser in the world. But as Dr. George W. Field, of Bangor, from whom I got the tale, remarked: 'No thanks were due the jackass for the benefaction.'

The second variety of praise and blame is of the sort that is unjust. Dr. Francis G. Peabody showed me a Charleston, South Carolina, daily paper, which contained one of his then recently published discourses, and, it may be added, one of rare worth and distinction, that had been preached by a Presbyterian minister of that city and printed as his own production. Doubtless this preacher received a world of praise for his mighty effort; how he felt on receiving it has not been recorded, but may be imagined. Literary thieves, lay as well as clerical, know where to go to get marketable goods. Many years ago — to be exact, it was in 1911 — Dr. Peabody, in publishing a volume entitled, 'Sunday Evenings in the College Chapel,' dedicated his book, in a poem of exquisite truth and beauty, to President Charles W. Eliot. The lines appeared in 'The Bar Harbor Weekly,' under another name; and this thief got not only a great volume of unearned praise, but a tidy sum of money for the supposed fruit of his genius. Stealing is a rare offense among ministers, either in the form of other men's thoughts or the contents of their purse. It is not an altogether unknown offense in its literary guise, and may fittingly represent, when skillfully done, one kind of unjust praise.

Unmerited praise, to an honest man, is one of the most painful experiences. To be praised for doing what one knows he has not done, for abilities or learning that he does not possess, for influence that he does not wield, is a keen and lasting distress. One of the best preachers I have ever known, to whom preaching was the noblest opportunity to do good to men's minds, invariably was overtaken with depression after his service, and words of praise for what he had said, and the way he had said it, seemed to him utterly unmerited, and became in those moods, the cruelest affliction. One Sunday after service this preacher was returning home when he met Dr. Alden, long a secretary of the American Board. 'What have you been doing, Brother Field,' said Dr. Alden, 'to make you look so miserable?' 'I am miserable,' replied Dr. G. W.

Field, 'because I tried to preach on God's love for mankind, and because I made such an utter failure in the treatment of this transcendent and glorious subject. What have you been doing, Brother Alden, to make you look so happy?' 'I have been preaching,' answered Dr. Alden, 'on the everlasting punishment of the wicked in hell, and I had a glorious time.'

Unmerited praise makes an honest man, layman or minister, extremely unhappy. An associate of mine, of fine intellectual quality, of true culture, strong and most lovable character, whose father was one of my good friends, had a tendency, which he later completely subdued, to shirk hard work. This I told his father, who replied, 'That boy always was lazy,' to which the mother who heard it answered, 'That boy has not a lazy bone in his body.' When I repeated this praise to my associate, he shouted: 'Good for my mother; I stand by her even when I know that she is lying.' When Herbert Spencer was in this country, a great dinner was given him in New York, at which many significant speeches were made, and the most significant and eloquent of all was by Henry Ward Beecher. Afterwards a pompous and enormously conceited physician ran up to Beecher with this exclamation, 'Beecher, you are the greatest man in the world,' to which Beecher replied, with biting sarcasm, 'My dear Doctor, you have, for the moment, forgotten yourself.'

The victorious general must often feel the injustice of the praise showered upon him. What would Hannibal have been without his Numidian cavalry, Cæsar without his Legions, Napoleon without his armies, Wellington without the men of many nations that fought under him,

Grant without the Army of the Potomac? The only view
which makes at all reasonable the applause that goes to
the triumphant commander is that which regards him as a
symbol of the army that fought under him; the men now
dead or disbanded get nothing; their commander, living or
dead, gets everything. This is in the highest degree unjust,
and it loses this character, as I have said, only when the
commander is regarded as the impersonation of his army.
Every successful preacher, in his narrower sphere, has the
same feeling. There are the men and women who give
character to his church, who make strangers welcome, who
render the fellowship in which they stand an object of
desire on the part of other substantial persons, who organize the activities of the fellowship to which they belong,
elevate its standards of thought, service, and giving, whose
high manner and spirit fill it with dignity and attractive
grace. What could the most eloquent and persuasive
preaching do without this great body of men and women?
Such a fellowship would be justified in saying to its minister, although it could not by any possibility be induced to
say it, 'Without me ye can do nothing.' Let any most
gifted man become the preacher, in a civilized community,
of a synagogue of Satan, and it will be clear that he must
first change the character of his church before self-respect-
ing and aspiring men and women will go near it. No one
can be more keenly aware than the successful preacher,
who is himself an honest man, that the praise which he
receives belongs as much to his people as it does to him.

On one occasion when the steamer on which I was to sail
from Liverpool to Boston was about to move down the
river, a gentleman rushed up to me on the deck, shook

my hand violently, and said: 'I can never forget that magnificent sermon you preached last Sunday, in Spurgeon's Tabernacle, on the Second Coming of Christ in the Flesh, and I must, before you sail away, thank you for it with all my heart.' There was no time to mention the man's mistake, to expostulate or explain; he was going, and in a moment he would be gone. I must be courteous, and I simply shouted after him: 'You are welcome; All good be with you.' I have often thought of this incident in receiving thanks for what other men had done, in being praised for what I could not have done, in being taken for what I was not, and never could have wished to be. Nothing remained but Cordelia's mood, under this shower of unmerited applause: 'Love and be silent.' I never preached in Spurgeon's Tabernacle, would not have been allowed to enter that pulpit; and if I had, I could not have preached on the Second Coming as other than the grandest of all spiritual processes, and if my unknown friend had heard me, he would have been bored if not disgusted with my doctrine. 'Love and be silent.' Hail and farewell to all who overpraise us or give to us the praise that others should receive, who applaud because they understand us to mean what we do not mean, or to be what we are not, and would very much deplore if we were.

When Charles W. Eliot was praised for achievements as President of Harvard University, by members of the Massachusetts Historical Society, he replied truly that he could have done nothing without the group of distinguished men, then teachers and scholars in Harvard University, who served under him. The group would have accomplished little or nothing without this great leader; still, it was as the incomparable leader of a group of great men in the college, and in the corporation, that he prevailed. It is always so. The individual, while a force in himself, must be enriched and reënforced by his human environment before his life can become availing. 'He could not do many mighty works there because of their unbelief' is the negative expression of the truth that I have been asserting, and in these words just quoted we see that it applies even to the highest. 'The could' and 'the could not' are in the keeping of the group, the whole with which one labors.

As to unjust blame, every minister has had his share of that. When I was a young minister I became profoundly interested in one of the vilest persons I have ever met. I invited him to come to see me in my home. I walked with him every day, I won him to the regular worship of the church of which I was minister, and it did seem, after six months of intense sympathy and friendly help, that I had succeeded in starting this man in a better way of living. One evening while I was preparing for service, he appeared at my home, forced his way in, insulted and terrified the servants. I was hastily summoned to face a man madly intoxicated, and who, with something like the hiss of a snake, charged that I was to blame for his condition. This was more than I could stand. I flung him round the room, then against the door, and finally out into the street, all the while saying things which corresponded fairly well with this series of actions. I believe that this was the best sermon that young man ever heard; it did me good to deliver it, and I hope it did him good to receive it.

The favorite charge against free-thinking ministers is that they have no sense of the superlative value of the

Bible, no love or honor for the person of Jesus, no real faith
of any kind; that they are in fact atheists. It is held that if
they would only speak their real thoughts they would pro-
nounce all religion in general, and the Christian religion in
particular, utterly unreal. Another charge, by other minds,
frequently takes a more cynical form. It is said that ministers are hired to air certain traditional beliefs; that if
they could get as good pay for denying as they do for
affirming the truth of these beliefs, they would sooner deny
than affirm. On this ground men are advised to pay no
attention to an address or a lecture or a book by a minister. He has contracted for a certain set of opinions, and he
must keep his contract or lose his job. All this is, of course,
rank injustice, the issue of ignorance and passion. No sin-
cerer body of men exists, such is my experience, than the
ministers of religion. They may be without adequate
learning, insight, general intellectual power, but they are,
for honesty and courage, unsurpassed by any other class
of men known to me. Their judgments are less influenced
by their environment and come more directly from the
heart than is the case with the vast majority of even good
men.

Sometimes the disrespect thus shown for the minister of
religion, in certain rough quarters, receives a stinging rebuke. A Bishop of Ripon, England, was showing several
ladies over his place among whom there happened to be also
a wealthy Englishman of the type I have been describing,
who lost no occasion for grossly profane speech during
the rather protracted interview. The Bishop heard this
broken torrent of profanity as if he had not heard it. At
length the man's better nature got hold of him, and, as

apology to the Bishop, and to the ladies of the party, he offered this: 'Your Lordship must know that I am a plain man, that I call a spade a spade'; to which the Bishop calmly replied: 'You do? I am surprised; from your manner this afternoon I should have inferred that you would call it a damned old shovel!'

Here I must relate what, after all, may have been a just judgment upon me. When I boarded my steamer in Liverpool for home in 1901, I found in my room the worst-looking human being that I ever set eyes on. He was an Austrian, with small weasel eyes, low receding forehead, head as if it had been shaved, small and ugly; in fact, experts told me that he looked the twin brother of Skeats the burglar, a gentleman unknown to me. I knew that I had to room with this man for nine days and nights, and I had considerable unspent money in my possession. I went to the purser and told him that I had a hundred dollars; that I felt that I should like to deposit it with him. He was very kind, took my money, and gave me a receipt for it. This did not altogether put my anxieties to rest. 'Do you know my room-mate, Mr. Purser?' I inquired. 'Indeed I do. Dr. Charmatz, of Carlsbad. He has just been here on a similar errand and with feelings similar to your own.' So much for appearance. This man I found to be in every way a gentleman. We became fast friends, and corresponded annually till his death. He was a consummate master at the piano, and, on the evening of the concert for the benefit of the families of lost seamen, outshone all others by his brilliance. He was a poor sailor, and I ministered to him in medicine and human comfort. He had been bitterly disappointed in love, and gaining confidence in me, told me the whole sad story. I could not much blame the lady, although I sincerely pitied him in the depth and bitterness of his sorrow. If I really am his double in appearance, I have to add that I was infinitely happier at the point where he tragically failed. Peace to his fine soul, now freed from a body fitted, not for the abode of the spirit of a nobleman, but for that of an assassin.

Sometimes one suffers from a kind of injustice of another sort. From him that hath not shall be taken away that which he hath or seemeth to have. I had the honor to be a member of the first Board of Preachers to Harvard University, appointed by the President and Fellows and the Board of Overseers, to conduct the new system of voluntary prayers. Our chief was Professor Francis G. Peabody, and his staff consisted of Edward Everett Hale, Phillips Brooks, Alexander McKenzie, and last of all, as one born out of due time, George A. Gordon. I was young, inexperienced, unknown; Hale and Brooks were men of national repute. We had hours, each minister, during his term of service, in which we gave interviews to inquiring students. The first term Brooks had a hundred callers, and so noted it in the 'Ministers' Book.' Hale had eighty, Peabody had sixty, a very large number considering the fact that he too was, in comparison with Brooks and Hale and McKenzie, a young man; McKenzie had thirty, and I had two. My two, in one respect, were of more interest and higher distinction than all the others, and this distinction I wrote into the 'Ministers' Book' thus: 'I have had during my term of service two, and only two callers; one inquired the way to the Bursar's Office, and the other the way to the Kingdom of Heaven.' This entry was for years the source

of much amusement among the preachers, and lifted itself
out into the public mind of the university. It served, in
this way, to cover my humiliation for the ghastly scarcity
of my callers. I was proud of my two men and the fame
they brought me. Judge, therefore, of my chagrin, in reading 'The Recollections' of Washington Gladden, when in
telling this story I found him ascribing it to Phillips
Brooks. 'To him that hath shall be given, and he shall
have in abundance, but from him that hath not shall be
taken away that which he seemeth to have.' Even under
this grand generalization, my bereavement of my one poor
distinction seemed to me a piece of cruel injustice. I have
found in Dr. Gladden's failure in memory a symbol of
much that passes for history. It is accepted as fact, not because it is true, but because no one living knows better.

By far the most significant forms of praise and blame
come to the minister, in the way of unconscious influence,
from the exalted character of many of the men and women
with whom he is in fellowship. Pericles was profoundly
wise when he concluded that if Athens were filled with
worthy images of the gods and heroes, and with temples of
beauty and splendor, the men and women who lived in the
presence of this universal display of high excellence would
be constantly exposed to an influence, a judgment, that
could not but refine and exalt the mind. Fill the environment of a young minister with great and beautiful characters, and he cannot but live, as it were, in the presence of a
perpetual Judgment Day, or, at least, a Judgment Day,
mediated all unconsciously, and lifting his thoughts to the
Grand Assize, not as to something terrible and overwhelming, but as to the supreme disclosure of the friendship of
God for the spirit in him.

Such praise and blame, such silent judgments of approval and disapproval I have found, unconsciously uttered, by the noble characters I have lived and worked with, in my missionary parish in Temple, Maine, in my parish in Greenwich, Connecticut, and in the Old South Church in Boston. In each, all that was best in me was called for; and when my available best was inadequate, as it frequently was, I was made to know it, in the kindest way, by the silent but piercing judgment of human excellence, and in hope of something better from me when life should become deeper and worthier. I can think of no form of education more potent than this or more significant as a light upon the office of human society at its highest, and the nature and wonder of the moral universe in which men live. There is in the Franconia Notch a sheet of water called Echo Lake. If one is a superb singer let him go there about sunset, and sing clearly and slowly:

> 'Nearer, my God to Thee,
> Nearer to Thee!
> E'en though it be a cross
> That raiseth me;
> Still all my song shall be,
> Nearer, my God, to Thee,
> Nearer to Thee!'

and listen as the great mountains return his voice magnified, and the song glorified, with this silent, implicit encouragement: 'You are in the right path; that is the song to sing; that is the way to sing it; go on and do still better.' Let another sing a ribald song, with a voice harsh and torn with discords, let him sing it into the great receptive heart of the mountains, and the ribald song will come back, and all the singer's discordant tones with it, and with this implicit judgment: 'You are on the wrong path; that is not the song to sing; that voice is unfit for song; go learn a better song; go and change your voice from discord to melody; begin a new career in lyric substance, in lyric manner, in lyric instrumentation.' This Echo Lake seems to me a symbol of the moral world and universe in which we live. We are singing the one song or the other every day into the Infinite Deep of space and time, and the heart of Human Society, singing the song of faith or the song of filth, singing with a voice melodious and grand or with a voice all discord, all harsh with cruelty and wrong, and back come to us every day, repeated in our own consciences, from the miraculous moral order in which we find ourselves, our song and our voice, and with them the judgment of approval or disapproval, not as a finality, but as part of the benignity of God, a revelation of the divine education of mankind: 'Go on with your lyric life; you are singing the right song; sing it better and lift your soul into higher power.' And on the other side: 'You are all wrong in lyric substance, in lyric instrument, in lyric purpose and spirit. Pause, learn to sing the song of faith, the song of a sacred humanity, the song of beauty and joy.'

Such is the highest form of praise and blame; such judgment is the hope of the world; it is an expression, perhaps the highest, of the friendship and benignity of God, the grace of the Lord Jesus Christ. Such is the Judgment Seat of Christ in whose presence we live our life. The austere kindness of it, its everlasting benignity, is in the fact that it is a revelation of our relation to reality, and always with the possibility and hope of a nobler and happier relation to reality.

We are conscious that we live in a hostile environment, but, truly seen, man's environment in its ultimate purpose and spirit is never hostile, is forever friendly. A great poet tells this tale of wonder in words of equal truth and beauty:

'Here eyes do regard you,
In Eternity's stillness;
Here is all fulness,
Ye brave, to reward you;
Work, and despair not.'

CHAPTER XXI
EDUCATION THROUGH FRIENDSHIP

FRIENDSHIP has, from earliest times, seemed to noble minds one of the sacred possessions of life. There are the ancient traditions of the friendship of Ruth and Naomi, David and Jonathan, Damon and Pythias. There is the essay of Aristotle, profound, subtle, far-reaching, in which friendship is seen to be indispensable to life, and the statement made, 'without friends no one would wish to live, even if he were in possession of every other good.' There is the eloquent discourse of Cicero upon 'Friendship,' in which many good things are said; for example, that 'friendship can only exist between the good'; that 'virtue is first, and friendship next' among our best possessions. There is Emerson's rarely beautiful essay on the same subject, in which truth and tenderness are put down as essential to friendship, magnanimity, rare natures, rare likeness and unlikeness, reverence and due silence; a truly faithful description of the friendship which existed between Emerson and Carlyle, one of the noblest in the entire century to which these extraordinary men belonged.

It may be an oversight on my part, but I have missed, in all these classic traditions and discussions about friendship, that which seems to me the chief thing in it, its educational power. From of old, friendship has been known as a superlative joy, a luxury for the minds that find themselves in profound accord, that are gifted with emotional responsiveness, each to each. This is, without question, one great and precious part of friendship, but in a world so apt to blind and discourage the seeker after high character, there would seem to be in friendship something worthier than the mere indulgence of happy emotion. Even if it be true that the happy emotion is inseparable from friendship, it must be said that it is still possible, and indeed necessary, for friends to disengage from this emotion the ideal that one holds in his intellect and character for the other. The great friend is first of all a standard to which we look, and by which we measure ourselves, a standard for character, service, aim, and passionate desire. The great friend is the great educator. This comes first; that he gives happiness, emotional volume, and glow is secondary. It is of this secondary value of the friend that Burns sings with such warmth of emotion:

> 'All hail, ye tender feelings dear!
> The smile of love, the friendly tear,
> The sympathetic glow!
> Long since this world's thorny ways
> Had numbered out my weary days,
> Had it not been for you!
> Fate still has blest me with a friend
> In every care and ill.'

This is as beautiful as it is true; but what Burns needed above all things else were friends whose character should hold for him the heavenly vision, whose life should draw him into the stream of their own great endeavor, whose influence over him should liberate the best forces in him, and guide him in the most difficult of all enterprises, the conduct of life.

My great friends have not been 'thrillers,' but standard-bearers; not primarily sources of happy emotion, but examples of what I should aim at and achieve, more of a just and benign judgment unconsciously but habitually rendered, than a satisfaction to feeling. In one line or another, they have been among the best of educators to me. Here I place my great teachers George H. Palmer, William James, William Watson Goodwin, all Harvard men, and others, too numerous to mention. I met in them always good will, but the good will always came through moral intelligence. I had their sympathy, but I had something better, their judgment upon the doings of my mind and spirit, unconsciously rendered perhaps, certainly after I left college, but forever there, and this was the highest service which these great friends did or could do for me. To allow a barren intellect or a bastard purpose to pass uncondemned is surely a poor sign of friendship. From the friends I have just named I received no such shabby treatment. 'Speaking the truth in love'; 'ye shall know the truth, and the truth shall make you free,' are the motto, idiom, and style of all that deserves the sacred name of friendship.

Charles W. Eliot, President Emeritus of Harvard University, I count the strongest and most influential friend I have ever had. At a dinner given him by the Philosophical Department, at which I had the good fortune to be present, William James said he owed to President Eliot the opportunities of his life. It was a graceful and a true confession. It is one that a thousand distinguished men might make, and many others, good and brave, of little or no distinction. President Eliot was able through a half-century of time to give to capable and aspiring men the chief opportunities of their life; and one can imagine the stores of happiness that came to Mr. Eliot in this way. The discernment, the good will, and the ability thus to dispose lives in noble opportunity were all of them united in him, and greater happiness, or a more useful service to the community, one can hardly imagine.

For many years President Eliot was a kind of perpetual Judgment Day to me. When, on June 15, 1878, at nine o'clock in the morning, I first met him, by appointment, this was the impression he made upon me. No one could have been kinder or more considerate; at the same time, something in his look and bearing said plainly, 'I am observing you; you must prove your worth.' All through college, whenever I happened to meet the President in the Yard, he would stop and speak kindly to me, but the keen observer and the just judge invariably communicated with me on those exhilarating occasions. They were a joy, but a sober joy. When I left college for Greenwich, I carried with me a sense of Mr. Eliot's special interest, but again in the form that good things, yet unaccomplished, were expected of me; accompanied with clear, cold hope, and sincere but not over-emotional good wishes.

I can say with William James that I owe the chief opportunity of my life to President Eliot. He it was that brought my name before the committee appointed by the Old South Church to find a new minister for that church, and his certificate as to my intellectual capacity exercised a decisive influence over the committee. When I met Mr. Eliot after coming to the Old South Church, he was extremely kind, and truly sympathetic with me in the hurricane of accusation and in the unhealthy publicity through which I had then passed; but once more the greatest value to me of Mr. Eliot's friendship was the relation of his mind and character to mine, in judgment. Nothing worthy of praise had yet been done, and therefore no praise was given. A splendid opportunity confronted me, and I had to measure myself against it. Time alone could show whether Mr. Eliot's hope in me was well founded or vain. Something in his bearing, a rare combination of sympathy and austerity, told me that I had to settle the question as to whether it should be hope well placed or mistaken, and this was the greatest service that even he could then or at any time afterward do for me. The story of forty years of growing intimacy is a long one, an epic of dignity and beauty in my career; it cannot all be told, the heart of it has been already told, a heart of light and fire. President Eliot lived and served in the light of the highest standards, and he could accept as friends only those who were willing, and in dead earnest, to do the same. Silently, invariably, unalterably his influence upon me has been that I must strive, in the best sense, to do my best, and thus to justify his great confidence in me, first as a young man, and then all through the strenuous years of my ministry in Boston. He knows well my admiration for his intellect, my affectionate reverence for his character, and my grateful appreciation of his influence, and I have, as a working hypothesis, a deepening assurance of his affectionate interest in me and my family. No emotional explosions have ever occurred between us, none are likely to occur; but that which is highest in man's relation to man has been ever-present, a judicial mind filled with grace and truth, something calmly objective, just and altogether lovely.

I insert here part of a carefully prepared estimate of

President Eliot as an educator, read before the Unitarian
Club of Boston, March 15, 1924, as a necessary comple-
ment to the sketch I have given of my personal relations
with this great man. In speaking of Mr. Eliot's services to
American education, I said:

I place first his conception of the university as the expression
and instrument of world mind, contemporary and historic. The
total intellectual achievement of mankind must be made acces-
sible in the university; the mind of the race at its best must be
brought to bear upon the mind of the student; all the great things
that have been thought and done by the most gifted peoples
must find representation and expression here. Nothing of art,
letters, science, wisdom, history, religion, of high distinction,
can be disregarded. The university is the organ of the mind of
the world, historic and contemporary, at once its sympathetic
and critical mediator. This conception of education through the
mind of the world at its best was brought into American academic life by President Eliot; it is, I think, his greatest achievement. It meant the beginning of the end of meagerness and pro-
vincialism in American education; it meant self-discipline in the
light and freedom of the best thought of the world; it meant
many other things of high value which I may not now mention.

President Eliot once said to me that he never had an original
idea, not one; to which I beg to reply that he never had an idea
that went forth from his mind without the stamp of his individuality upon it. Every idea that came to President Eliot from the
outside, in passing through his mind grew so astonishingly in
luminousness, vitality, availability, and fruitfulness that its orig-
inator, whoever he may have been, would have been unable to
recognize his own child. Originality is a word that should be
carefully and sparingly used. There is, indeed, little of absolute
originality among men. The great mind is always a mind in society, and our relations one to another are so intimate and subtle,
and form such a network of mutual influences, that no intellect,
however gifted, could or would wish to free itself from the group
or whole with which its activities are inset. Originality has, however, another meaning. Whoever gives an idea greater depth,
vitality, scope, availability, and effective power must stand forth

as an original mind and character. In this sense President Eliot stands in the history of American education, for strength and originality, without a peer.

I place in importance next to that mentioned President Eliot's conception of the glory of the teacher's vocation. He had the courage to announce early that the teacher must be a teacher. Great learning is worthy of deep respect, and should be encouraged; productive scholarship is still worthier of high regard, and should be fostered; the vocation of the teacher, one who can make the student aware of his power, who can draw forth that power, push it into fullness of activity, the teacher, enlightener, maker of mind and character, is worthiest, and should be held in highest esteem. This President Eliot did, against a body of opinion that would have dismayed a man less valiant and strong. It was a common criticism of Eliot's administration, in my younger days, that he killed off the really great scholars and put in their places mere intellectual striplings. Those same striplings, like Palmer and James and Royce, changed the character of Harvard College, changed the character of Harvard University, and made it, under its administrative leader, the academic center of America. In time these same striplings became great in learning and in productive scholarship, whose works gained the attention of the world. But ever and always the teacher was supreme, the man whose intellect and character went into the life of his students, and thence into the biological stream of the world, to work there as a saving grace to the end of time.

Next to this I put President Eliot's discovery that among a thousand or two thousand students there are diversities of gifts. It had long been observed that some men excel in languages, others in mathematics, others still in the physical sciences, and still others in the view of the whole, in the synoptical gift, which Plato said is one grand characteristic of the philosopher. This ancient observation never came to anything, nor was it analyzed into its final form. This President Eliot did. He saw that there were these diversities of gifts, that they were natural, that they should be conserved and subjected to the best training, chiefly because society had need for all of them. The elective system did not originate in the sense of the impossible breadth of modern knowledge; it originated as a device to favor the conservation to society of all the distinctive gifts in select and promising youth.

The impossible breadth of modern knowledge strongly commended the system, helped it to gain headway, made friends for it everywhere, but its origin was in the discovery that young men differ enormously in their natural aptitudes, and that these are all good, and when conserved and trained, vastly enrich society with able and useful servants.

One more achievement of moment I must mention, and that is President Eliot's contention that it is the privilege of the university to look beyond its order, and to endeavor to discover promising intellect under academic misfortune. He was as strong as any one could be for the maintenance of just rules, and orderly procedure; at the same time he was ready to modify or amend, or cancel all rules that while they tend to keep the unfit in college conspire to keep the fit out. Here surely is a glory of his administration that shall not fade, that he, the man of privilege, should have felt and advocated the sacred obligation on the part of the University to be a discoverer of mind, to think less of rules than of promising youth, to adopt in education the principle of the greatest of all educators:

'The Sabbath was made for man, not man for the Sabbath.'

I speak not as a novice. It will be seven and forty years in June next since I first saw President Eliot. Adequate general recognition of his genius and services came to him late. There was a battle to be fought, a victory to be won before that could be, and for many years a strong body of sincere but unenlightened opinion obstructed his path. Before he could win he had to face depreciation and disparagement. Merely a good business head was the characterization that I first heard of President Eliot; this was followed by the reserved admission that he had some high moral qualities; much later he came to be recognized as an intellect remarkable for depth, penetration, critical and constructive force, and because of early discipline in scientific method, working with rare precision and extraordinary prevision; finally, the whole community discovered that he had a soul, that he was a profoundly religious nature, a truly great representative human being.

One of the best and greatest of my friends was Phillips Brooks. During the stress of college days I found two preachers who spoke to me as no others did, Dr. A. P. Peabody, of Harvard, and Phillips Brooks. Dr. Peabody was a wise and good old man, of great beauty of character, of the utmost sincerity, in whose sermons I found light and delight. I felt exactly as one of my classmates did when he said: 'It is easy for me to believe, when Dr. Peabody reads the Ten Commandments, that God wrote them with his own hand on the tables of stone.' This classmate was a Unitarian, and I was a Trinitarian, but we both responded at once to the wisdom of this man of God, and to the appeal of his strangely awkward but fascinating personality. He went about in the College Yard, and among the students, the unconscious embodiment of divinity. The college tradition was that no student, however wicked, was ever found who did not respect and trust Dr. Peabody. He was altogether the most revered and loved member of the Harvard faculty in my time.

The stories told of him were numerous enough; how he would go to the post-office for letters, and would be unable to tell his name to the clerk. Once at Communion Service in Appleton Chapel — which I never missed, it was always a service on the heights — Dr. Peabody became so engrossed in the prayer before the distribution of the Cup (an exercise which was always a kind of rapt meditation), that when he closed his prayer he did not know where he was or what to do next. He looked upon the congregation with the strangest expression in his eyes, of trouble and inquiry, then, making no progress toward clearness, he gave out a hymn. Professor Bowen went to his assistance, located the revered Doctor in his service, after which we made port without further mishap. I thought this a strange and in-

deed an almost incredible thing to happen to a sensible
man till some years ago I narrowly escaped doing very
much the same sort of thing.

Dr. James DeNormandie, who succeeded Dr. Peabody
as minister of the Unitarian Church of Portsmouth, New
Hampshire, has told somewhere a Peabody anecdote of a
different sort. He was walking, in his usual extremely awkward manner, with Mrs. Peabody on his arm. The Portsmouth street was very slippery; down went Dr. Peabody
pulling down with him Mrs. Peabody, and rolling over her
into the gutter. When he was able to rise, and after he had
assisted Mrs. Peabody to her feet, he said to her: 'My dear,
let us be thankful that all this happened over against So-
and-So's house. She is so big a liar that if she should say
she saw it, nobody will believe her.' His temper was hot,
swift to rise, swift to fall; he was full of wisdom, piety, and
goodness; he was one of the happiest of men, first, because
he was one of the healthiest, and second, because his delight was in the truth and beauty of the world, and in the
prosperity of human beings. I rejoice in the memory of
this wise and good friend, in whose radiant sincerity I had
so deep a trust.

Judged by any standard Phillips Brooks was one of the
very greatest of American preachers. I did not meet him
till 1884, the year that I began my work in the Old South
Church. From 1878 I had been one of his most enthusiastic
admirers. I went to Trinity Church from Cambridge, with
unbroken regularity for two years, and I had a seat in a
pew in one of the galleries. There I listened Sunday after
Sunday to sermons of torrential eloquence, outpourings of
the preacher's mind and heart, as he was seeking for him-

self surer standing in the truth of God, and stronger purpose to serve his Kingdom. For imaginative sweep, for
volume and refinement of emotion, for rapidity, pathos,
sympathy, and grandeur of utterance, I had never before
heard such preaching, and I have never heard its equal, in
the qualities named, from any preacher since. Phillips
Brooks was then in his physical and mental prime, and
there was a hurricane quality in his speech that I have
known in the speech of no other human being. His eloquence was as unconscious, as multitudinous, as tremendous, as the play of the ocean upon the shore after a northeast gale. There were the moments of lull, followed by the
thundering return of tides and waves, and this seemed to
be going on over wide and wild expanses, as far as the eye
could see. Two of his sermons of that time, both delivered
without notes, one on John the Baptist, the other on Meeting Angels on the Way, were the best that I ever heard
from him or any other preacher. Usually, Brooks's extempore sermons were intellectually unsatisfactory. He made
to me this profound criticism upon himself, when speaking
without notes: 'When I am interesting I am vague; when
I am definite I am dull.' His written sermons, which he
delivered with great freedom, were as a usual thing far
above the level of those preached without notes. But there
were exceptions, and the two I have named were, for ideas,
energy, and beauty of expression, and for vast tumultuous
power, beyond any others to which I have ever listened.

Brooks's voice was not naturally great. It was hollow, a
kind of weird whisper, which rose to piercing power only
under the expanding force of emotion. He was the best
example I have ever known of the influence of character

upon the natural qualities of the human voice. This naturally rather ordinary voice became quick with the visions and sympathies of a great soul; it took on the character of the man to whom it belonged; it became a swift and beautiful instrument in its master's service; when deepened to its utmost one could feel the vibration in it of the world's pathos and tragic hope, and when raised to its highest it became an irresistible appeal to the hero that slumbers in the nature of every human being.

Brooks was an inspirational preacher, the greatest of all American preachers here. He did not teach; he was in too great haste to deal with ideas as such; the worth of an idea for human character was the object of his search, and when he found an idea that meant moral light, new range of motive, consolation, and hope, he rushed his idea at once into the service of life. For systems of theology he had little regard; for the organization of ideas into an order under which men might live at peace with their own minds, and through which they might consider the being of all things, he had slight esteem. When I mentioned to him the intellectual grandeur of Jonathan Edwards, his reply was: 'Oh, yes: a brooding kind of a creature, nothing more.' Brooks was supremely great in one thing, in finding and in uttering the human value of the ideas of Christian faith. Wide reading in history, a knowledge of all the really great books in the literature of the world, a sympathetic attitude toward all the arts except music, a man of subtle insight and of imaginative sweep, and one of the purest and loftiest souls that ever lived, made the preaching of Phillips Brooks what it was, a witness for God, the invisible world, and the true humanity of man as beheld in the Divine humanity of Jesus, of surpassing loveliness and power.

For nine happy years we were friends. For fifteen years I was open to his influence, and I should like to note here the nature and the limits of this influence. For moral tonic, for inspiration in the early evolution of Christian character, for the vision of what the Christian preacher should be and what he might hope to achieve, it would be difficult, if not impossible, for me to overestimate my obligations to Phillips Brooks. To this should be added the charm of his companionship, the lofty grace of the friendship with which he more and more honored me. That he ever contributed to my intellect any idea that I had not previously received from other sources is simply not true. I was in quest, from early manhood, for an order of ideas, a house of faith to replace the Calvinism in which I had been brought up, and which had gone to wreck. In my search for suitable ideal material, in the plan of that new house of faith, Phillips Brooks gave me no help, he contributed nothing. I am therefore in no sense his disciple; I am far more truly a disciple of F. D. Maurice with whom I lived, through the forty volumes of his works, for more than twenty years. Nearer the truth still is the statement that the men who did most for my mind were my college teachers, G. H. Palmer, William James, W. W. Goodwin, and others, who by different paths led me to first-hand acquaintance with the great original minds in European history, with whose help and opposition I came at length to find myself, and frame for myself my own account of the amazing world in which I was living. What John S. Mills said of his intellectual relation to Carlyle is true of my relation to Phillips Brooks. His influence upon me, which for many years was very great, 'was not as philosophy to instruct, but as poetry to animate.' My debt to this great friend was a debt of character and not of intellect.

The way in which our friendship began is interesting. Having heard this great preacher for two years and more, I read in 'The Golden Rule' what I considered a mean review of 'The Candle of the Lord and Other Sermons,' in which the reviewer absurdly charged Brooks with the repetition in this volume of what he had said in a previous volume, and added the grave charge of literary theft from the famous Scottish preacher Dr. Chalmers of the idea contained in his discourse, 'The Expulsive Power of a New Affection.' To this review I replied at length in the same paper, finding it easy to refute the charge of unreasonable repetition, and wholly easy to dispose of the charge of plagiarism. The article closed with a sincere and warm tribute of personal admiration for this kingly man. I have not seen the article since it was published, and I hope it is not offensive in its expressions of grateful appreciation and profound respect. At any rate, it brought me the following note from Brooks, wholly beautiful as it seemed to me then, and as it seems to me now, marking the beginning of what was later to become a friendship of deep and exalted happiness.

233 CLARENDON STREET, BOSTON
Nov. 17, 1881

DEAR MR. GORDON:

I thank you truly for the kind words of your note and also for the cordial expressions of your article. I wish that I deserved them better, but I know you will believe that I am devoutly glad of your assurance that some of the things which I have said have sometimes helped some of my brother-Christians. In such gladness as that there is plenty of humility.

May I send you my most earnest Godspeed for your work.

I hope that we may meet some day, when you are in Boston. I should count it a great favor if you would come and see me.

Meanwhile pray allow me to count myself

Your friend

PHILLIPS BROOKS

REV. GEORGE A. GORDON

Here comes a response to a note from me sent to welcome Brooks back to Boston.

July 2, 1886

DEAR MR. GORDON:

I thank you with all my heart for your kind note of welcome. It is good indeed to know that you care where I am. I shall work the better and more happily for your good friendly words.

Ever affectionately yours

PHILLIPS BROOKS

What I then considered Brooks's best book, that on 'Tolerance,' impressed me so much by its insight into a tangled subject, by the noble breadth of its discussion and spirit, that I ventured to write to him in terms, I doubt not, of warmest, if not wisest praise. Here is his reply:

April 29, 1887

DEAR GORDON:

Oh, if my little Book were only half or quarter of what your kind note says. But for the moment I believe that it has some good in it, and am happy!

Thank you a thousand times for your kind note. It was so good in you first to think it and then to say it.

Ever faithfully yours

PHILLIPS BROOKS

The older part of the community will recall Mrs. Ward's novel 'Robert Elsmere,' and the wide ferment which it occasioned among religious people in this country. I sent to Brooks a copy of my address, which the Old South Society had printed, and here is his response:

December 20, 1888

MY DEAR GORDON:

These be good words which you have said about Robert Elsmere, and I, for one, thank you for saying them. It is good that the All Sufficiency of the book should be exposed and pricked. Then let it stand for what it is worth. There are better and worse books on every hand but since this one happens to have caught the public ear, let us not go about scared as if the heavens had fallen.

Thank you especially for what you say about Christianity being greater and deeper than the Miracles.

With best Christmas wishes
Ever sincerely yours
PHILLIPS BROOKS

The following note will be read with pleasure:

January 13, 1890

MY DEAR GORDON:

I enjoyed my visit to the Old South very much and I am sure that the Congregation at Appleton Chapel had a good time. So that at least one minister and one people were happy, which is perhaps as much as can be expected of two services.

Now the next thing is Lyman Abbott's consecration whither I shall go under your kind care on Thursday morning. My brother's house where you have promised to call for me is at 209 Madison Avenue.

I thank you for letting me come last night.

The check shall go into next Sunday's Foreign Missionary Collection at Trinity and so the little Episcopal heathen thank you.

Always faithfully yours
PHILLIPS BROOKS

This note will be welcome as a sign of the writer's exalted and wonderful sympathy with the joyous side of life:

Tuesday morning, June 3, 1890

DEAR GORDON:

Hail to your marriage morning! I greet you, as the sun does, with my beamingest smile.

I knew there was something which we did not speak of yesterday, but I could not think what it was. It was the license! Of course you have got it, but if you hadn't, how horrible! Will you send it to me now or give it to me at noon?

God bless the Day!

Your friend

PHILLIPS BROOKS

My congratulations went at once to Brooks upon his election to the office of Bishop of his Church in Massachusetts. I knew it meant that we should see less of each other, but I rejoiced for the whole diocese, and at the same time, for the religious life of the Commonwealth. His answer to my note was this:

May 4, 1891

MY DEAR GORDON:

I welcome a greeting from my brother across Copley Square. I cannot tell whether it is a welcome or unwelcome thing that has come to me; at least, there is this that is unwelcome about it, that I shall not be at Trinity Church, and so shall not be geographically as near to you. But I am sure that nothing can separate my cordial affection from one whom I so sincerely love.

May we have the joy of working together for many long, happy years.

Yours most affectionately

PHILLIPS BROOKS

The brief note which follows is a sample of the playfulness and humor so characteristic of Brooks. The Reverend Mr. Temple, then chairman of the Congregational Ministers' Meeting, wanted very much indeed an address from Phillips Brooks, upon the troubled theological mind of the times, and particularly of the community of Boston. Almost certain as I was that Brooks would decline the invitation, at the urgent request of the Reverend Mr. Temple I gave him a note of introduction to Dr. Brooks, in which I ven-

tured to express my belief that such an address from him
would do much to clear the air, and establish better relations among all types of thinking ministers. Temple was
politely received, gently but swiftly dismissed, and the
note below dispatched to me:

Sept. 26, 1890

MY DEAR GORDON:

You are very good to send me this pleasant note seconding
Temple's Folly. I cannot do the awful thing he wants, but I
thank you as much, perhaps all the more, for thinking that I can.

Affectionately yours

P. B.

Before the convention at which a bishop of the Episcopal Diocese of Massachusetts was to be chosen, and when
it had become known that Phillips Brooks was to be a candidate, much was made by way of objection to him because
of the fact that he had shared in a Good Friday Service in
the Old South Church, with its minister, and with a Unitarian minister and a Baptist. At the request of my friend
Dr. Leighton Parks, I wrote to the 'Churchman,' stating
that the responsibility for the service, and those invited to
share in it, was mine, and mine alone. Dr. Brooks was
simply one of our guests on that occasion, and his responsibility began and ended with his own words. When next
I saw him, we had considerable amusement over the fact
that I had been electioneering for him. I challenged his
charges, and said that I had written the truth and nothing
but the truth. This he at once agreed to, but he added that
I had not told the whole truth. 'You asked me,' he continued, 'if you should invite a Unitarian, and I answered,
by all means, and that Unitarian should be Brooke Her-
ford.' 'That,' I replied, 'was my business, and no Episco-

palian, living or dead, had anything to do with it.' The
union Good Friday meeting, established at the suggestion
of Brooks in 1889, continued for eleven years; then it became a permanent service in the Old South calendar, a
service with which his revered name must ever be associated. The mixture of absolute reverence and humor in
Brooks was unique. We met in the robing room of the Old
South Church, he and Parks, and others. I always appeared with the Prayer Book, and I always used it, out of
respect for our Episcopalian friends who came from Trinity
and Emmanuel Churches, to worship with us, and Brooks
poured forth an extempore prayer, at the close of the service. I suppose I looked serious, and somewhat awkward,
in my handling of the Prayer Book, in anticipation of the
service, which gave rise to a humorous remark of Brooks
on one occasion just as we were about to enter the pulpit,
and which nearly upset me: 'Look at Gordon and his anxiety. That Prayer Book will kill him yet.' It did not kill
Gordon, but the remark of his friend Brooks nearly destroyed his gravity for that sacred hour. The letter which
follows, the last to be given here, will show the depth of his
interest, even when overburdened with his labors and cares
as Bishop, in the service which was established at his suggestion.

January 12, 1892

DEAR GORDON:

I thank you with all my heart; and I will certainly come on the
evening of Good Friday; if I can change an appointment which
I thoughtlessly made for that evening.

I have no doubt that I can arrange it. I will try at once to do
so and will let you hear as soon as I know the result.

It will be good indeed to look forward to the rich and happy
service.   Your sincere friend

PHILLIPS BROOKS

I have never lived so intensely in any man's life as I did in the great friendly soul of Phillips Brooks. I knew him as I have known few other men, and the more intimately and deeply I came to know him, the finer, the more just, the more stainless he seemed to me to be. He had but one infirmity, so far as I could discover, and that was impatience, especially with foolish religious people. Even then, lion-like though he was, he could not be more than abrupt, or threatening, and this would issue in benediction before the fool got far away. A whole world of exalted and happy memories remain with me about this illustrious human being. I spoke my estimate of him, 'Phillips Brooks as The Messenger of God,' from the text, 'Let me go for the day breaketh,' the Sunday following his death. This sermon was published, and the proceeds from the sale, which was large, went to the Monument Fund, and the fund for the erection of the Phillips Brooks House at Harvard College. Only once have I printed anything about him since that time. With a few rare exceptions I found so much emotion and so little real insight in what was written and printed about Brooks that I have chosen to be silent. Even here that silence is scarcely broken when so much waits and pleads for utterance. Thirty-two years and more have passed since that solemn Monday morning when Boston awoke to the reality that 'the beauty of Israel was slain upon her high places.' His majestic presence passed; his still more majestic spirit abides, and I have been all through these silent years 'disturbed with the joy of elevated thoughts' because of the continued reality of his soul.

I find in my journal, September 2, 1919, the following

entry, and with that I shall close this brief interlude upon
one of the dearest of friends and best of men: 'Just before
I awoke for the day I had a delightful dream about Phillips
Brooks. He was calling upon us, as was his custom. He
looked like himself only he had become very old, but it was
old age crowned with radiance; with exquisite kindness and
moving grace he said, "Gordon, it is a long time since we
have had a good talk together." "Yes," I replied, "both of
us are busy, each absorbed in his own bit of work. There
is no change of feeling between us, only there has been
these many years, no opportunity." He added: "There is
a chair awaiting you in my study; do come and let us have
a long, long talk together." Then I awoke, and behold it
was a dream, a dream whose glow shall not fade; it is in
memory a perpetual daybreak.'

Phillips Brooks was many things. He was a large and
beautiful mind, a man of cultivated and rich intelligence,
a majestic presence, a consummate gentleman. But these
qualities do not account for him. All these are incidental
if the real thing is not added, that he saw the divine world,
that he dwelt there, that he loved it and drew his wisdom
and fire from it, that he came forth from it to declare with
inexpressible joy and pathos its openness to all souls, that
he went back after each message, each service, to that divine world as his home. There, in my judgment, is the secret of Phillips Brooks, the source of his spirituality, fascination, endless interest for men, the wonder and the beauty
of his character, the fountain of the grace that made his
presence a hallowing influence in Boston, and wherever he
went.

Another great friend who must be named was Dr. Theo-

dore T. Munger, of New Haven. Dr. Munger had been
known, in a quiet way, for many years, as one of the finest
minds in the Congregational Fellowship, but not till the
year 1882, when he published his 'Freedom of Faith,' did
he become a recognized religious leader over the whole
breadth of the country. That position he maintained till
his death in January, 1910. He had been for a generation
of years a wide and wise student of the thoughts of serious
men, and he had grown into full possession of what was his
distinctive and rare gift, a seer in the sphere of the spirit,
before publicity came. When it came he was ready to meet
it, and abundantly able to sustain it. The last third of his
life was the happiest because it was life at its climax and
without any anticlimax. His influence as a writer was
wide, and of the most quickening sort. He was an orderly
thinker, but not a systematic one; bred in the school of
Bushnell whose ablest disciple and critic he was, he cared
little for logical processes; for him vision was the greatest
quality in the thinker, and this quality was met by the self-
attesting nature of moral and spiritual truth. I have called
Munger a disciple of Bushnell; this is hardly fair. Munger
was an original and independent mind, and he was in certain respects superior to Bushnell; in the freedom of his
mind from the New England divinity this was altogether
evident, in the breadth and consistency of his outlook
upon the world, in his sense of the imperfection of all our
theories about things divine and human, and in his large
expectation for theology and faith from the union of science and religious faith. Munger's mind was one of incessant ferment; his motto might well have been, 'When that
which is perfect is come, that which is in part shall be done

away.' Everything done hitherto was for him provisional; the future was infinitely alluring, and the hopes of science of every kind lay there. Munger loved Bushnell, understood him better than most men, saw clearly what was incidental and passing in his writings, brought into the bright light of day his method of spiritual experimentation and adventure, the new path on which he was moving, the new spirit that possessed him, and he admired with all fullness of heart Bushnell's courage, his character, and his genius. Munger's book on Bushnell is one of the best of its kind; in it he pays the great man the noblest homage, that of critical appreciation.

For two and twenty years Munger and I were among the closest of friends. We wrote each other often and at great length on the theological questions of the day. We differed in type; we differed in opinion a good deal; neither in any case changed or modified a belief or conviction of the other; yet the constant attrition of mind with mind put edge upon both, and our debates brought into clearness the wide expanses of thought which we held in common, and the peculiar possessions which each had won by his own toil, and which neither would surrender to the other.

Munger was a good deal of a pantheist, I not at all. He was continually emphasizing the law of identity which runs through all things, and I, while recognizing identity as one great aspect of life and the universe, was forever emphasizing difference. One afternoon on our return from those great rocks east of New Haven, Mrs. Munger being with us, full of charm as she always was, Munger started off on his identity business, declaring difference to be nothing. I saw my opportunity. There, a little way in front of us, was a homely and shabby woman with a filthy red shawl round her, the image of all that one misses in a splendid woman, and my remark was, 'Munger, if difference is utterly unreal, and identity is everything, you take that old woman with the red shawl and I will see Mrs. Munger home. I see real difference here, and I infinitely prefer this expression of it.' This brought forth a burst of laughter, and so the debate ended, with this consequence, that Munger never said 'identity' to me again.

Munger's home was my home for all those happy years on my annual visits to New Haven. A more hospitable home there never was. The faculty of the theological school would call, in the evenings, in a body, with members of the philosophical faculty added, and at times members of the classical department, especially Professor Seymour, the Greek scholar. Munger was the recognized friend of all these men, and they came to greet me, primarily, as his guest. Professor Fisher would open the fullness of his historical stores, and point them with delicious tales of New England divines. Critical questions would be started by B. W. Bacon, F. C. Porter, and Williston Walker; ultimate considerations of philosophy and theology by Ladd and Stevens. Then we would get down to business as to the obligations of the intellect to the Christian faith of the day and hour. Here Munger and I would have our turn. These meetings, for freedom of mind, for fullness of heart, for richness of reminiscence, for intellectual play, for friendly and happy fellowship, are without parallel in my experience. Dull such conversations might seem to be; strangely enough, they were not so. The young people of the Munger household and other friends remained with us, and saw the play end and the curtain fall, often as late as eleven o'clock, or later, with evident delight at the comic features of the drama, and without perception of the tragic aspects of the show, — motion and no progress.

That such books as those of Dr. Munger should pass out of the religious mind, simply because they were written a generation ago, is indeed a tragic thing. His books, 'Lamps and Paths' and 'On the Threshold,' have no equals in the religious literature of to-day for the class of persons to whom they are addressed, and his greater books, 'The Freedom of Faith' and 'The Appeal to Life,' carry a message to young men in preparation for the ministry, and to thoughtful laymen, which they should be slow to miss. The substance is great and the style is high and fine. It would seem as if the science of theology were to-day in danger of becoming like a quarry hole, with heaps of dirt and plenty of water to match, where neither granite nor marble is found or much expected, where the digging goes on merrily one knows not why, except that it is the fashion of the scholarship of the world. There is the Book of the Acts of the Apostles, a simple account of the beginnings of Christianity, by a sincere and good man, who loved the religion of Jesus and His disciples, and looked at the whole movement in the light of his time, told his story and recorded his judgments as they honestly rose before him. Was the Book written in Aramaic? Is it a translation as we have it? Was it published by its author, or is it a posthumous work? All these questions are interesting to the technician, and some grain of certainty in the answer to be given to them may be arrived at A.D. 6000. Assemble a hundred scholars of equal learning and judgment; let them tell us what their opinions are about the Acts of the Apostles, and we shall find Babel in their decisions. Some questions are unanswerable; how long will it take learned men to discover this fact? They are unanswerable and incidental. If they were answered to the satisfaction of every scholar, they would not have the weight of an autumn leaf upon the genius, ideals, and powers of the Christian religion. Some questions are unanswerable in philosophy, but the endeavor to answer them is essential to the continued life and activity of the human mind. No such dignity can be claimed for the critical and historical studies that to-day almost monopolize the sacred science of theology. I am sorry that I shall not live to see a revolution which I firmly believe will come, a revolution in which the records of religion shall have their sovereign value as the symbols of great religious experience. Much may be said in defense of the technician's point of view, from the fact that the religious records of Judaism and Christianity have been subjected for centuries to unhistorical treatment, and considerable good has surely come in rolling back the cloud of unpurified tradition. Let the surgeon do his work, but let him not forget that he is operating on a living patient, and that he is working for life and not for death. Much more needs to be said upon this subject, but the times are not ripe. The scholar, critical and historical, is joined to his idols; let him alone. He has a speculative intellect, and a human heart, too, although he is an expert at concealing both.

Among many valuable letters from Dr. Munger in my possession I select two, the first as showing the growth of our friendship through debate, the second as showing how full of stimulating praise he could be to a writer twenty-three years his junior. A terrible debate and its reactions explain the first letter:

NEW HAVEN, 202 PROSPECT ST.
Jan. 17, 1899

MY DEAR FRIEND:

Mrs. Munger and I have been in a remorseful state of mind ever since you left. You came to us fresh and strong, and you left us weary and probably as pessimistic as you are capable of being. We take the blame to ourselves.

First; we gave you lemonade to drink; that was Mrs. Munger's mistake; and second I let Blank in on you; that was my fault; worse than that, it was my crime; I was a treacherous host and went over to the side of your enemy and added my stabs to his. But what else could be expected of one pantheistically inclined as I am? You are aware — if not, almost any orthodox work on Theism will inform you — that a pantheist is incapable of morality, has no sense of right or wrong, truth or honor, and hence is as liable to do one thing as another. This explains why I turned traitor to my guest and sided with a man it would be impossible to side with except on pantheistic principles.

And then Monday morning; — how we abused you — shut you up in that den, forced you to listen three hours and then having squeezed the life out of you, sent you home. I repeat — we are full of remorse.

But there are redeeming features: you did us lots of good; you brought Boston to us where we hope to go when we die; and you gave me a crumb of comfort over Bushnell which I shall feed on discreetly.

But I am writing chiefly to tell you why Fisher did not call and what he said. I met him in the car yesterday P.M. He planned to come to the house, but he went to see Dr. Harwood after dinner — Harwood is a great invalid — and he stayed too late. But he spoke of your sermon in unqualified terms of admiration; and he gave me the whole line of thought. It is the first time this year he has spoken in this way. It confirmed my fear that you will become a popular preacher. Cannot you arrest the tendency? Think how miserable you will be when the people always expect you to be interesting; and if you are not, will rend you in pieces. Do as I do; preach in an ordinary way, and be happy between Sundays.

We are eager to receive your promised letter and so learn how you came out of your three days of New Haven life. Don't tell us that you have la grippe; or that you will never visit us again. Next time everything shall be as it ought to be — no lemonade, no Blank, no manuscript criticism, but only the best possible of everything.

With all messages of love and remembrance to Mrs. Gordon and yourself from us all.

Affectionately yours

T. T. MUNGER

In this second letter the immemorial but delightful belligerency between Yale, of which Munger was a graduate, and a preëminent one, and Harvard, my Alma Mater, comes out in strong light. Munger was in error when he supposed the freest possible criticism, so long as it was responsible and expressed in the language of a gentleman, had any tendency in Boston to shorten one's day or render one unacceptable. Altogether the reverse is true, as I here proudly and gratefully acknowledge:

NEW HAVEN, 202 PROSPECT ST.

May 1, 1903

MY DEAR FRIEND:

I have just finished reading your paper on Emerson — at one sitting. The page is black with under and side scoring. I am rather too much under the spell of it to write calmly, but at the present moment I am under the impression that it is the best thing you have ever done; also that it is one of the best pieces of criticism I have ever seen — keen, brilliant, weighty and profoundly true; also that it is most timely and even providential. There will be, this month, a flood of appreciation of Emerson that will make us forget Plato and Jesus and Franklin and Geo. Washington, and most of the other great men who have ever lived, and require us to ascribe everything uttered or invented or done on the continent the last half century to Emerson.

Your tremendous paper will change a good many sentences in these tributes before they are made. Yours is the first thorough, comprehensive estimate of Emerson I have ever seen — because it touches outside relations and fixes his place in them.

The most valuable part of the paper, to my mind, is the summary of the other influences that have shaped things, compared with which Emerson's is but slight. I enjoyed this not only because it is true but because it is such a blow between the eyes at the unendurable Harvard conceit (I put this in to pay you off for your fling at Yale; I like to even up matters). The next best thing — to me — was your relentless exposure of his defects as a great constructive thinker; and next your explanation of the reasons why, though one may admire him greatly, as I do, especially as a poet, he has so little fructifying influence over one. I rejoice in your courage of plain speaking. How all Boston shivered when it read your 'hit or miss' sentences! Your last division is so generous and so splendid that you will come out about even, and be suffered to remain in Boston.

Affectionately yours

T. T. MUNGER

Even when most beautiful, the close of life brings a deep sense of pathos, as the close of the day, when the sun sets like a lovely, radiant eye red with weeping.

Too frail to endure even the company of a friend of two and twenty years' standing for the usual visit, I dined with Dr. Munger and his family. For his sake I left early. He perceived at once the unusualness of this procedure. He accompanied me to the door, asking with an unforgettable expression of anxiety in his eyes, and with utmost, tremulous tenderness: 'There is no change, is there?' He stood outside his door, followed me with the same affectionate gaze till I disappeared in the solemn beauty of the starlit evening. That was my last vision of this friend till the day break and the shadows flee away.[1]

In my profession I have found a host of friends. It is true that in my own denomination the older ministers were

[1] Quoted from my Memorial Sermon on Dr. T. T. Munger, in B. W. Beach's *Life of Dr. Munger.*

critical, a number of them in Boston and the vicinity being unable to see in me any good. Generally they were kind, and our personal relations were unaffected by theological differences. There was one exception, an old minister who never forgave me for a look, and who ever afterward refused to recognize or speak to me. Dr. Thompson, of the Eliot Church, Roxbury, was this person, a scholar, a man of keen intellect, and of unusual general ability, but fanatical in his attachments and in his aversions, of a highly nervous temperament, and of a temper somewhat difficult for even the grace of God to subdue. At a council called to dismiss a minister, Dr. Thompson was moderator. The praise of the departing minister was so lavish that a member of the council inquired why it was, if this minister was so praiseworthy, the church had called for his resignation. The reply from a representative of the church was that the minister was so conservative in his theological opinions that the young people could not endure his teaching. At this point I caught Dr. Thompson's eye, and I sent toward him a smile with a good deal of sarcasm and mockery in it. The effect was like an electric shock; the old man straightened up and stiffened in his seat, and he gave me a look which plainly meant, 'I am done with you forever.' I had been called a destroyer of the church on account of my liberality; here was a conservative turned out because the youth of the church wanted light which he could not give. These were the circumstances in which a sardonic look earned me the scorn and hatred of this imperfectly sanctified Christian. Dr. Thompson has the distinction of being the only minister I have ever known who was thus controlled by the temper of a fanatic. I believe that he could have

practiced vivisection upon heretics with unmeasured satisfaction, and felt that he was doing God service. Agree with
him, praise him, follow his lead, entertain him and pay him
homage, and he was one of the most charming of men.
Withhold all this and there was

'A laughing devil in his sneer.'

He was the only malicious minister I have ever known, the
only ministerial enemy I have ever had. He had my prayers and sympathies then, and he has them now.

My ministerial contemporaries of all denominations I
have found delightful men, and many of them enlightening.
The Ministers' Club of Boston and vicinity had in its mem-
bership such distinguished leaders as Dr. William F. Warren, Borden P. Bowne, Joseph Henry Thayer, Andrew P.
Peabody, Alexander V. G. Allen, and that saint among
radicals, Charles A. Dole, Apostle of the Absolute, as heedless of contradictions in the path of his thinking as the
Chicago Limited is of a head-on hurricane. Dole was one
of our acutest minds, resourceful, so made that he could
not be changed from without even by the Holy Ghost of
Reason, but only from within, if at all, by the force of personal experience. Dole and I fought for five and twenty
years over our opposing creeds; neither ever had the
slightest influence upon the other except that we drew together in an ever deeper and devouter friendship. To Dole
I am indebted for my clearest views of the two varieties of
the Unitarianism of the last forty years, the type of Unitarianism that has much in common with modern Trinita-
rianism, between which there may be a gradual and an important approach, and the type of Unitarianism to which
I must say, 'God bless you and good-bye.' This excellent

club had an important part in my theological education. I
was somewhat beyond the susceptible age when two strong
men joined the club, William W. Fenn and Daniel Evans,
both learned and vigorous thinkers and influential teachers.

One anecdote about an illustrious guest of the club at
one of its meetings, Edward Everett Hale, will be enjoyed,
both by the reverent and the profane. The essay of the
evening gave rise to a discussion on creed subscription.
Dr. A. V. G. Allen contended, in a calm and scholarly way,
for breadth and freedom of interpretation. One could believe that Mary was a virgin in the sense that one believed
that one's mother was a virgin before the sacrament of
marriage. Hale sprang into the debate, but in the warmth
of his temper and the newness of this method of interpretation, he could not hold his ground against the subtlety of
Allen. Allen's reasoning he could answer in only one way,
by a burst of passionate feeling thus expressed: 'I'd be
damned before I subscribed to any creed in that way!'
The meeting broke up in roars of laughter and in ultimate
universal friendliness.

My younger brethren in the ministry, after my parish
and the loyal devotion there, have been one of the greatest
consolations of my life. They have, many of them, been
members of my congregation while in college or the Divinity School, and they have remembered me with a kindness which I have been unable to understand, but which I
have prized beyond words, after they have left Cambridge
and Boston and become men of consequence to the religious life of our country. These men have read my books,
and given me to know that I had a share in the equipment
of their minds and characters for the work to which they

were called. Thousands of letters have gathered, during these forty years, from this great host of gallant friends, and they have become, in memory, a garden of unfading, ever-blooming flowers. No matter if I have not deserved this, there is the garden, and there are the deathless flowers. What I had to give I freely gave these young men; they have returned more and better than they received. Their remembrance is like great music.

Next to a minister's family is his parish. The educational side again comes before me. When called upon to join in marriage exalted and happy youth, when invited to christen the child that is the rapt possession of a noble mother, when bereavement asks for light in darkness and for hope in death, the minister receives the mightiest of all incentives to find a metaphysic adequate to the quality and the ideal of normal human life. All that is great in the speculative thinking of the world, all that is most sacred in the religious teaching of the world, the sovereign insights of Jesus into the consubstantiality of God and man, the essential spiritual being of the Infinite and the finite, start into life, offer themselves as light and consecration, when a minister stands in the presence of the ideal demands of the awakened humanity of man. How any minister can be other than a profound thinker, other than an endless metaphysician, when moved upon by the tides of human love and sacred solicitude, is something that I cannot understand. In no other profession is there an opportunity so incessant or a motive so vital, so majestic, toward real thinking, toward the endeavor to ground the humanity of man upon the being of the Eternal Lover of man. To be under the perpetual call to think, preach, pray, serve, up to the level of life's truth and beauty, as these lie in the consciousness of good men and women, is a privilege, an educational advantage which the minister enjoys in a measure known to no other class in the community. Let there be everlasting scorn for those who say because a man is a minister he cannot be a thinker; let there be the same scorn for those who meekly accept this indignity.

I have learned much from the business and professional men with whom I have been intimate in the Old South Church, particularly from their habits of mind and methods of arriving at conclusions. During the eighteen years in which I was a member of the Board of Overseers of Harvard University I had an opportunity to observe closely the mental procedure of lawyers, physicians, and men of business, all eminent in their respective callings. The lawyers were admirable in debate; they were skillful dialecticians; their keenness in the detection of flaws in the methods of doing things and of unconstitutional proposals was unmatched, and their temper both in success and in defeat was always exemplary. They were apt to see only one side of the case they were handling, to make special pleas, to address the Board as if it were a jury, and to talk too much and too often. The physicians were usually exact in the statement of fact, accurate in drawing inferences, sound in the series of judgments by which they reached the practical conclusion. In all this they were models. Their fault was that they were apt to take it as personal disrespect when the Board rejected their counsel. I note it as a fault that is apt to go with authority. The great physician is an authority; his prescriptions are commands; and he is justly indignant if these are not accepted at once and without question. In general deliberation and debate something, often only a mere shadow, of this professional tendency, would follow these able and admirable men. Business men were accustomed to go at once for the facts in the case; they were keen and sure and swift in practical judgment; their object was to get the wise thing done and without delay. Their fault was that they hesitated to stand alone, they paused when disunion touched their ranks, they were somewhat wanting in independence and moral courage; like certain predatory animals they loved to hunt in packs. The great qualities which I found in the lawyers, physicians, and men of business in the Board of Overseers, I have found, without their defects, in the same classes in my congregation. No receptive mind could witness, as I have done, the sure judgment and reasoned opinion of these men, all leaders and highly responsible thinkers in their several callings, without constant revision of his own intellectual processes. For many years I have regarded the business world as a great university, and I have seldom known an honorably successful business man who had not gained through his vocation two things of transcendent worth, a highly trained intellect and a strong and true character. I have been under great obligations to the Committee of the Old South Church, and the Standing Committee of the Old South Society. They have supported me by their enlightened and enlightening judgment in whatever worthy thing I have undertaken to do, and with the authority of their character. The chairmanship of the Standing Committee of the Society has been held in succession by three men — Joseph H. Gray, John Wells Morss, and Edward B. Bayley — over the entire length of my ministry, and their confidence and friendship have been one of the comforts of my life. The same tribute is due their associates on that great responsible committee. The Church Committee is renewed from time to time, thus allowing a large number of men to share in administrative work. The deacons and the clerk are permanent officers. We have had three clerks, all able, all devoted, all friends and helpers of the minister. Much fun used to be made at the expense of the traditional deacon, so much so that it required a certain measure of moral courage for a first-rate man to accept this office, interwoven as it has been with humorous and sometimes ridiculous associations. With one exception, the deacons with whom I have had the honor to serve have been representative of the best talent and the highest character in the Old South Church, men of great public spirit, governed in an extraordinary degree by an enlightened religious purpose, leaders, and recognized as worthy to be leaders, in the whole noble endeavor of the church. Men of ability all of them, men of high ability some of them, men who have used the authority gained by their acknowledged worth and public service to strengthen the hands and cheer the heart of their minister, the living among them deserve my utmost thanks, and the dead a sacred place in a grateful memory.

For five and thirty years we had as a member of the congregation Justice John W. Hammond, of the Supreme Court of Massachusetts. He was a man for whom respect and love were universally felt among us. His humor was full of charm and ever-flowing. One Sunday after service he came to me, with assumed gravity and anxiety, and said: 'I want your preaching to be searching, but do you

think it is fair to point to me as you did this morning when
you uttered that tremendous sentence, "Old men go to the
Devil, *and you and I* are on the way"?' This remark is too
good willingly to allow to die. Another remark, and this
time the wisdom came almost from the 'mouth of babes
and sucklings.' I had said, in the course of my sermon,
that I was inclined to think that Christians were sometimes among the most foolish people that the Almighty
ever made. The mother of the family who heard it, in re-
peating at the dinner table this wild utterance of the minister, was greeted with the outcry from her son, a boy of
tender years, 'Mother, dear, that was most untactful of
Dr. Gordon; there might have been a Christian in the congregation!'

It may seem strange that I have said nothing of the
women of the church. That is because time would fail me
to do justice to them. For liberality of opinion, freedom
from inherited bias where that bias was limitation, grasp
of essential Christianity, insight into the heart of things,
and general large and hopeful outlook, the women have
been with few exceptions always the peers, and frequently
the superior, of the men. This was emphatically true of
the generation of men and women that called me to the
Old South Church. For elevation of mind, personal dignity, immunity from gossip, that worst vice of the tongue,
devotion to good causes, and availing sympathy with me
in every noble endeavor, the women of the Old South
Church have won my highest admiration and my affectionate respect.

About Dr. Merrill, head-master of the Boston Latin
School, I have a precious memory to recall. Dr. Merrill was

born in September, 1833; I was born in January, 1853,
nearly twenty years afterward. One day he told me this:
'For the first five years of your ministry here I thought
you were leading this church absolutely astray.' Nobody
could have inferred that this was his conviction from his
behavior. He was as loyal, as sympathetic as if he had
been completely satisfied with the minister. He then
added: 'I can now see that you were right all the time and
that I was wrong.' Can this be paralleled? One may be
able to parallel it, but one cannot surpass it in the history
of any church in Boston. There was the magnanimity of
the man, his moral greatness, his nobility.

Another great friend remains from whom a word of
grateful remembrance cannot be withheld, Samuel Johnson, long connected with the firm of C. F. Hovey & Company in Boston. He was a great citizen, a great character,
a great Christian. But for him my strength and courage
would have failed me, in the dark beginnings of my ministry in the Old South Church, when like Milton I felt that
I had

> '. . . . . fallen on evil days,
> On evil days though fallen, and evil tongues;
> In darkness, and with dangers compass'd round.'

In the fifteen years of our friendship I never had from
Mr. Johnson one word of criticism, one utterance that was
not warm with purest affection, one look that was not the
smile of friendliest regard. Under his wise conservative
manner he was a profound and precious radical. He knew
that the Christian Church had been loaded for centuries
with mountains of incredible stuff, with no more essential
relation to the mind and heart of Jesus, and the high man-

ner of His spirit, than the profanity of a mule-driver. The
first scare I gave the Old South, after my examination, was
a sermon I preached on the American Board in 1887. The
sermon was afterwards published in 'The Christian
Union,' now 'The Outlook.' There was dismay at the un-
sparing refutation of the arguments of the traditionalists,
the unmerciful exposure of their fallacies, especially the
fallacy that belief in everlasting punishment for those who
die without the knowledge of Christ in this world is essential to the existence of foreign missionary endeavors, and
all this accompanied with scorn for the attempt to lord it
over the free mind of the churches. After the service Mr.
Johnson met me with a lovely smile, saying: 'Well, we
have made up our minds not to send you out as a foreign
missionary, because we need you here.' This man's integrity, judgment, perfect self-control, although possessed
of a warm temper, his easy control of other men, because
of his enlightened mind, and because he was wholly disinterested, all became a sacred study to me. He had the
qualities of a great man, and by admiration of them I
hoped sometime to win a share in his worth. His affection
for me was of surpassing loveliness; the sound of his voice
in parting when vacation came, and in bidding me welcome when I returned to my work, was to me like sacred
music, soft, rich, a melody coming from the divine in man's
heart. We sailed together, fished together, bowled together
once each week for twelve radiant years, and when we
parted for the last time, it was without tears, but with
such a look on his face, and I doubt not on mine, as nothing
in human speech can describe, as only reverential silence
may hold as one of her immortal secrets.

When I had Samuel Johnson to urge me, and to accompany me, I went to the greater conventions of the Congregational order. We went together to the meeting of the American Board at Springfield, Massachusetts, in 1887. That was the wildest of all the denominational meetings that I ever attended. The question up for debate was this: Shall young men, however spiritual they may be, be allowed to go forth as missionaries of the American Board, who hold that for the dead who never had a chance to believe on Christ in this world, there will be an opportunity in the world to come? To me the whole business was so preposterous, such a mere matter of miserable detail, that I could not be serious over the great meeting. The excitement was something appalling; the absorption in the pending issues made the corporate members and the congregation oblivious to everything else, however startling and impressive. In the opening of the morning session the former Governor of Massachusetts, Washburn, fell dead from excitement. A pause was made, a hymn sung, the dead man was carried out, and in five minutes all thought of what had happened was wiped out of the mind of the assembly. The debate lasted eight hours, with a recess of an hour for refreshments, which were needed; and it must be said that in all that long debate not one unworthy word was spoken by any debater; over all the heat and fury the power of Christian character and good manners was supreme. Mr. Johnson insisted that I should take the Old South into this debate, and where from six to ten men rose to speak when the previous speaker had finished, I was recognized by the presiding officer, wholly through the influence of Mr. Johnson. I could do nothing but play the humorist over the triviality of the question at issue. In doing this I well remember the grim looks that greeted me from veterans who thought that I made light of a matter of life and death. I could not change a single shade of an opinion, but I could poke fun at the fanatical conservatives, make them hot with holy rage, and this I did with considerable satisfaction.

The greatest effect of a humorous incident upon all present came in a speech by Dr. Edwin Pond Parker, of Hartford. He sprang into the debate, and, while usually deliberate and slow of speech, he was now a whirlwind on fire. He claimed that the public did not know what the American Board had become so crazy over. To illustrate, Parker continued, two men met last evening in front of this very hall in which we are now gathered. One addressed the other thus: 'These religious people have jewed us out of our fun on Sunday, they have jewed us out of our liquor, and I'm blamed if this American Board ain't talking about Prohibition after death.' The effect was a thunderstorm of applause and laughter, continued, as it seemed, for minutes, and recurring again and again. There were a few more serious speeches, but the end was evidently near. The work had been done, not by logic, but by laughter, inspired by Him, I cannot doubt, of whom it is written, 'He that sitteth in the heavens shall laugh.'

My associate ministers have been the Reverend Dr. Allen E. Cross, who served with me from 1901 to 1911; the Reverend Willis H. Butler, whose term of service was seven and one-half years; the Reverend Archibald Black, who did not remain in Boston long enough for her people to know him, but who left with me an enduring memory of personal kindness; and the Reverend Boynton Merrill, the present associate minister. Each of these men had his own distinctive excellence, each contributed much to the life of the church, and to all of them I am under permanent obligation for their assistance and their high-minded comradeship. Dr. Cross had a distinctive literary gift much appreciated by many of our people; he was and is a poet as well as a preacher. A more loyal and lovable soul I have never known. Mr. Butler was a man of noble presence in the pulpit, one of the most effective preachers from manuscript that I have heard, a man of much independence and dignity, resolute in service and enduring in his friendship. Mr. Black remained with us only a little over one year, not long enough for him to disclose his power. The present associate minister, I must not praise except to say that he seems to me essential to the continuance of my ministry and the new life of the church. So much I may be forgiven for saying, especially when I add that so much more in the way of grateful acknowledgment might justly be said. I never distribute words of recognition among four very different individuals without recalling an experience of Samuel Johnson, the friend of whom I have been writing. The occasion was some high social affair, one of excellence, whose character and triumph were due to a group of able and delightful women. Mr. Johnson and his young friends called for a speech in response to 'a toast to the ladies' from a gentleman who had been married four times, hoping to get some youthful merriment out of this gentleman's embarrassment. They were mistaken. Mr. Jones was equal to the occasion, and, taking his own experience as guide, replied thus: The first Mrs. Jones in her distinctive excellence was the most wonderful woman he had ever seen; the second Mrs. Jones was totally unlike her predecessor, but in her own line of excellence she was unmatched; the third Mrs. Jones (whom he always spoke of as the former Mrs. Jones) was a complete contrast to the other two, but in her worth she was absolutely unapproached; while the fourth and present Mrs. Jones united the truth, beauty, and worth of three glorious women whom she had succeeded. I may not go so far as this in praise of my present beloved associate, the Reverend Boynton Merrill. I simply let suggestion do its perfect work. The record for calls upon the people of the Old South is still held by the Reverend Warren S. Archibald, of Hartford, who as a special servant of the church for one year made in eleven months more than a thousand visitations. He has left a memory for knightliness of spirit and beauty of influence which we should like to surpass, but which so far we have been unable to do more than barely equal.

Education through friendship is the subject of this chapter. It has been a delight to write it. Long as it is, it is still marked by incompleteness, and a host of friends who have been round me all these years, enlighteners and gladdeners all, have received no recognition or mention. Two there are in this multitude to whom I must express a word of special gratitude. John Wright Buckham, theologian in the Pacific School of Religion, has set what he considers, in his kindness, my contribution to theology in the grandest perspective. He has done me the honor of a careful study of my books and of associating my work with some of the ablest of my older contemporaries and with the succession of the mighty dead. Himself a penetrating and productive mind, whose work is on the highest level both for substance and form, I find it impossible to repress this expression of grateful obligation to him. The other friend is Joseph Fort Newton, beloved by the whole ministerial profession, a man as brilliant as he is generous, of whom I can never think but with grateful affection. The great multitude must remain nameless. Let them be described as the high and bracing atmosphere of my days, as renewing my strength with their vitality, and cheering me ever onward with the sunshine and beauty of their influence. The details of all lovely days, sunrises, noons, and sunsets, no memory is large enough to hold, no imagination subtle enough to reproduce, but the spirit in the whole beauty of the world abides, through its effect upon intellect and character. So it is with the circle of our friendship; 'nameless here forevermore' they live in the mind and character they have helped to make and to bless.

If this were a confession of faith I should name as my first, last, and greatest friend, Him of whom it is said that he thus addressed his disciples: 'I have called you friends.' Christianity is friendship glorified through Jesus of Nazareth and lifted into the life of God. I invite a great and noble heretic to speak for me here the universal feeling and conscience of all Christian men and women:

'O Thou great friend to all the sons of men,
Who once did'st come in humblest guise below,
Sin to rebuke, to break the captives' chain,
And call thy brethren forth from want and woe,

'We look to Thee; Thy truth is still the light
Which guides the nations, groping on their way,
Stumbling and falling in disastrous night,
Yet ever hoping for the perfect day.

'Yes, Thou art still the Life; Thou art the Way
The holiest know; Light, Life and Way of heaven!
And they who dearest hope and deepest pray,
Toil by the Light, Life, Way, which Thou hast given.'

CHAPTER XXII

PROSPICE

A KINSWOMAN of mine, considerably younger than I, recently wrote that she had nothing to look forward to but death. This seems to me to be a deplorable and a wholly unnecessary state of mind for a healthy human being at any age. Good mothers, in their old age, show human nature as it should be and as it may become in all, by moral discipline. They live spontaneously in their children and grandchildren; in this way the channel of individuality that might otherwise run dry is flooded with great and lovely tributaries from the abundant heart of youth. While in health who ever saw a good mother or grandmother without zest in life, without ability to transcend and ignore the fading flower of her own existence?

It is true that the individual as such counts in this world only for a few brief years; it is also true that every morally decent individual, in the service of his fellowmen, transcends his simple earthly individuality, and lives, in one way or another, in the life of his race, in the being of the Eternal Silence. He will at once acknowledge his frailty and brevity as a citizen of time; he will do this with candor and humor. In the Old South Church there are two black marble tablets, on which are dimly inscribed the names of the fifteen ministers who, having finished their labors here, have gone to their rest. To the unaided eye these names are invisible, mere shadows on the wall, fitting symbols of the shadows that these ministers and their congregations have become to the men and women of to-day, pathetic, and at the same time humorous, tokens of the fate awaiting the present minister and his people; shadows on the wall all are destined to become in due season.

Even the immortals are doomed; they are granted a reprieve by time, but not a pardon, not a release. They are still held for extinction because involved with the fate of the planet. If the ship founders in mid-ocean there can be no survivors, and when in the depths of space this globe founders, the immortals will have done their work, and will share the same fate with the rest of mankind. Plato, surely one of the immortals, had a poor opinion of this whole time-world. 'For the mind in which there is lofty thought, and the vision of all time and all existence, do you suppose it possible that to this mind human life seems anything great?' Here is one of the high Greek analogues, so often found in Plato, to the Apostle Paul's sovereign contempt for time: 'The things which are seen are temporal, but the things which are not seen are eternal.' Shakespeare, another of the immortals, took the same ultimate view of the fate of all things earthly:

> 'The cloud-capp'd towers, the gorgeous palaces,
> The solemn temples, the great globe itself,
> Yea, all which it inherit, shall dissolve,
> And, like this insubstantial pageant faded,
> Leave not a rack behind.'

This being admitted once for all, the healthy mind in old age refuses to dwell upon it. The raft on which Odysseus sailed might be wrecked or sunk, but under the protection of the goddess Athena this sailor was always able somehow and somewhere to make land. The soul of man

is such a mariner; it is in league with the Eternal by its
purpose and destiny, and whatever may become of the
material raft on which it is sailing the voyage of time, in its
nature it is something that seas cannot overwhelm nor
floods drown. They are near-sighted metaphysicians who
do not discern that individuality has its ground in the will
and purpose of the Absolute Spirit. It is either this or
nihilism, and healthy minds refuse to entertain the idea
that spirit is subject to the scythe of time. When Browning asserts that 'Man has forever,' he means that man is
essentially spirit, that spirit is of the being of the Deity,
and that its individuality is grounded in His Eternal Will.
The one without the many and the many without the one
lead to nothing; the Eternal One in the many spirits that
He has created from Himself is the reality that has meaning and that endures. Wise old men hold fast this faith;
with Cicero they end their discourses upon Old Age in the
vision of the endless future; with Emerson they aver: 'I
have heard that whoever loves is in no condition old. I
have heard that whenever the name of man is spoken, the
doctrine of immortality is announced; it cleaves to his constitution. The mode of it baffles our wit, and no whisper
comes from the other side. But the inference from the
working of intellect, hiving knowledge, hiving skill — at
the end of life just ready to be born — affirms the inspirations of affection, and of the moral sentiment.' Healthy
minds refuse to brood upon the fate of our earth; they pass
to the eternity of truth and beauty and goodness, not in
the abstract, whatever that may mean, not for God or the
Absolute Spirit alone, but also for all rational beings, in all
possible worlds. There is a kingdom of truth and beauty

and goodness in this world, the most precious possession of mankind. Here that kingdom has one phase of its development; its consummation is beyond time. Here and now the love which it creates for itself in unselfish hearts, the service which it inspires, the sacrifice which it induces and makes easy, constitute the zest and joy which time can neither give nor take away.

There are moods, especially in old age, when one is ready to exclaim with Edmund Burke: 'What shadows we are, and what shadows we pursue.' Even so, healthy minds are swift to remember that shadow is always the witness to substance. Where there is no substance there is no shadow. The essential good of human beings is the central reality of the world. That, under many aspects, physical, economic, political, scientific, artistic, philosophical, and religious, is the one thing that gathers round it the loves, sympathies, hopes, endeavors, and prayers of all heroic souls. All romance, all comedy, all tragedy have their meaning here. Arthur and his knights, in their speech, adventure, achievement, prosper or fail in the light of essential human good. The progressive triumph of the essential good of mankind is the sovereign romance of history; it is the delight of noble minds, a delight in which the old may indulge as freely as the young, one in which age may forget the havoc of time, and again, with Emerson sing,

> 'Love wakes anew this throbbing heart
> And we are never old.'

The comedy of the world is seen in the farce to which life turns when its perspective of values is all wrong, when it crowns the beggar passion king, and makes the kingly passion slave or clown. Behind the comedies of Aristophanes and Shakespeare is the perpetual farce of the sensuous life broken loose from the control of moral ideas. Rich men in their palaces, with nothing in their minds to match this magnificence, fashionable women engaged in the hopeless endeavor of making brass pass for gold, the brainless of both sexes, because of some accidental advantage trying to convince the world that they move it, the witless, humorless, heartless human creatures who walk in a vain show, constitute a pageant forever passing before wise old eyes, a pageant which, at times, fills one with indignation, but the greater part of the day, with amusement. These bubbles will burst, and, although other bubbles will be blown, the unbroken process of bursting carries with it not only healthy amusement, but also increasing illumination. The bubble business breaks down at length and is seen not to pay. Comedy passes into tragedy, in life, and in the parables of Jesus which are true to life, the comedy of the man who built his house on sand, with no thought of the coming storm, the comedy of the man felicitating himself on the fortune he had made, upon whose door the hand of death was already present, the comedy of Dives in his mansion clothed in purple and fine linen, faring sumptuously every day, who had no care for the beggar at his gate, no least dream of the place of torment toward which he was driving. In life, as in the teaching of Jesus, it is often true that the first phase of tragedy is comedy, the last phase of comedy, tragedy.

Old sinners, worn out with their folly, creeping into the House of God, like mendicants seeking shelter from a blizzard before nightfall, I have seen all along the years, witnesses all of them to the play that was not worth the candle, to the good times and the sport that dried the heart to a desert. The lover of comedy has a Don Quixote and his world before him to the end of his days, something of inexhaustible interest, and, when rightly regarded, full of hope. It is a tough business, but this is a tough old world, and it is true that the moral fool, man or woman, may be made wise; laugh at him long enough and loud enough, and he is likely to come to himself. Few human beings can long endure their way of life when they know that it has made them objects of merriment and ridicule. Laughter I put among the redemptive forces of the world, and wise old men have amazing capacities here. Cervantes is one of the heroic representatives of the power and consolation of laughter; I maintain that laughter is both recreative and redemptive; it makes spring in the mind and puts a new face upon the world.

The heart of tragedy, as the Greeks saw with unerring insight, is in mistake. Truth and falsehood, beauty and deformity, good and evil are engaged in a conflict mostly in midnight darkness. Jesus is here in profoundest sympathy with the Greek seers, because He has His eye, at a yet greater depth, upon the tragedy of the world. 'If thou hadst known in this day, even thou, the things which belong unto peace!' To mistake truth for falsehood, beauty for deformity, good for evil, is tragedy at its utmost depth, and this form of tragedy runs through all history. Here is our hope. Because our deepest woe issues from mistake, because the darkened mind is still set upon what it conceives to be good, the expectation of ultimate triumph is reasonable; it is in the nature of man. Educate the mind, educate the feelings, educate the will, and the confusion of essential good with apparent but unreal good will vanish, and the livery of heaven which essential evil assumes, in which it cheats poor mortals, will fail to conceal the devil within. Man's soul, by its constitution, and by all the forces of experience, is on the side of the educator and prophet of essential good. He may fail; he will die and pass out of the memory of his kind; his cause cannot fail, no weapon formed against it can prosper. As of old it is still true, 'As the rain cometh down and the snow from heaven and returneth not thither, but watereth the earth, and maketh it to bring forth and to bud, that it may give seed to the sower and bread to the eater, so shall my word be that goeth forth out of my mouth. It shall not return unto me void, but it shall accomplish that which I please, and it shall prosper in the thing whereto I sent it.' The optimist has the only adequate insight into the nature of man, into the ultimate character of the universe. Good is man's object; made as he is, nothing else can he aim at or desire; his mistakes are vast and tragic, but they bring illumination; his will is set again, and this time upon clear essential good; thus, out of the tragedy of human lives, out of the tragedy of the world, comes, like a slow, long-deferred sunrise, the radiant assurance of the eventual triumph of truth over falsehood, beauty over deformity, goodness over evil. In this vision old age may rejoice and serve till its last hour. Luther's great words stand fast: 'His Kingdom is forever.' Our New England hymn makes music in the evening of life no less sweet than in the morning, 'I love Thy Kingdom, Lord'; human life at the first and at the last is at its best only when it endures 'as seeing Him who is invisible.' For such a mind the long eonian

night, with its conflict, its tears and blood, is already past;
the great answer is at hand:

> 'I feel not the red rains fall,
> Hear not the tempest at all,
> Nor thunder in heaven any more.
> All the distance is white
> With the soundless feet of the sun.
> Night, with the woes that it wore,
> Night is over and done.'

THE END

INDEX

INDEX

Abbott, Ezra, 178.

Adams family, the, 37.

Alden, Dr., Secretary of the American Board, 278, 279.

Aldrich, Thomas Bailey, quoted, 34.

Alexander, English philosopher, 244.

Allen, Alexander V. G., 320, 321.

American Board, meeting of, 329, 330.

Anarchy, due to the lifting of authority, 239, 240; in philosophy, 240; among Biblical scholars, 240, 241.

Angier, Reverend Luther H., inspires Gordon, 143, 144; his voice, 144, 145; his eloquence, 145; friendship of, 148, 149; assists at Gordon's marriage, 263.

Angier, Mrs. L. H., 147–49.

Archibald, Reverend Warren S., 332.

Aristotle, had no conception of humanity, 103; his 'Politics,' 157; identity of phrase in 'Politics' and in Paul's 'Letter to the Galatians,' 201; preëminence of, 205–08, 260; on friendship, 290.

Art, as inspiration to imagination and sentiment, 151.

Athens, Pericles's description of democracy in, 96, 97.

Athletes, Scottish and American, 126, 127.

Athletics, the bearing of, upon the life of youth, 120, 121; overexertion in, 121; competition in, 121, 122; a premoral religion, 122, 123, 129, 130; Scottish, 124–27; wholesomeness of, 128; demand temperance and a clean life, 128; induce to hero-worship, 128, 129.

Augustinianism, 251.

Authority, from, through anarchy to insight, 239, 240.

Autobiography, discouragements to the writing of, 9–11; justification of, 11; things important for, 11–13.

Bacon, B. W., 313.

Ballad, Sir James the Rose, 70, 71; Chevy-Chace, 87.

Barbour, Dr., 236.

Barnet, Sandy, 50–53.

Bayley, Edward B., chairman of the Standing Committee of the Old South Society, 324.

Beach, B. W., quotation from his 'Life of Dr. Munger,' 318.

Beaton, Lewis, teacher, 83, 84.

Beecher, Dr. Edward, 237.

Beecher, Henry Ward, 279.

Beecher, Lyman, anecdotes of, 232, 236, 237.

Benedict, Mr., 219.

Bennachie, 13.

Berkeley, George, 258.

Bible, exercises in, in school, 80; speaks for itself, 214; as literature, 257.

Black, Reverend Archibald, associate minister at Old South Church, 330, 331.

Blackie, John Stuart, poem on the immigrant, 132.

Blame, foolish, 276, 277; unjust, 282–85; coming as unconscious influence, 286–89.

Books, 152–57, 160, 162.

Booth, Edwin, 157, 158.

Bosanquet, Bernard, 'Contemporary Philosophy,' 240.

Boston, orthodox atmosphere in, 213.

Boucicault, Dion, 159.

Bowen, Professor, 298.

Bowne, Borden P., 320.

Brooks, Phillips, 146, 147; congratulatory letter to Gordon, 262, 263; Gordon married by, 263; calls on